THE I TATTI
RENAISSANCE LIBRARY

James Hankins, General Editor

LANDINO

POEMS

ITRL 35

CRISTOFORO LANDINO
✦ ✦ ✦
POEMS

TRANSLATED BY

MARY P. CHATFIELD

THE I TATTI RENAISSANCE LIBRARY
HARVARD UNIVERSITY PRESS
CAMBRIDGE, MASSACHUSETTS
LONDON, ENGLAND
2008

Series design by Dean Bornstein

Library of Congress Cataloging-in-Publication Data

Landino, Cristoforo, 1424–1504.
[Poems. English & Latin]
Poems / Cristoforo Landino ;
translated by Mary P. Chatfield.
p.   cm. — (I Tatti Renaissance library ; ITRL 35)
Includes bibliographical references and index.
ISBN 978-0-674-03148-7 (cloth : alk. paper)
I. Chatfield, Mary P.   II. Title.
PA8540.L3A2 2008
808.81 — dc22   2008033807

Contents

꽃§?꽃

· CONTENTS ·

vi

· CONTENTS ·

vii

· CONTENTS ·

BOOK III

· CONTENTS ·

BOOK I (EARLIER REDACTION)

MISCELLANEOUS POEMS

Introduction

☙❧

Among the many famous artists, writers, and philosophers whose names embellish the memory of Lorenzo de' Medici's Florence, that of Cristoforo Landino (1424–1498) shines with a particular luster. As the best-known humanist to give courses at the University of Florence devoted to the poetry of that city's most illustrious poets, Dante and Petrarca, and as the first Florentine of his century to write a commentary on the *Divine Comedy*, he today stands out as a great teacher in an era famous for its philosophers, historians and poets. Pupil himself of the literary scholar Carlo Marsuppini, he went on in his turn to teach perhaps the most famous philosopher of the era, Marsilio Ficino, his own brilliance outshone by the greater brilliance of his remarkable pupil. In recent years, thanks to the efforts of several American and Italian scholars, Landino's ground-breaking pedagogical work has begun to achieve the recognition it deserves, and his reputation as a humanist-teacher more fully appreciated.[1] His Latin poetry, however, deserves to be better known.[2]

Landino was born in Florence in 1424 to a family of modest means. Although he mentions, in a poem to Bartolomeo Scala (1.24), three relations of whom he was very proud—an ancestor who fought at the battle of Campaldino; his great-great-uncle Francesco Landini, the famous composer and organist; and his uncle Gabriele, a learned Camaldolese monk—his parents, lacking both money and powerful connections, placed him at the age of ten with a notary in order to learn law. He was not happy in this career. As he wrote to his friend Bernardo Nuti, "See how poverty's evils make me give up the Muses, / and master unwillingly the laws of the forum" (er1.21, 3–4).[3] It is no surprise that in 1439, as soon as he had finished the prescribed course of law, he returned to Florence and began to study literature at the University (or Studium) of Florence under Marsuppini. He may well have had guidance from the historians Leonardo Bruni and Poggio Bracciolini as well. Certainly he feasted on the literature of the past and thrived, giving himself over to the writing of Latin elegiacs and taking for his "Laura," his poetic inspiration, a young Florentine beauty whom he called Xandra.

Both his studies and his writing prospered, so much so that the notary with whom he had been placed in order to learn law helped finance his time at the university. In 1441 he took part in a vernacular poetry contest, the famous *Certame coronario*, reciting the prize-winning poem that had been composed by his patron, Francesco d'Altobianco degli Alberti. Landino later composed a poem of his own for his patron (er1.48), which begins "Greathearted man," and goes on to praise Francesco's beneficence and honorable example, acknowledging the older man's moral and intellectual influence on him. This poem seems to have happily impressed the Alberti family, and Landino was drawn temporarily into the orbit of Leon Battista Alberti. Leon Battista must have had little to offer as a patron, however, as Landino later changed the dedication of his first book of poems from Alberti to Piero de' Medici, son of Cosimo, whose patronage was to prove crucial after the death of Marsuppini. The Alberti connection bore other fruit, however, and in 1459 Landino married Lucrezia di Alberto di Aldovardo degli Alberti, a union which produced seven children.

Meantime a battle was waging at the Studium as to who would take the chair held by Marsuppini, whose death in 1453 Landino had marked with a long and moving elegy (3.7).[4] Known as the "universal professor" from the range of his teaching, Marsuppini had given lectures on rhetoric, poetry, and both Greek and Latin philosophy. In the contest over who was to succeed him, support for the great Greek humanist John Argyropoulos was led by Donato Acciaiuoli and Alamanno Rinuccini, while allies of the Medici backed Landino. Several other candidates, including Francesco da Castiglione and Bernardo Nuti, were proposed as well. In a Solomonic decision the professorship was divided, with John Argyropoulos taking the chair of philosophy, Francesco da Castiglione that of Greek, and Landino that of rhetoric and poetry. Although the division of the professorship had been funded as early as February 1455, and there is a record that he was already giving public lectures on Dante, Landino did not take up the chair until 1458.[5]

He received a salary of 100 florins to start, an amount which gradually rose to 200 florins in the 1460s and to 300 florins in 1485. The last increase put him among the best-paid humanities professors of his day, no doubt a testimony to the fame he had earned with the publication in 1481 of his *Commentary on Dante*. By that time also he had become a firm friend of Bernardo Bembo, the noble Venetian diplomat and bibliophile who moved easily among the humanists and philosophers who composed the intellectual circle of the Medici.

The *Three Books of Xandra*, which constitute the bulk of Landino's poetic *oeuvre*, were completed by 1460, and the individual poems that make up the cycle can often be dated by contemporary events to which Landino makes reference. The rest of his poetic work consists of poems which he omitted when changing the dedication of the first book of *Xandra* from Alberti to Piero de' Medici, and poems written from time to time during his years as a teacher. Six of these were written to Bernardo Bembo between 1475 and 1480 when Bembo, twice on embassy from Venice, was resident in Florence. These suggest a likeness of interests and temperament (Landino comes close to teasing Bembo in some passages), even love of a strictly Platonic kind (see Appendix), which offers an illustration of how, during the Renaissance as at other times, eminence in the life of the mind could erase class distinctions.

Once Landino assumed his professorship he immediately began the great work of teaching for which he was valued and honored over the next four decades. We know that in 1459–60 or 1460–61 he gave a course on the *Odes* of Horace, in 1461–62 on the works of Juvenal and Persius, in 1462–63 on *Aeneid* I-VII, and in 1463–64 on the later books of the *Aeneid* and probably on Vergil's other poems as well. In 1464–65 he taught Horace's *Art of Poetry* and other texts concerned with rhetoric and poetics, and in 1465–66 Cicero's *Letters to His Friends*. The courses on Vergil and the *Odes* of Horace were repeated between 1467 and 1471, and during this time too he taught a course on the *Canzoniere* of Petrarch; in 1473–74 he repeated the course on Dante that he had given before becoming a professor. These courses, honed and polished with each repetition, made him "the academic authority *par excellence* in literature for almost forty years,"[6] and the quality of their scholarship and penetration drew to him pupils of the caliber of Marsilio Ficino and Lorenzo de' Medici. His early biographer, Angelo Maria Bandini, says that Landino was *summus interpres et illustrator* (the best interpreter and commentator) of the Tuscan authors, considering them vital to a complete education and urging everyone to read Dante, Petrarch, Boccaccio, Bruni, and Alberti.[7]

Like Salutati, Bruni, and Poggio before him, Landino sought a bureaucratic appointment along with his academic one and counted on his favor with the Medici to achieve it. In 1458 he tried but failed to secure a position at the chancellery, complaining to Piero de' Medici when he did not get it.[8] In 1464–65 he tried again, this time appealing to Lorenzo de' Medici, and once again met with failure. In 1467, however, he was made chancellor of the Guelf party, and in 1483 he received the post of secretary to the chancellery, holding that position until he died. In 1498, the last year of his life, he received a pension and retired to Borgo alla Collina, a little village near his ancestral town of Pratovecchio, where he died shortly afterward, on September 24. He is buried in the parish church, where his mummified body was on view as late as the mid-nineteenth century.[9]

In his brief biography of Landino in *Centuriae Latinae* Craig Kallendorf emphasizes the need to see Landino's career as a whole.[10] As the Medici moved to transform the city of Florence, with its history of fierce republicanism, into an ever less-disguised principate, Landino was among those who praised them most ardently. Yet his greatest neo-Latin work, the *Camaldulensian Disputations*, shows how eager he was to have humanists participate in and guide the decisions of the powerful. For Kallendorf, "Landino's work bears the mark of the tensions of his time. It was difficult to perpetuate republican traditions of liberty . . . while at the same time being eulogist of the Medici."[11] As we read his poetry we can sense these tensions, even in the earlier poems, and we can also see that the critical methods which Landino brought to bear on both classical and Florentine authors and, indeed, on contemporary Florentine painters, were already taking shape in his mind when he wrote the *Three Books of Xandra*.[12]

The meticulous work of collecting and collating all of Landino's poems from manuscript and printed sources was undertaken in the 1930s by the great Italian philologist Alessandro Perosa.[13] His text, which the interested reader may consult for important variant readings, is the one followed for this translation. Perosa preserved the existing, broadly chronological arrangement of the poems as much as possible, so that those reading the text from beginning to end can follow the development of Landino's sensibility as a poet and as a proud citizen of Florence.

The original first book of *Xandra* comprised fifty-three poems and was begun sometime in 1443, for Landino writes in 1.2, 15–16: "When first I recognized . . . the eyes of Xandra . . . I had scarcely added thrice five years to four." It must have been completed in early 1444, as the poem that directs the book to find Alberti (1.15) says that he is to be found in Rome, where he lived from September 1443 onward. In this volume the poems Landino chose to omit from the first book of *Xandra* when he rededicated the work to

Piero de' Medici follow, in a separate section, the collection in three books which had circulated in manuscript form by 1460. These earliest poems include many to a number of different young women — Xandra quite often to be sure, but also Gnognia, Bice, Tubia, and Lucretia. In these poems he portrays himself as a young poet playing the field, who can sigh many times over a disdainful and unapproachable beloved, but who can also make ribald jokes about his friends' mistresses and complain about his poverty. While he chose to put one poem to Alberti in the rededicated first book, perhaps because of its Catullan echoes and clever hendecasyllables, he omitted other poems that made reference to Alberti or his family, as well as other poems that undercut his self-presentation in the three-book cycle in other, less obvious ways.

The second and third of the *Three Books of Xandra* were in circulation before the rededicated and now shortened first book (see 1.1.5–6), but, with the exception of the opening dedication and the closing *envoi*, both to Piero de' Medici, the later form of the first book maintains its chronological integrity. The dedicatory poem proclaims that its book — chronologically the first — has hidden itself for "thrice five years," so we may assume that Landino had completed the finished version by late 1459 or early 1460. His omission of twenty poems, the most juvenile of his *juvenilia*, from the rededicated book suggests that he had moved into a new phase of life, which indeed he had: he was now married and had taken up his teaching duties at the Studium.

Hence the *Three Books of Xandra* chronicle Landino's life, loves, friendships, interests and growing political awareness from his late adolescence to his middle thirties, and they illustrate, though sometimes in a still rudimentary form, the ideas and feelings that were to govern his thinking and teaching for the rest of his days. Ranking with his idealized passion for Xandra is the depth of his feeling for his native city, an idealized patriotism which seems to rise almost as much from devotion to the great writers of Florence as from admiration for the city's love of liberty. The two are never far apart: a poem ("To the City of Florence," 2.23) which begins with an encomium to his adopted city moves seamlessly, after thirty lines, into the praises of Xandra. And as if to illustrate the complexity of both Landino's position and his thought, a similar encomium to Florence ("To Antonio Canigiano on the Beginnings of the City of Florence," 3.3) ends in fulsome praise of Cosimo de' Medici. The grand stories of Florentine resistance to oppression that his former mentor, Bruni, had recounted in his *History of the Florentine People* could not blot out the reality that when Florence was not fighting for her liberty, she was at the mercy of class, factional, and party strife. To the man who brought stability, peace, and an end to the ravages of such divisions all honor was due. The loss of liberty need never be mentioned, especially if that man was a wonderfully generous patron of the arts.

In their progression the books illustrate the poet's coming of age. While the first book deals primarily with "the pricks of gentle Venus" (1.3.25), often in forms which imitate or recall poems by Catullus, Horace, and especially Propertius, the reader can discern, in the names of those to whom many of the poems are addressed, the friendships which Landino had formed with budding humanists and public servants. He is proud of his heritage and, in by far the longest poem of the book (1.24), he describes with evident satisfaction the musical accomplishments of his great-great-uncle, Francesco Landino, accomplishments made all the more astonishing because of his lifelong blindness. The one poem that is not about himself either as client, lover, or friend is a four-line epitaph for Bruni. This is the book of a very bright young man who is not over-shy about putting himself forward and who seems to be almost enjoying the pangs of a love that can never be requited.

The second book shows the beginnings of a greater seriousness. Lovesick longings for Xandra, with whom he had by then been enamored for four years, are sandwiched between poems of gratitude to Piero de' Medici, whom Landino addresses frequently as his Maecenas. But other concerns appear as well. He writes against greed, in praise of a sojourn in the country, and most movingly, about the death of Nuti's young sister, Lisa, as if in her own voice (2.12). The longest poem in the book (2.23) begins with a reprise of some of the great moments in Florentine history before breaking down into a "tender song" to Xandra. This "breaking down" (if the poet is not simply echoing a pose of Propertius) seems to be a kind of realization on Landino's part that his gift is not for epic poetry, though he often says he longs to write in a loftier strain.[14] The poem crystallizes this moment of self-knowledge whose light shines forward through the rest of the book. The final poems, with two exceptions, offer a narrative of Xandra's immanent departure for Rome, her leave-taking, the poet's hurried journey after her, his vision of how Rome reacts to his beloved, and a finale in which he forgets himself and his passion and looks at the ruins of ancient Rome with horrified and sorrowful eyes.

That finale prepares us for the greater maturity and public awareness that characterize the third book. What Landino calls the Aragonese War—in fact an intermittent war with Milan, Naples and the Pope that ended with the Peace of Lodi in 1454—is at the forefront of his thoughts as the book begins. The praise for Cosimo which dominates the opening poem flows in gratitude for "his invincible heart" when others "stir up war against us" and for what has been accomplished "by Medicean wealth, by their loyalty and strength." Although the third poem begins with a brief history of the founding of Florence by a group of Sulla's veterans— for his was "a Florence which prided itself on its affinities with republican Rome"[15]—it moves quite easily into an encomium to the Medici family, beginning with Vieri di Cambio, and hurries quickly on to Cosimo, whom he calls "another Aristides, another Cato." Here is the embodiment of those tensions, alluded to earlier, which Kallendorf finds throughout Landino's mature critical work—the voice which can speak so eloquently of the Florentine love of liberty but which can glide seamlessly into sincere praise for the man who was the virtual ruler of the city and who had forced his compatriots into an alliance with the Milanese tyrant, Francesco Sforza, against the wishes of the Florentine *popolo*.

Placed between poems of praise for Cosimo's conduct of affairs and further descriptions of the Aragonese War itself is the first of the two deeply personal poems in the third book: a eulogy for his brother, killed near Montepulciano (3.4). In it Landino draws on one of the most tender passages in the *Aeneid*—Evander's farewell to his son, Pallas (*Aeneid* 8.560–583)—to illustrate the depth of his own and his family's grief. In it too he employs to great effect a technique he had first used in his poem on the death of Lisa Nuti. By putting most of the poem in the voice of his dying brother, Landino is able to describe a scene he himself never witnessed and to validate his brother's heroism with the latter's own words. The other poem in this book which seems to rise from the poet's heart is the eulogy for Marsuppini, the great humanist, whom Landino calls the "poet-teacher" of Florence (3.7). In this, the longest of his poems, Landino paints a scene of deep civic grief. As the great and near-great of Florence and her allies move in solemn procession behind Marsuppini's bier, the voice of Calliope describes his literary achievements. Finally, Landino himself offers his tribute to the man whose exceptional learning and magisterial ability served as his model. Almost as if he were a Vergil to the Dantesque spirit of his teacher, Landino in words leads the soul of Marsuppini to a joyous welcome by his literary peers in the groves of Elysium, where Dante, Petrarch, Boccaccio, and Bruni, "his own Tuscans," await him in their verdant and secluded spot. As he was to do throughout his teaching career, Landino here fuses the world of the classic Latin writers with that of fifteenth-century Florence and makes the vernacular literature of the latter the natural heir of the great works of republican and Augustan Rome.

As if the poet had now found his public voice, the remainder of the third book is devoted to more formal concerns. A series of epitaphs for great Florentines (and, surprisingly, one on Queen Tamyris) is followed by poems in praise of Cosimo de' Medici as *pater patriae* ("father of his country"), the Acciaiuoli family, and the humanist and manuscript-hunter *extraordinaire* Poggio Bracciolini. The penultimate poem, on the death of Cosimo's little grandson Cosimino, sounds a somber note once more, giving the third book its particularly elegiac cast, as if in saying farewell to his brother, his teacher, and his patron's young grandson, he was also saying farewell to his own youth and to the sense of invulnerability which accompanies it.

The group of poems titled *Carmina varia* are of special interest because, except for one special mention, they contain no reference to the woman who was the centerpiece of his earlier work. Instead, in a series of elegies to Bernardo Bembo, Landino brings to vivid life the passion which Bembo conceived for Ginevra de' Benci, providing a poetical counterpart to the portrait of that remarkable young woman that Bembo commissioned from the young Leonardo da Vinci.[16] Here Landino uses his friendship to direct Bembo's feelings toward platonic, rather than sexual, delights. Here he enacts in his modest verses what he believed was true of all great literature: that it exists to praise virtue and condemn vice.[17] Furthermore, since the function of literature to Landino was to describe a life moving through successively higher virtues toward the *summum bonum*, he seems to be asserting that his humble elegiacs would do their best to conform to that ideal.[18] It is in that spirit of sublimation that the one mention of Xandra occurs. In the sixth poem Landino looks back over the thirty years in which she has been his muse-mistress, and reminds Bembo (Var. 6.21–25) that "if any lover is won by loveliness alone / he's mounting insecurely on an unstable step." But "if anyone loves a noble mind or a keen wit / and a heart filled with a variety of goods, /

he pursues a loveliness which age cannot taint," and arrives through this higher passion at a state in which his love ranks with those described by Homer, Vergil, and Petrarch.

A few other poems follow, including a touching account of the death of Michele Verino, Landino's student and the son of his old friend Ugolino Verino, but the serene beauty of the final poem about Xandra unquestionably marks the true close of Landino's poetic life. All the rest is simply a coda. Xandra's beauty of soul has shone in his heart for "six times five years" and, as he solemnly professes, "this will hold / while my spirit lives, while my memory lasts."

I have been supported in this endeavor by my children and by many friends and colleagues. Professors James Hankins, Craig W. Kallendorf, and E. J. Richards have been particularly generous with information and encouragement. But towering over all have been the unstinting gifts of wisdom, time, and thoughtful concern from my brother, Michael Putnam. I offer this book to him in heartfelt thanks.

NOTES

1. Most important are the works of Cardini, Field, Kallendorf, and Lentzen, for whose works see the Bibliography.

2. On his Latin poetry, see particularly the articles of Charlet, Coppini, La Penna, Murgatroyd, and Tonelli cited in the Bibliography.

3. In this volume the following reference system has been adopted: the *Xandra* is referred to simply by book, poem, and line number, so *Xandra*, Book I, poem I, line 1, is 1.1.1. References to the earlier redaction of *Xandra*, Book I, are preceded by "er," so er1.12.1 is the first line of the twelfth poem in the earlier redaction. References to the *Miscellaneous Poems* are preceded by "Var," and references to the *Doubtfully Ascribed Poems* are preceded by "D."

4. Arthur M. Field, "The *Studium Florentinum* Controversy, 1455," *History of Universities*, 3 (1983): 31–59.

5. Arthur M. Field, "Cristoforo Landino's First Lectures on Dante," *Renaissance Quarterly*, 39.1 (1986): 16–48.

6. Craig W. Kallendorf, "Cristoforo Landino," *Centuriae Latinae*, ed. Colette Nativel (Geneva: Droz, 1997), 478. The entry on Landino in *The Encyclopedia of the Renaissance*, vol. 3 (New York: Charles Scribner's Sons, 1999), 378–80, is also by Kallendorf.

7. Angelo Maria Bandini, *Specimen Literaturae Florentinae saeculi XV in quo . . . Christophori Landini gesta enarrantur* (Florence: Rigaccius, 1747), 218, 229.

8. Alexander Perosa, *Christophori Landini Carmina omnia* (Florence: L. S. Olschki, 1939), 187.

9. Augustus J. C. Hare, *Florence* (London: George Routledge and Son, 1925), 242.

10. Kallendorf, *Centuriae*, 478ff. See also Roberto Cardini, "Landino e Lorenzo," *Lettere Italiane*, 3 (1993): 361, where he describes Landino as "il maggior teorico e critico di quella rifondazione su base humanistico della lingua e della letteratura italiana, che va sotto il nome . . . di 'umanismo volgare'" (the major theorist and critic of that re-establishing, on a humanist foundation, of the language and literature of Italy that goes by the name of 'vernacular humanism').

11. Kallendorf, in *Centuriae*, 478–79.

12. Craig W. Kallendorf, *In Praise of Aeneas: Vergil and Epideictic Rhetoric in the Early Italian Renaissance* (London and Hanover: University Press of New England, 1997), Chapter VI, *passim*. For a brief assessment of Landino's art criticism see Michael Baxandall, *Painting and Experience in Fifteenth Century Italy* (Oxford: Oxford University Press, 1972), 114–115.

13. For the criteria used in editing and dating Landino's poems see Perosa, *Carmina omnia*, xxxvii–lvii.

14. 3.1.1–6. See Propertius 2.1, 3.2–3, 3.9, among other poems where Propertius claims that his style is inadequate for the heroic verse asked of him by Maecenas, but also promises to do his best to celebrate the glories

of Rome. For Landino's role as a reviver of Propertian elegy and as the fountainhead of a tradition of Florentine elegists, see the useful article of D. F. S. Thompson on Propertius in the *Catalogus Translationum et Commentariorum*, ed. V. Brown et al., vol. 9 (Washington, D.C., forthcoming), and the works of La Penna and Coppini cited in the Bibliography.

15. Deborah Parker, "Commentary as Social Act: Trifone Gabriele's Critique of Landino," *Renaissance Quarterly*, 45 (1992): 241. For a full discussion of the myth of the founding of Florence by Sulla's veterans see Giovanni Cipriani, *Il mito etrusco nel rinascimento fiorentino* (Florence: Olschki, 1980).

16. See the articles of Fletcher and Walker cited in the Bibliography and the notes to Var3.

17. Kallendorf, *In Praise of Aeneas*, 133.

18. Kallendorf, in *Centuriae*, 481.

XANDRA

LIBER PRIMUS

: I :

Ad Petrum Medicem

Qui nunc censuram mavult tolerasse legentum
    terna olim potuit lustra latere liber;
namque pudens, gnarusque sui sapienter ineptas
    in lucem nugas noluit ire suas.
5   Nunc tua cum videat geminos per limina fratres
    audere in doctas saepe redire manus,
ipse etiam Medicis se Maecenatis in aula
    sperat honoratum posse tenere locum.
Qui faciam si magna tui clementia suadet
10   tristia ne docti iudicis ora tremat,
si nimium petulans, nimium te, Petre, superbus
    effugit obscurae sordida tecta domus?
Ergo eat: at turbae morsus si quando malignos
    senserit et turpes in sua terga notas,
15   heu, cupiet rursum spretas intrare latebras
    et semel invisos ultro redire lares;
sed si forte sacro felix se fonte lavabit,
    qui fluit e Medica, lucida lympha, petra,
tunc lautus, nigras vertens in candida mendas
20   rumores de se negliget ille malos.

BOOK I

To Piero de' Medici

A book which once hid itself for thrice five years
    now wishes to endure the judgment of its readers;
for, being shy and wisely insecure, it did not wish
    its awkward trifles to come out into the light.
Now because it sees its twin brothers daring often   5
    to go back across the threshold into learned hands,
it too hopes to take an honored place
    in the palace of the Medici Maecenas.
What should I do if your great clemency persuades it
    not to shake at the stern gaze of a learned judge,   10
if too impudent, too proud, it flees to you, Piero,
    from the lowly roofs of a humble dwelling-place?
So let it go: but if it ever feels the spiteful nips
    of the crowd and the marks of shame upon its back,
alas, it will yearn to find the hiding place it spurned   15
    and willingly return to its hated home forever.
But if by happy chance it bathes beneath the blessed spring
    which flows in clear waters from the Medicean rock,
then, washed clean and its dark defects turned purest white,
    it will shrug off the evil whisperings of the crowd.   20

: 2 :

Ad librum

Si te Pierides, vatum si tutor Apollo,
    vivere, parve liber, saecula longa velint,
hos fuge, quos nullo quondam violaverit arcu
    neve suis facibus usserit asper Amor;
5   namque negant veniam tristes qui fronte severa
    censuraque graves mollia verba notant.
Si quis at hamatis transfixus corda sagittis
    pertulerit nostri vulnera cruda dei,
hic veniamque dabit simul et miserebitur ultro
10   nec feret in nostris lumina sicca malis;
nam semel indignas furias expertus amantum
    asseret in terris durius esse nihil.
Praesertim ignoscet nimium iuvenilibus annis;
    semper enim haec aetas digna favore venit.
15   Vertere Gorgoneae nam cum me lumina Xandrae
    in silicem primum sic potuere novam,
ternis addideram lustris vix quattuor annos.
    Nec bene dum noram quid sit amare malum:
quid mirum, telis facibusque armatus, inermem
20   tironem adduxit in sua iura deus.
Vos igitur, nostro quos experientia damno
    admonet in caecos cautius ire dolos,
principiis obstate: licet. Nam fixa medullis
    flamma semel numquam vellier inde potest.
25   Nec lectae prosunt Haemi de montibus herbae,
    Pontica nec magicis gramina cocta focis,
nec quae Dulichiis mutarunt corpora nautis
    carmine Circaeo noxia philtra valent.

: 2 :

To His Book

If the Muses and Apollo, teacher of the poets,
    wish you to live long ages, little book,
flee from those whom the harsh god Love has never
    wounded with his bow or burned with his torches;
for they who, gloomy and severe in their appraisal,   5
    criticize tender words, will refuse you any pardon.
But if a man, his heart pierced by sharp barbed arrows,
    has suffered the bleeding wounds of our god,
he will at once grant pardon and will pity besides
    and not look without moist eyes on my misfortunes;   10
for a man once tried by the ignoble passions of a lover
    will declare that on earth there is nothing harder.
He will forgive much to youthful years especially,
    for through noble favor this age always makes its way.
When first I recognized that the eyes of Xandra,   15
    like a Gorgon's, could turn me to a thing of stone,
I had scarcely added thrice five years to four,
    nor did I know then what an evil it was to love:
what wonder that the god, armed with spear and torch,
    took an unarmed novice under his lawful sway.   20
You, therefore, whom experience warns by my injury
    to venture more carefully into hidden snares,
stand firm from the beginning: it's allowed. For once the fire
    is nailed into your heart, it can never be drawn out.
Herbs gathered from the mounts of Haemus do no good,   25
    nor Pontic plants cooked on witches' hearths,
nor are noxious philters woven with Circean spells,
    which changed the bodies of Ulysses' sailors, of any avail.

Carmina Tartareo Manes Acheronte reducunt,
30   carminibus segetes arva aliena petunt,
carmine montanos redeunt in flumina fontes,
        carmine destituunt sidera noctis iter;
sed licet ipsa suis redeat Medea venenis
        atque addat quicquid Thessala cantat anus,
35   non tamen auratis semel ah, confixa sagittis
        ad sanum posthac corda redire queant.

∴ 3 ∴

Quo tempore amore oppressus sit

Nunc, age, dum tacitae sub nigra silentia noctis
        fundere iam lacrimas vel sine teste licet,
huc Erato duros dum nos solamur amores,
        huc assis, nam tu nomen amoris habes!
5   Hic libet, heu, primae tempus meminisse iuventae,
        cum vacuum tanti pectus amoris erat,
cum poteram totas securus stertere noctes
        et ridere miser si quis amator erat,
necdum turbabant moestum suspiria pectus,
10   ore nec a tristi salsa fluebat aqua.
Heu, quis tunc fueram, quis nunc! An vertere mentes
        ius tibi, proh, tantum, saeve Cupido, datur?
Tu mea servitio pressisti colla nefando
        ut primum dominae vidimus ora meae;
15   nam neque mortalis facies nec lumen in illa
        quale sub humana fronte micare vides,
quod si pace licet, Superi, mihi dicere vestra,

6

Magic has returned dead souls from blackest Acheron;
    through magic, crops have taken root in foreign fields;   30
with magic, streams return to their old mountain springs;
    under magic's spell, the stars will quit their nightly paths;
though Medea herself with her poisons should return
    and add whatever the old Thessalian woman chants,
still, once pierced through, ah! with those gold-tipped arrows,   35
    hearts can never more return to their former health.

: 3 :

When He Was Crushed by Love

Now come, beneath the silence of the dark, wordless night,
    while one may at last without a witness pour out tears,
come hither, Erato, while I ease my remorseless passion;
    come hither, for you have the name of love!
Here willingly one remembers, ah, the days of early youth,   5
    when the heart was free from so great a love,
when I could snore away in security whole nights
    and laugh if some wretched lover was at hand,
while yet no sighs disturbed a saddened heart,
    and salt tears did not besmear a gloomy face.   10
Alas, who was I then, who am I now? Have you the right,
    brutal Cupid, to alter minds so very much?
From the first moment I saw my mistress's face,
    you pressed upon my neck a wicked slavery,
for one sees in her neither mortal features, nor eyes   15
    like the ones that flash from a human face,
and if, by your leave, gods above, I may say this,

visa est caelestes voce preire deas.
Quin et tempus erat quo iam sub vere tepenti
20   pectora nostra solent igne calere novo —
aurea Phrixei nam tum per vellera signi
        maxima lux mundi, sol agitabat equos —
cum sua nascentes depingunt floribus herbae
        prata novis foliis cum viret omnis humus,
25 cum Veneris placidae stimulis excita volucris
        demulcet querulis frondea rura sonis,
cum desiderio tauri concussa iuvenca
        consortem viridis quaerit habere tori,
cumque ovis irrigua nimium lascivit in herba
30   atque gregis sequitur sima capella virum,
omnia cum rident suavi respersa lepore
        et tenet in terris aurea cuncta Venus;
tunc tua me primum certissima, Xandra, sagitta
        fixit et in pectus duxit amoris iter,
35 tunc primum insolitos mens nostra experta furores
        coepit venturis tristior esse malis,
tunc mea libertas miserum me prima refugit
        et coepi duro subdere colla iugo,
tunc primum sensi quae insania verset amantes,
40   sub specie mellis quanta venena latent,
quid sperare queant, quid sit magis usque timendum,
        quae levitas miseros nocte dieque premat.
Ex illo semper maduerunt lumina nobis
        tempore nec gratus venit in ora cibus.
45 Fulmine quid rapido figis fera corda Gigantum,
        Iuppiter? Est maior poena paranda malis.
Quisquis stelliferum contendit scandere coelum
        tentat et in superos bella movere deos,
hic facibus duri subito inflammetur amoris

she seems to surpass the heavenly goddesses with her voice.
Indeed time was when, as the warming spring drew near,
    my heart was wont to glow with newborn heat—   20
for then the sun, greatest of the world's lights, begins
    to drive his horses through Aries' golden fleece—
when the growing plants paint the meadows all with flowers
    while all the earth grows green with new leaves,
when stimulated by the pricks of gentle Venus   25
    plaintive bird-song soothes the leafy countryside,
when the heifer, smitten with yearning for the bull,
    longs to possess the mate of her green bed,
and when the sheep capers wildly in the damp grass,
    and the snub-nosed she-goat stalks the male of the flock,   30
when all Nature laughs, bedewed with sweet charm
    and golden Venus embraces everything on earth;
it was then, Xandra, that your most sure arrow
    first pierced me and made a path for love into my heart;
then first my mind, having suffered this strange madness,   35
    began to grow ever sadder at evils to come,
then did my liberty first flee from wretched me,
    and I began to bend my neck to a hard yoke,
then I first felt how madness whirls lovers round,
    and how much poison hides beneath the honey,   40
why they can hope and they can fear overmuch,
    what inconstancy plagues the wretches day and night.
Since then my eyes have been ever wet with tears,
    and food comes into my mouth tastelessly.
Why pierce the wild hearts of Giants with your swift bolt,   45
    Jupiter? A greater punishment awaits such evils.
Whoever attempts to climb up to the starry heavens
    and aims to make war upon the gods above,
let him be set afire at once by the torches of harsh love

50 et dominae teneat sub iuga colla suae:
tunc sciet Aetnaeos onus hoc anteire labores
  et cupiet potius Pelia saxa pati.

∶ 4 ∶

Ad Bartolomeum Opiscum Scalam

Quaeris cur nostros macies contraxerit artus
  inque dies crescat pallor in ore mihi,
cur placidus miseros relevet non somnus ocellos,
  cur lacrimae a facie fluminis instar eant?
5 Ah nescis quantae vexent mea pectore flammae,
  nec, mi Scala, vides quid sit amare malum.
Quod si te certa deus hic violare sagitta
  coeperit, et faculis urere corda novis,
tunc Tityi duros poteris ridere dolores,
10 vulturis et saevi rostra putare iocos,
Tantaleaeque voles potius succumbere sorti
  oraque Tartarei terna videre canis,
quam semel insano mentem vitiare veneno
  et sentire quibus ignibus urat Amor.
15 In me tela volant, in me sua fulmina taedas
  concutit, inque dies durius instat Amor.
Tu tamen infando nondum, mea Xandra, furori
  succurris: moriar, si mihi lenta venis.
Quae tibi, quae laus est, quae gloria tanta misellum
20 perdere me? Damno stant mihi fata tuo;
quis roseam faciem, quis cygnea colla manusque,
  si peream, vel quis lumina nigra canet?

and let him keep his neck beneath his lady-love's yoke: 50
then he will know this burden beats Etnaean labors
    and will wish rather to endure Pelion's rocks.

: 4 :

To Bartolomeo Scala

You ask why my limbs are shrunken and wasted
    and day by day my face grows ever more pale,
why serene sleep does not relieve my wretched eyes,
    why tears flow down my face like a river?
Ah, you do not know what flames seethe in my breast,   5
    nor do you see, Scala, what an evil it is to love.
But if the god began to outrage you with his sure arrow,
    and burn your heart with unwonted flames,
then you could laugh at the cruel pains of Tityos,
    and think that the savage vulture's beak was a joke,   10
and you would rather suffer Tantalus' fate
    and gaze upon the hell-hound's triple mouths
than damage your mind once with this mad poison
    and experience the fires of burning Love.
Love's spears fly at me, at me he shakes his brands —   15
    his thunderbolts — and each day he hits me harder.
Still, my Xandra, you won't help my speechless passion;
    I shall die if you come to me too late.
What praise or glory do you gain by destroying
    a poor wretch like me? My ruin is your loss;   20
Who would sing of your rosy face, your swan-like neck,
    your hands or your dark eyes, if I should die?

: 5 :

Ad Xandram

Talia si nobis contingant munera, Xandra,
    ceperat Ascraeo qualia monte senex,
non ego, ut ille, soli pinguis mollissima culta,
    nec referam niveae fertile vellus ovis;
5   sed nova tam molli modulabor carmina voce,
    victus amore gravi, tam tibi dulce querar,
Xandra, tuum ut videam gelidum suspiria pectus
    fundere corque simul igne calere meo.
Tunc tua seu rigido quondam praecordia ferro
10   horruerint duro sive adamante licet,
victa tamen precibus tandem sic fatere nostris:
    Hic meus ingenti iam meret esse fide.
Splendida tum varii mutabunt ora colores
    et lacrimae in morem fluminis ore fluent.
15   Hoc mihi si detur, regum confusa valeto
    ambitio et quicquid Persica regna tenent;
nam quid, Xandra, tuae possum praeponere formae,
    dummodo, quod cupio, sit tibi cura mei?
Viderunt nitidas per florea prata Napaeas
20   Naiades et vitreos cum subiere lacus,
at quae tam flavos crines collegit in auro
    spargere vel ventis per sua colla dedit?
Unicus in Veneris resplendet Lucifer orbe,
    qui tamen occiduas, Hesperus, intrat aquas;
25   at dominae nitida si quis sub fronte tuetur
    aspiciet gemini lumina Luciferi.
Nec certet Sidon Sarrani muricis ostro,
    purpureus superet ut sua labra color;

: 5 :

To *Xandra*

If such gifts fell to my lot, my Xandra,
    as the old man received on the mount of Ascra,
I wouldn't tell, unlike him, of farming tenderly
    the fertile soil or the rich fleece of snowy sheep;
but overcome by weight of love, I'd versify new songs   5
    in a tender voice, Xandra, I'd make soft plaint to you,
so that I'd see sighs pouring from your icy breast
    and your heart burning with a fire like mine.
Then, though your breast were inflexible as iron,
    unyielding as adamant, still you would at last   10
confess yourself finally overcome by my prayers:
    This is what my great and loyal trust deserves.
Then varied colors will come and go in your shining face
    And tears like a river will flow down your cheeks.
If this were given me, then farewell, anarchic schemes   15
    of kings and anything the realms of Persia may contain;
for what could I put ahead of your beauty, Xandra,
    as long as (what I yearn for) you care for me?
When they rose up from their glassy pools, the Naiads
    glimpsed the neat wood-nymphs in meadows full of flowers,   20
but who among them binds such tawny hair with gold
    or offers it to the wind to toss along her neck?
Lucifer uniquely shines in the orb of Venus,
    while setting, as Hesperus, in western seas,
But anyone who gazes at my lady's gleaming brow   25
    will see eyes similar to twin Lucifers.
Let not Sidon try with its purple Tyrian shell
    to surpass the rosy color on her lips;

nec putet aequales et densos vincere dentes
30   egregium quamvis India mittat ebur.
Mollius haec cygnis cantat; sed nec sua cygni
     colla tamen Xandra candidiora gerunt.
Quod si quis partes poterit vidisse latentes
     invidiam summo concitet ille Iovi.
35   Haec mea perpetuis exurunt pectora flammis,
     haec eadem vitae dant alimenta meae!
Quis neget hoc monstrum? Sola est in pectore flamma,
     quae vitae causa est, quae mihi causa necis.
Sed monstrum in terris nihil est iam maius amante,
40   nullum natura ius in amante tenet:
solus amans magno misere frigescit in igne,
     aestuat horrenti frigore solus amans!
Ah quotiens stupui cum, crasso in carcere clausus,
     vescerer aethereis, iam salamandra, cibis;
45   obstupui posset propria cum sede revulsus
     spiritus in dominae vivere corde meus.
Prodigiosa fides, et quod ventura iuventus
     confictum falsis iam putet esse iocis,
terrenos artus, quamvis iam spiritus illos
50   liquerit, absenti vivere mente diu.
Ergo animo duplici vivis tu Xandra, meumque
     exanimis vita corpus inane tenet.

: 6 :

Ad Xandram

Xandra mihi tantum quondam crudelis amata
     quantum dilecta est femina nulla viro:
en erit ulla dies qua tu succurrere nobis

nor though India sends its finest ivory should it think
    it can surpass her even, close-ranked teeth.   30
More tender than the swan's are the songs she sings
    but no swan can match the whiteness of her neck.
And if anyone should have seen the parts she hides,
    he would arouse the envy of highest Jove.
These places burn my heart with relentless fire,   35
    yet likewise give me nourishment for life.
Who will deny it's unnatural that in my heart
    a single flame can be the cause of both life and death?
But on earth there's nothing more unnatural than a lover,
    for Nature holds no rights over someone who loves: 40
the lover alone freezes wretchedly in a hot fire,
    in shivering cold, only the lover burns!
How often have I been amazed when, locked in a dark prison,
    I've fed like a salamander on ethereal food;
I have been astounded that, torn from its own place,   45
    my soul could live on in my mistress's heart.
You must trust in marvels (something which youth to come
    might think was fabricated from lying jests),
that earthly limbs, though the breath of life has left them now
    may live long with their mental powers absent.   50
Therefore, you, Xandra, live with doubled soul,
    while soulless life keeps my body empty.

: 6 :

To Xandra

Once cruel Xandra was loved by me
    as no woman ever was loved by a man;
will the day ever come when you would comfort me,

et tumidos fastus ponere, Xandra, velis?
5   Anne ferox cursu semper perstabis eodem
      nec disces animum flectere saeva ferum?
Sed quid me macero, miserum? Sperare quid ultra
      fas puto? Iam subito, iamque puella vale!
Dum licuit tecum felicia tempora vixi,
10   laetitia pleni dumque fuere dies;
nunc vertis mores: ergo et vertenda voluntas.
      Esto quoque. Iam nobis, iamque puella vale!
Te tamen et coeli sanctissima numina testor
      me invitum faciem linquere, Xandra, tuam.
15   Sed tua me feritas moliri talia cogit:
      cedendum nobis. Iamque puella vale!
Ah quotiens flebis misere quotiensque rogabis
      ut redeam lacrimis, insidiosa, tuis.
Sed nil proficies: neque enim tolerare superbos
20   amplius est fastus. Iamque puella vale!

⋮ 7 ⋮

Seni senarii ad imitationem Petrarcae

Iam satis extremo fuerit servisse furori,
dum vigil insomnes poteram perducere noctes.
Sit satis heu frustra tantos tolerasse labores
ni cupiam hanc omnem vitam traducere luctu,
5   postquam sperata privas me, Xandra, quiete
atque iubes tota sic, o, lugere iuventa.

Ah quot nostra tulit, norunt dii, Xandra, iuventa,
quam tu perpetuo vexasti saeva furore!

Xandra, and put aside your swelling pride?
Or will you always stick defiantly to the same course, 5
   savage one, and never learn to bend your fierce spirit?
But why torment my wretched self? Do I think it's right
   to cling to further hope? Now, right now, girl, farewell!
When it was allowed, happy seasons I lived with you,
   and then my days were ever full of joy; 10
now you change your ways: so my will must change as well.
   Let it be also. Now, right now, girl, farewell!
Still, I call to witness you and the holiest gods of heaven
   that I leave your presence, Xandra, unwillingly.
But your ferocity drives me to undertake such measures; 15
   I must give way to you. And now, girl, farewell!
Ah! how often you'll weep miserably, how often ask
   through your tears, you scheming girl, that I return.
But it will do you no good; for I can no longer bear
   your disdainful arrogance. And now, girl, farewell! 20

: 7 :

A Sestina in Imitation of Petrarca

Once it was enough to serve you in the height of passion,
while in my wakefulness I could pass sleepless nights.
It might be satisfactory to have borne in vain such suffering
if I wished to pass my whole life in sorrow and grief,
after you robbed me, Xandra, of any hope of peace 5
and had bidden me thus to grieve, ah, my entire youth.

Ah, Xandra, the gods know how much I endured in youth,
how cruelly you harassed me with everlasting passion!

Ergo quod restat, placidae donare quieti
10　　fas erit, ac reliquas levius producere noctes,
insanum cum sit tam duro tempora luctu
conterere et nulla requie donare labores.

Morte olim tantos placuit finire labores,
atque id fecissem prima, fera Xandra, iuventa;
15　　sed spes semper erat posse hoc tua flectere luctu
pectora: nam numquam duxi talem esse furorem,
qui vel nostra dies vel posset pectora noctes
perdere et aeterna mentem privare quiete.

Sed postquam tecum stultum est sperare quietem,
20　　nec mihi tam duro sunt praemia digna labori,
has statui curae meliori impendere noctes;
quodque pudet prima non perfecisse iuventa,
nunc faciam. Tu, Phoebe, tuo mea corda furore
incute; nam tristes cupio nunc ludere luctus.

25　　Praeteritos referam laeto iam tempore luctus,
te duce, Phoebe. Tuo vati da, Phoebe quietem,
da mentem mihi, Phoebe, novam sanctumque furorem
inspira, ut vanos valeam enarrare labores,
ut nostris edocta malis ventura iuventa
30　　teque, Cupido, dies fugiat, teque, improbe, noctes.

Cur unam de mille mihi saltem, improba, noctem,
qua mihi tam tristes licuisset ponere luctus?
Huic ego praeteritae pensarem dura iuventae
tempora et hanc solam possem preferre quietem
35　　cunctis, quos olim pro te, mea Xandra, labores
excepi, duro correptus corda furore?

Therefore, it will be right to grant to tranquil peace
what remains, and pass unburdened my remaining nights,   10
since it would be madness to waste time in such hard sorrow
and give no reward of rest to my suffering.

Once I would have liked to end by death such suffering
and I would have done it, cruel Xandra, in early youth;
but there was always hope your heart might bend to my   15
    sorrow,
for I never reckoned there could be the kind of passion
that could destroy my heart both by day and night
and deprive my thoughts of everlasting peace.

But since with you it's foolish to ever hope for peace,
and no worthy recompense exists for such cruel suffering,   20
with worthier concerns I've decided to pass my nights;
things it was shameful to leave undone in early youth
I'll do now. You, Apollo, strike my heart with your passion;
for now I long to make poems of my gloomy sorrow.

With you as my guide, Apollo, I'll look back on past
    sorrow   25
in an hour of joy. Apollo, grant your poet peace.
Give to me a new mind, Phoebus, and inspire holy passion,
that I may say farewell to my tale of empty suffering,
that, having learned my lesson of woe, my remaining youth
will flee from you, perverse Cupid, every day and night.   30

Why, perverse girl, was I allowed for just one night
in a thousand to load myself with such miserable sorrow?
For this would I have purchased in my former youth
hard times? Might I not have preferred this lonely peace,
my Xandra, to all I once endured for you in suffering,   35
my heart in the grasp of unrelenting passion?

19

Sed prius Aeolio crescent sub vellere noctes,
atque labor Phoebi poterit sibi ferre quietem,
quam furor aut luctus sinat hanc laetam ire iuventam.

: 8 :

De Alphonso claudo amatore

Tres amat Alphonsus, quamvis sit claudus, amicas;
    sed sunt diversis (hoc dolet ille) locis.
Ambrosii prima est— ut ait— post limina divi:
    pulchra licet, lusco nupta puella seni;
5   in Transarnina spectabis classe secundam,
    inter Carmelos Spirituamque domum;
incola Galphundae nunc tertia, Braccia quondam
    castra sequens, turmis vix satiata decem.
Has ergo octipedis fervent cum sidera Cancri
10   vix una cunctas luce videre potest;
nam mane incipiens dum latum circinat orbem
    vix valet hinc sera nocte redire domum.
Ergo cum venient angustae tempora brumae
    et breve per spatium sol agitabit equos
15   unam sat fuerit sibi tunc si viset amicam
    ire vel intorto desinat ille pede.

: 9 :

De theologo contionatore luxurioso

Insanis totam rumpit qui vocibus aedem,
    pulpita quique manu concutit atque pede,

But the nights shall lengthen under the Aeolian Fleece,
and Apollo's work shall bring its own peace
before passion and sorrow shall admit joy to my youth.

: 8 :

Alfonso, the Lame Lover

Alfonso loves three mistresses, even though he's lame;
    but they are (and this is painful) in different places.
The first, he says, lives behind the church of Sant' Ambrogio:
    She's a pretty girl, though married to a one-eyed old man;
You will spot the second among the Oltr'arno crowd,   5
    between the Carmelite church and Santo Spirito;
the third lives in Galphunda now, but once she was a Braccian,
    a camp-follower, scarcely satisfied by a squadron.
Hence, when the stars in eight-footed Cancer are glowing,
    he can scarcely see all these women in the daylight;   10
for though beginning early in the morning to make his rounds,
    he can barely get back home in the wee hours of the night.
Therefore, when the season of scanty winter comes
    and the Sun drives his horses through a short space of sky,
he must be satisfied to see but one mistress   15
    or give up going round on his twisted foot.

: 9 :

A Dissolute Theological Demagogue

There's a man who shatters the whole church with his ravings,
    and who strikes the pulpit with hand and with foot,

qui furit, exclamat, strepit, intonat omnibus unum
    luxuriae crimen turpius esse ferens;
5   hunc, moneo, vitate virum: licet ore rotundo
    Chrysippi ritu tristia verba cadant.
Nam modo vittatae deprehensus virginis aula
    vix valuit missa carpere veste fugam;
et nisi sublimi quod lapsus fune fenestra est
10   cantanda a pueris fabula nota foret.

: 10 :

Ad Lupum

In Transarnina cunctos se vincere classe
    asserit antiqua nobilitate Lupus:
hoc alii rident cum nec domus ulla paterna
    sit sibi, nec patriam dicere possit avi.
5   Nobilis attamen es; nam tota nullus in urbe
    Bardorum quam tu bardior esse potest.

: 11 :

Ad Bernardum

Ne doleas versu quod epistola nostra secundo
    claudatur, quoniam tu breviora facis!

who rages, shouts, roars and thunders, all to maintain
    that the single sin of lust is the worst of all;
I'm warning you, avoid this man: for, though smooth of   5
      tongue,
    words as gloomy as Chrysippus' pour out of him.
For just now, caught flat in the chamber of a nun,
    he just barely got away, leaving his clothes behind;
and if he'd not slid down from the high window on a rope,
    children would be singing a familiar song about him.   IO

: IO :

To Lupo

In Oltr'arno Lupo swears that he beats everyone
    in his class for his old and noble birth;
everyone else mocks him, since his father doesn't own
    a house nor can he name his grandfather's native land.
Still, you *are* noble, Lupo; for in this city of fools   5
    no one is more distinguished for his foolishness.

: II :

To Bernardo

You shouldn't be sorry because my letter closes
    at the second line, since yours is even shorter.

: 12 :

Ad Aldam

Esse tuum dicis quem dant unguenta colorem,
    Alda. Quod emisti, quis neget esse tuum?

: 13 :

Ad Leonem Baptistam Albertum

Ibis, sed tremulo libelle gressu,
nam cursus pedibus malis negatur;
verum ibis tamen et meum Leonem
Baptistam, Aonidum decus sororum,
5   antiqua Aeneadum videbis urbe.
Quid stas? Quid trepidas, libelle inepte?
Cur non sumis iter? Timesne tanti
forsan iudicium viri subire?
Nil est quod timeas. Legit poetas
10   doctos ille libens salesque laudat
leves et placidos probat lepores;
sed nec raucidulos malosque vates,
quamvis molliculi nihil bonique
candoris teneant, fugit severus:
15   laudat, si quid inest tamen modeste
laudandum, reliquum nec usque mordens
coram carpit opus, bonusque amice
secreta monet aure nigriora,
quae tolli deceant simulque verti

24

: 12 :

To Alda

You say your color is the product of an ointment, Alda.
    Since you've bought it, who'll deny that that color is yours?

: 13 :

To Leon Battista Alberti

You will go, little book, but with tremulous step,
for passage is denied to wicked feet;
still you will go and you will see my Leon
Battista, glory of the Aonian sisters,
in the ancient city of Aeneas' sons.   5
Why do you stop? Why tremble, silly booklet?
Why not take up your journey? Are you afraid
perhaps to submit to the judgment of such a man?
There's nothing to fear. He reads learned poets
with good-will and praises their witty trifles   10
and gives approval to their gentle sallies;
but even harsh-voiced and unlovely writers,
who in their weakness grasp nothing fine or bright
that man's severity does not avoid:
he praises with restraint, if there is aught to praise   15
and never finds fault in public bitingly
with the rest, but good as he is, advises
in friendly fashion in one's secret ear,
which uglier poems ought to be excised

20   albis carmina versibus. Suumque
       non hunc grande sophos decensque lusus,
       quamquam utroque valet nimis diserte,
       non Alberta domus facit superbum:
       cunctis est facilis, gravisque nulli.
25   Hic te, parve liber, sinu benigno
       laetus suscipiet, suisque ponet
       libris hospitulum. Sed, heus, libelle,
       audin, nequitiae tuae memento!
       Quare si sapies severiores,
30   quos ille ingenuo pios pudore
       multos composuit, relinque libros,
       et te Passeris illius querelis,
       doctis sive Canis iocis Hiberi,
       argutae lepidaeque sive Muscae
35   extremum comitem dabis: superque est
       istis si potes ultimus sedere.

: 14 :

Quaerit qua perturbatione sit affectus

Si non vexat amor, quidnam mea pectora vexat?
    Pergite Pierides, dicite quaeso, deae!
Vel mihi, quid sit amor qualisve, referte Camenae,
    si mala tot nobis congerit asper Amor,
5   si dulcis, dulci cur tot permiscet amara,
    dulcia vel qui dat, si sit amarus Amor,
aut mihi si flammae consumunt corda volenti,
    unde igitur nobis tanta querela venit?
Invito vel si comburunt ossa calores

and which turned to neater verses. He does not 20
claim great wisdom or apt wit as his own
though exceedingly accomplished in both;
the Alberti name has not made him haughty:
He is indulgent to all, severe to none.
This man will happily take you, little book, 25
in his kind embrace, and put his little guest
among his own books. But, dear me, little book,
be mindful, do you hear, of your vices!
Wherefore, if you're wise, leave aside the many
pious and overly severe books which he has 30
gathered out of noble self-respect,
and offer yourself as the last companion
to the laments of that Sparrow, or the learned
play of the Spanish Dog, or the amusing
pleasantries of the Fly; it will be enough 35
and more if you can sit the last among these.

: 14 :

He Wonders Why He Feels Such Disquiet

If love does not afflict, why does it afflict my heart?
    Come, goddesses of the Pierian spring, tell me why!
Or answer me, Camenae, what is the nature of love,
    if harsh Love can heap such evils upon me?
If it is sweet, why does it mingle bitter with the sweet; 5
    who gives this sweetness, if Love is bitter?
If flames devour my heart of my own free will,
    whence come my many cries of pain?
If passion consumes my bones unwillingly,

10   quid misero tantum proderit usque queri?
        Talibus, heu, fragili in lembo me fluctibus aequor
           iactat et in scopulos iam ruit ipsa ratis.

: 15 :

Ad Theoplasmam Francisci Castilionensis amicam

Parce, precor, tenero suavique puella poetae,
      Castilionensi iam, Theoplasma, tuo,
nec perdas per quem post fata novissima vives,
      quique tuo faciet te superesse rogo.
5   Hic canet errantes per candida colla capillos,
      sidereos oculos, oscula digna deo,
atque genas roseas, vultum incessumque decorum
      pectora brumali candidiora nive.
Ast ita si miserum pateris, Theoplasma, perire
10   nulla tuo cineri fama futura venit.

: 16 :

Ad se ipsum

Hactenus o lusi, satis est, lasciva Camenae
      carmina, plusque satis me malus ussit amor!
Nunc meliore lyra, divae, meliora canamus,
      nam satis atque super me malus ussit amor.
5   Dicamus coelum, coeli dicamus honores,

what good will it do for a wretch to complain?   10
The sea, alas, tosses my frail craft upon such waves,
   and even now my bark is rushing towards the rocks.

: 15 :

To Theoplasma, Mistress of Francesco da Castiglione

I beg you now, Theoplasma, lovely girl, to spare
   that young and charming poet from Castiglione;
don't destroy the man through whom you'll live forever,
   and who, as your poet, will make you outlive the pyre.
He will sing of the hair straying round your shining neck,   5
   your eyes like stars, your kisses worthy of the gods,
your rosy cheeks, your look and the lovely way you walk,
   and your breasts fairer than the snows of wintertime.
But if, Theoplasma, you let him die thus wretched,
   no future renown will ever come to your ashes.   10

: 16 :

To Himself

Thus far, O Muses, I've played enough with wanton poems,
   and wicked Love has burned me even more than enough!
Now, goddesses, let me hymn better things with a better lyre,
   for wicked Love has burned me enough and more.
Let me tell of heaven, let me tell of heaven's glories,   5

sitque mihi lacrimas promere posse pias.
Et tandem pigeat tantos sumpsisse labores
    in cassum; pigeat paeniteatque mei.

: 17 :

Ad se ipsum

Quid facis infelix? Quidnam Landine miselle
    te iuvat ad flammas addere ligna tuas?
Quid laqueum texis quo mox capiaris et amens
    iam referas dextra vulnera facta tua?
5 Desine iam vanos tibimet nutrire dolores,
    desine iam gratis tanta subire mala.
Pone modum lacrimis et quae deperdita cernis
    perdita iam ducas, paeniteatque tui.

: 18 :

Epitaphium in Leonardum Arretinum

Hic cui frondenti nectuntur tempora lauro
    Romanae linguae dos, Leonardus, erat;
qui Florentini descripsit gesta Leonis,
    transtulit et Latiis dogmata Graeca viris.

and make it so that I can weep godly tears at last.
And make me ashamed to have taken on such sufferings
   in vain; make me both ashamed and penitent.

: 17 :

To Himself

What are you doing, unhappy man? Why, pray, Landino,
   wretch, do you love to add fuel to your fires?
Why do you weave snares by which you soon may be caught,
   and in madness wound yourself with your own right hand?
Give over now this nursing of unavailing sorrow,   5
   give over tolerating such evils for nothing.
Put an end to tears, and what you see has been lost
   call it lost now, and be penitent.

: 18 :

Epitaph for Leonardo of Arezzo

Here lies Leonardo, gift to the Roman tongue,
   whose temples are bound with the laurel ever-green;
he wrote of the deeds of the Florentine Lion
   and translated Greek philosophy for the Latin world.

: 19 :

Ad Xandram

Non ita gavisus Phrixeo vellere Iason
    cum cecidit magico Martia turba sono,
nec pius Aeneas cum iam defessa carina
    tangeret optatos, regna Latina, locos;
5   non ita gavisa est monstris erepta marinis
    Andromade, matris crimine facta rea,
atque ego sum, posito cum post fera proelia bello
    firmavit sancto foedere Xandra fidem.
Nam quibus, heu, curis quantoque urgente dolore
10   hactenus urebat pectora nostra calor,
nec mihi, Xandra, iugum collo exturbare licebat,
    flectere nec lacrimis aspera corda piis.
At nunc iste dies longe felicior omni
    venit, quem nobis lactea gemma notet;
15   candidus iste dies quo tu mitescere nobis
    coepisti et vultu spem meliore dare.
Illa quidem fuerat nox pergratissima Nautae
    qua potuit dominae concubuisse suae,
gratior at nobis et toto carior aevo
20   iste dies fuerit quo mihi laeta redis;
nam tandem risum recipis, vultumque serenas,
    rugaque de tota fronte repulsa fugit,
nec dedignaris nostros audire labores,
    nec potes auditis dura manere diu.
25   Discite, contempti, quantum patientia possit:
    frangitur assidua victa puella prece;

: 19 :

To Xandra

Jason was not as happy with the fleece of Phrixus
    when the martial band fell down at a magic charm,
nor pious Aeneas when his tired boats touched
    at last the longed-for shores of the Latian kingdom;
Andromeda, made to answer for her mother's crime,   5
    was not so happy to be saved from sea-monsters,
as I am, since Xandra made peace after our cruel battles
    and confirmed her good faith with a sacred treaty.
For till now, alas, passion burned my breast
    with such anxiety and insistent sorrow,   10
and I was not allowed to wrench your yoke from my neck,
    Xandra, or to soften your hard heart with loyal tears.
But now that day has come, far happier than any other,
    a day I shall mark with a milk-white stone;
that bright day on which you began to soften   15
    and, with a kindlier glance, began to give me hope.
That night was of all the most delightful to Nauta,
    really, when he could go to bed with his mistress,
but to me more pleasing and dearer than an age
    will be that day that you returned to me in joy;   20
for at last your smile's come back, your countenance is
        clearing,
    and its frown has fled, wholly banished from your face,
and you do not disdain to hear of my sufferings,
    nor can you long remain unmoved by what you've heard.
Learn, abject souls, how much patience can do: 25
    my girl is tamed, conquered by unceasing prayers;

praecipue nostris lacrimis mea Xandra movetur
    et lacrimis victas praebet amica manus.

: 20 :

Ad Philippum de amica

Cum matutine peteres pia sacra, Philippe,
    Luciae venit pulchra Ginevra simul,
nuda pedes, inculta comas, sine lege togata,
    candelasque decem relligiosa ferens.
5   Quae postquam ingressa est ornati tecta sacelli
    effuditque preces ad simulacra deae,
substitit atque vagis oculis, cervice reflexa,
    inter mille viros te studiosa legit.
Inde abitum simulans, ut se coniungat amanti
10   praeteriens tacito te premit illa pede,
atque tuo lateri, turba ut compulsa, cohaerens,
    murmure depresso dixit: Amice, vale!

: 21 :

Ad Lucinam pro partu Xandrae

Ecce dies partus: properat Lucina puellae,
    casta fave, partus; advenit ecce dies!
Ergo laboranti, si vis me vivere, Xandrae
    des, precor, auxilium subveniasque pie.

my Xandra is particularly moved by my tears,
    and in tears offers her hand to be my sweetheart.

: 20 :

To Filippo about his Sweetheart

Early in the morning, Filippo, when you went
    to Lucy's holy rites, fair Ginevra came too,
barefoot, her hair unbound, her clothes all disheveled,
    bearing her ten candles most religiously.
After she had passed beneath the roof of that rich shrine   5
    and poured out her prayers to the image of the saint,
she stood with her neck turned, her eyes wandering about,
    and carefully chose you from among a thousand men.
Then pretending to leave, so that she might meet her lover,
    as she passed by she touched you quietly with her foot,   10
and clinging to your side as if pressed by the crowd,
    she said in a low murmur: Farewell, my sweetheart!

: 21 :

To Lucina on Behalf of Xandra in Childbirth

Now comes the day of birth; Lucina hurries to my girl:
    look with favor on this birth, chaste one. The day is here!
Truly, if you want to keep me living, give Xandra help
    in her labor, please, and relieve her, holy one.

: 22 :

Laudes Dianae

Candidae laudes, age, iam canamus
Musa, Dianae! Nemus illa, Manes
inferos, coelum colit et serenum,
      terna potestas.
5   O Iovis summi decus omne prolis,
virgo, quae fratrem modo nata diva
diligens partu relevas parentis,
      lucida Iuno;
tu suis septem Niobem superbam,
10 ulta Latonam celeri sagitta,
filiis orbas prohibesque matris
      numina temni.
Nec tuos ausus temerare fontes,
cernere et nudas vetito Napaeas
15 lumine Actaeon, meritas refugit
      pendere poenas.
Nunc enim, prisca fugiente forma,
cornibus spargi comites stupebant;
hic sibi notis canibus revelli
20   viscera sensit.
Nulla sed maior tibi, Diva, venit
fama quam per te rudis insolenti
miles in partu, mea magna cura,
      Xandra supersit.
25 Tu meae partus dominae dolentis
mitigas, felix, nimios dolores;
tu sinu natum puerum benigno
      laeta receptas.
Digne nunc tali puer o parente,

36

: 22 :

In Praise of Diana

Come, my Muse, let's now sing praises
to Diana bright! She fosters her grove,
the spirits below, and tranquil heaven,
      a threefold power.
O virgin goddess, glorious offspring of High Jove,   5
you who, scarcely born, lovingly help to deliver
your brother in your mother's own childbirth,
      O Juno, bringer of light;
you deprive proud Niobe of her seven children,
avenging Latona with an arrow swift,   10
and keep the divinity of your mother
      from contempt.
When Actaeon dared to defile your pools
and to cast on your naked wood-nymphs
a forbidden glance, he did not escape from paying   15
      the deserved penalty.
For then, his former shape fleeing, his companions
were startled to see him sprouting horns;
and he felt his organs being torn out
      by his familiar hounds.   20
But no greater fame comes to you, goddess,
than that, through you, my special care, my Xandra,
like an untaught soldier, may survive, although
      unused to childbirth.
Blessed one, soothe the extraordinary pangs   25
of childbed for my suffering mistress;
with joy take her new-born child
      to your kindly bosom.
O child now worthy of such a mother,

30 quem nec alatus superet Cupido,
    sis, precor, matris decus et voluptas
            maxima matris;
    namque tam cunctos roseis labellis,
    candido vultu pueros praeibis,
35 quam parens cunctas superat nitenti
            fronte puellas.

∶ 23 ∶

Ad Bartholomeum Opiscum Scalam

Desine iam leges nostro praescribere amori,
    desine! Solus amor nescit habere modum.
Quis modus aut Myrrhae cum matris adultera facta est,
    aut quis Medeae finis, amice, fuit?
5   Quis modus aut Scyllae cum crinem dura puella
    exsecat infami regna paterna manu?
Solus amor vaccam ligno simulare dolato
    Pasiphen iussit furtaque ferre bovis;
Phyllida solus amor laqueo subnectit amaro,
10   dum tu Demophon fallis inique fidem.
Sed quid foemineos nunc est numerare furores?
    Adiicit hic superos in sua regna deos.
Nec puduit cygnum, paret cui regia coeli,
    induere et plumis spargere membra novis;
15 et crinitus oves ad flumina pavit Apollo,
    ut posset dominae se refovere sinu,
inque iubas abiit magnus Saturnus equinas
    vallibus Idaeis gramina pastus amans.
Nec matri deus iste suae, deus iste, pepercit:

whom winged Cupid may not surpass,   30
may you be your mother's honor, and her
        greatest pleasure;
for you will outdo all other children
with your rosy lips and glowing face,
just as your mother surpasses all young women   35
        with her bright countenance.

                              : 23 :

                         To Bartolomeo Scala

Stop laying down the law now about my love!
    Stop! Love alone knows not how to keep the mean.
Was Myrrha moderate when made her mother's adulterer?
    And what limits did Medea have, my friend?
What restraint did Scylla show when that hard girl   5
    cut the hair, her father's power, with infamous hand?
Love alone bade Pasiphaë to counterfeit a cow
    with hewn wood and take her pleasure of a bull.
Love alone binds Phyllis in its bitter snare
    while you, perverse Demophon, betray her trust.   10
But what now is the point of counting women's passions?
    Love annexes to his kingdom even the gods above.
He whom Heaven obeys was unashamed to become a swan,
    and cover his limbs with new-sprouted feathers;
long-haired Apollo pastured sheep by the rivers,   15
    that he might refresh himself in his mistress's lap,
and great Saturn, in love, vanished beneath a horse's mane,
    and fed upon the grass in the valleys of Mount Ida.
This Love, this very god, did not spare his own mother,

20 illius imperium sensit et alma Venus.
Ah quotiens Paphon, quotiens sua regna Cythera
    deseruit flammis iam calefacta novis!
Et modo Panchaeis demens errabat in agris,
    cerneret ut vultus, pulcher Adoni tuos;
25 et modo Myrrhea requiescens fessa sub umbra,
    pectore fusa tuo basia mille dabat.
Nec visum indignum niveos onerare lacertos
    retibus et duro ducere monte canes,
nec suus a puero poterat divellere conjux,
30 non Mavors, quondam maxima cura sibi.
Quin etiam montes ac turpia lustra ferarum
    praetulerat coelo praetuleratque Iovi.
Omnia formosum propter faciebat Adona:
    tantum nostra valet vertere corda furor!
35 Ergo, Scala, meo leges imponere amori
    desine; solus amor nescit habere modum.

: 24 :

Ad Bartholomeum Opiscum Scalam
de suis maioribus

Inquiris veteres ubi quondam, Scala, penates
    maiores norim composuisse meos.
Non ego Cecropia refero de stirpe parentes,
    nec domus antiquos Iulia praebet avos.
5 Nullus et egregios titulus mihi signat honores,
    quos inhiat laudis ambitiosa sitis.

40

and kindly Venus too felt his imperial power.   20
Ah, how often did she desert Paphos, how often Cythera,
    her own kingdom, heated again with new-made flames!
At one moment she wandered witless in the meadows of
        Panchaea,
    when she saw your face, O lovely Adonis;
at another, resting exhausted in the shade of Myrrha's tree,   25
    stretched upon your breast, she gave you a thousand kisses.
It did not seem shameful to load her snowy limbs
    with hunting nets and lead dogs over the rough
        mountainside,
Not even her husband, not even Mars, once her greatest care,
    could tear her away from that boy.   30
Indeed, she preferred the mountains and the lowly dens
    of wild beasts to heaven, preferred them even to Jove.
She did everything for the sake of her lovely Adonis:
    Such power has passion to transform our hearts!
Therefore, Scala, stop imposing laws on my love;   35
    love alone knows not how to keep the mean.

: 24 :

To Bartolomeo Scala
on His Own Ancestors

You asked me once, Scala, whether I knew where
    my ancestors had set up their household gods.
I do not go back to parents of Cecropian stock,
    nor does the Julian house offer me long-dead forebears.
No title marks me out with splendid honors   5
    which ambitious thirst for praise desires.

Tecta nec e Faesulis spectantur fulta columnis,
    nec regum nobis arca recondit opes.
Tu tamen alma meis priscas, Florentia, sedes
10   Spirituae classis non procul aede locas.
Est vicus Tusci Putei cognomine clarus,
    urbis qui in laevo moenia colle videt:
hic tu Scala meas cernes primordia gentis;
    quamvis parva, tamen hic monumenta patent.
15 Nam licet ex humili populo mea surgat origo,
    casta tamen semper et sine labe fuit;
nec Musis odiosa piis nec inutilis armis,
    nec venit haec patriae dissimulanda suae.
Hoc Campaldinae testantur funera pugnae,
20   tempore quo rubris fluxerat Arnus aquis:
namque huc Landinus, comitatus signa tribulum
    quae velis niveis nigra flagella notant,
sumpserat a proprio non aspernanda tribuno
    munera, dum caeso victor ab hoste redit.
25 Hic avus, o Francisce, tibi cui Musa canora
    arte dedit priscos aequiperare viros,
nec magis Aoniae gaudent Amphione Thebae,
    cum stupeant dulci saxa coisse lyra,
quam tua Tyrrheni soliti per templa, per aedes,
30   organa tam facili cernere pulsa manu.
Lesbous celeres cantu delphinas Arion
    permulsit, vitreas dum rate findit aquas;
at Rhodopes gelidis ducebat montibus ursos
    Orpheus et fulvos per iuga summa lupos.

I have no house held aloft by Fiesolan columns to admire,
    and no coffers hiding the wealth of kings.
For all that, you, dear Florence, put the ancient seat
    of my clan not far from the Church of Santo Spirito.   10
There is a famous quarter called the Etruscan Well,
    which looks out on the city walls from the left-hand hill.
Here, Scala, you can see the origins of my people;
    though small, their memorials are still evident here.
For though my descent derives from humble folk,   15
    yet it was always pure and incorrupt;
not averse to the holy Muses nor vain in arms,
    nor did it need to be disguised to my native land.
Their deaths in the battle of Campaldino attest to this,
    that time when the Arno flowed with blood-red waters: 20
for there a Landino, standing guard by his tribesmen's flag,
    which showed black whips drawn upon a snowy ground,
received from his own tribune gifts not to be despised
    when he returned victorious from the slaughter of the foe.
Here the Muses gave you, O my forefather Francesco,   25
    the skill to equal those men of old in artful song.
Aonian Thebes did not delight more in Amphion when,
        amazed,
    it saw rocks join together at his sweet lyre's sound,
than when in their shrines and churches the Tuscans once
        used
    to hear the organ played by so accomplished a hand.   30
Arion from Lesbos soothed with song the racing dolphins,
    while he cut through the green sea-waters in his boat;
while Orpheus led bears through the cold mountains of
        Rhodes
    and tawny wolves through their highest ridges.

35 Sed neque per silvas, neque per freta dulcius illo
        hactenus audisse iurat Apollo melos;
    quin et adoptiva Musam de stirpe parentem
        retulit et Musis dignus alumnus erat.
    Sed simul, heu, nulli superi Dii cuncta dedere,
40   nullus et ex omni parte beatus erit.
    Nam qui Sirenas superabat voce canoras
        damnata aeterna lumina nocte tulit.
    Non quia sic meritus fuerit: sed noscite quanta
        invidia livor infera regna premat.
45 Est inter Stygias Phthone deterrima nymphas
        tempora cui multus oraque pallor obit.
    Hanc pater et Stygiae Phthonem dixere sorores
        invida quod tristi fronte secunda videt.
    Haec patrias primis tenebras iam liquit ab annis,
50   ausa per excelsas aetheris ire plagas;
    namque potest hominum res si turbare secundas
        tunc fruitur proprio nympha maligna bono.
    Ergo forte trium perscrutans fata sororum
        audierat Lachesis talia voce dari:
55 Nascetur Faesula Franciscus origine tali
        Dircaeum quali vidimus arte Linum.
    Protinus tumuit dea saeva suisque
        supplicibus Clothon vocibus alloquitur:
    O dea, nam nulli vitae sub lumen ituro
60   te sine mortali ianua prima datur;
    Castalii quae sacra colunt Heliconides antri
        iam mira cupiunt arte parare virum.
    Et cupiunt et tanta illas fiducia cepit
        ut sibi, vel sine te, cuncta licere putent.
65 At tu ne quisquam quondam tua numina temnat,

But Apollo swears that he never heard any song,   35
    either in forests or on the sea, more sweet than his;
indeed, he counted a Muse as his ancestor, of his adoptive
        stock,
    and he was a worthy foster-child of them all.
But, alas, the gods above have given to no one all things
    at once, and no one shall be blessed in all respects.   40
For he who surpassed the melodious Sirens with his voice
    had eyes condemned to eternal night.
Not that he had deserved it; but you know how much
    envious spite seethes in the kingdoms of hell.
There is among the Stygian spirits the wicked Phthone   45
    whose ghastly pallor covers her face and brow.
Her father and her Stygian sisters so called her, since
    her gloomy face looks enviously on fortunate things.
From her earliest years she left her father's shadows
    and dared to travel the lofty regions of the upper air;   50
and if she can upset good fortune in human affairs
    then that malicious spirit enjoys her proper good.
Hence by chance, while searching the Three Sisters' fates,
    she had heard this proclaimed by Lachesis' voice:
"Francisco of Fiesolan descent will be born   55
    with such art as we saw in Linus the Theban."
Straightway the savage goddess swelled with rage
    and called to Clotho in a pleading voice:
"O goddess, without you the first passage for any mortal
    about to enter the light of life is never given;   60
those who dwell upon Helicon and adore the Castilian cave
    desire now to equip a man with marvelous skill.
They yearn for it, and they've become so confident that
    they think they'll be allowed all things, with or without
        you.
But lest anyone ever should despise your godly power,   65

ne lateat possit quid tuus orbe furor,
illius alterna damnabis lumina nocte:
    sit Linus, ut iactant, dummodo caecus eat.
Hac olim Thamyrim poena afflixere Camenae,
70   certaret cantu cum superare deas.
Hac nunc illarum poena afficiatur alumnus,
    sic tua qui spernat numina nullus erit.
Dixerat et partus maturi venerat hora
    atque tuam mater, Parca, petebat opem.
75 Ergo ades et puero reseras dum limen, adempta
    aetheris in lucem luce venire iubes.
Non tamen Aoniae caecum sprevere puellae,
    nec puduit molli saepe fovere sinu.
Musarum silvis, Musarum montibus olim
80   lusit, Musarum captus amore puer.
Quin et Pierias, Phoebo ducente, per umbras
    audivit sacros ex Helicone choros;
audivit varia modulantes voce sorores:
    haec ore, haec tibiis, concinit illa fide.
85 Atque hic disparibus nato distincta cicutis
    organa porrexit Calliopea suo,
atque ait: Ausonias, sume haec, i nate per urbes,
    i nostras laudes, nostraque facta cane.
Tanta hic carminibus tibi gloria surget Etruscis,
90   Thraicii quanta carmine vatis erat.
Nam mire Tusco vivens celebraberis Arno,
    Lydia qua fulvus temperat arva leo.
Nulla dies sacrum poterit subducere nomen,
    sed tua post maior funera crescet honos.

  lest it be hidden how your rage can harm the world,
you shall condemn his eyes to successive night;
  let him be Linus, as they boast, as long as he walks blind.
Once the Camenae inflicted this punishment on Thamyris,
  when he vied to surpass those goddesses in song.   70
Now inflict the same chastisement on their foster-child,
  so there will never be anyone to despise your divinity."
She spoke, and the proper time for his birth arrived
  and his mother began to ask for your help, Goddess Fate,
You come, therefore, and opening the doorway for the child,   75
  you bid him come into the light, robbed of light.
Yet the Aonian maidens did not reject the blinded boy,
  nor did they blush to hold him often to their tender
      breasts.
Seized by love of the Muses, the child frisked and played,
  now in their forests, now in the Muses' mountains.   80
Apollo his guide, he heard among the Pierian shades
  the holy songs that come, too, from Mt Helicon.
he heard the sisters making music in measure to varied
      sounds;
  this one with her voice, with a flute this other, that with a
      lyre.
And then Calliope held out an organ to her child,   85
  fashioned with hemlock pipes of unequal lengths,
saying: "take this, child, and go throughout Italy's towns,
  go sing our praises, go sing of our deeds.
Glory will shine round about you for your Tuscan songs
  as great as came to the Thracian poet through his.   90
For living by the Tuscan Arno, where the tawny lion holds
      sway
  in the Lydian fields, you will be splendidly celebrated.
No time will ever take away the reverence for your name,
  and after your death your honor will grow greater still."

95 Nec mater de te quicquam mentita: suisque
  egregiam verbis facta tulere fidem.
Namque Fluentini solus dum cantibus aedem
  pontificis celebras, Tuscia tota ruit;
teque rudes doctique simul, iuvenumque senumque
100 pectora divinis obstupuere sonis.
Sed nec tu fueras una contentus in arte
  cum posses veterum dogmata nosse patrum.
Nam solers rerum causas penitusque repostae
  naturae occultas tendis inire vias;
105 et quod terrenis oculis vidisse negatum est
  cernere mente parens Calliopea dedit.
Iamque tuum nomen duras transcenderat Alpes
  oraque complerat trans freta longa virum.
Quin et marmoreo moriens donare sepulcro,
110 quod nunc Laurenti templa vetusta tegunt;
templa tegunt quae mox Cosmus suffulta columnis,
  fornice sublimi conspicienda dabit.
Tunc licet aurato niteant laquearia tecto,
  et Faesulus multa splendeat arte lapis,
115 non tamen e media quoquam removeberis aede,
  nec volet hoc, doctis qui favet ingeniis;
nam favet ingeniis Cosmus quin luce carentum
  inviolata loco busta manere iubet.
Aeternum, Francisce, igitur per saecula vives,
120 et tuus Elysium spiritus arva colet.
Sed nec degeneres referet tibi fama minores,
  nullaque de turpi posteritate nota est.
Nam tibi germanus fuerat, cui cara nepotem
  progenies magna non sine laude dedit;
125 nam Gabriel quem sorte sua Camaldula legit

About you my mother never lied: and your deeds have shown   95
   the special trust that her words are due.
For when you alone made the cathedral church of Florence
   famous for its music, all Tuscany rushed to hear you;
and the ignorant and the learned, the hearts of young and old,
   were amazed at you and your heavenly sounds.   100
But you were not content with just one art,
   when you could also learn the creeds of the men of old.
For in your cleverness you strove to explore deeply
   the causes of things and the hidden ways of abstruse
      nature.
And because to see with earthly eyes was denied you,   105
   your parent Calliope gave you the gift of mental sight.
And now your fame had crossed beyond the cruel Alps
   and had filled the mouths of men across distant seas.
And indeed at death you are given a marble tomb,
   which the ancient church of San Lorenzo now enfolds;   110
that church encloses it which Cosimo will soon give,
      supported
   by columns and remarkable for its lofty vaulting.
Then, though a coffered ceiling shine beneath a golden roof,
   and Fiesolan marble gleam with abundant skill,
yet you'll not be moved from the center of the building,   115
   nor would he who is patron of learned minds wish for that;
for Cosimo, who shows favor to minds that are lacking sight,
   orders that your tomb remain in its place untouched.
And so, Francesco, you will live on through the ages,
   and your spirit will dwell in the Elysian fields.   120
Fame will bring you no unworthy descendants,
   and no baseness will brand your posterity.
For you had a brother, whose dear offspring
   gave him a grandson who is not without great praise.
For Gabriele, whom the Camaldolese Order,   125

Relligio, niveis conspicienda togis,
Ambrosio primos nutritus lacte per annos,
    roscida Gorgoneis antra subivit aquis.
Hinc fidibus proceres coeli laudavit et illos,
130   militiam summi qui meruere Dei,
qui nobis patriam, pro Christo vulnera passi,
    sanguine divinam iam peperere suo;
mox dum Parrhasiae, Pisano in litore, gentis
    victa Fluentino moenia Marte canit,
135   ante expectatum, iuvenilibus obrutus annis,
    deserit heu quanto proelia coepta pede.
Sic nobis, Gabriel, prima fraudate iuventa,
    complesti luctu saucia corda gravi;
nam tibi me Musae, tibi me patruelis origo
140   iunxit et ex uno sanguine ducta domus.
Tu me Musarum magno inflammatus amore,
    Cirrhaei impuleras scandere celsa iugi.
Te duce Permessi liquidas ad fluminis undas
    venimus et sacro tinximus ora lacu.
145   At nunc si Phoebus velit aspirare canenti,
    magnorum ut possim dicere facta virum,
si qui rauca canit gracili nunc carmina plectro,
    intonet altiloquo maior in ore sonus:
Cosmus et egregii cernent me pignora Cosmi
150   a patribus nusquam degenerasse meis.

notable for its white robes, chose for its portion,
fed on Ambrosian milk from his earliest years
    and entered caves dewy with the Gorgon's waters.
Hence he praised on the lyre those princes of heaven
    and those who have deserved knighthood from God on   130
        high,
who, having suffered wounds for Christ's sake,
    have begotten a heavenly country for us through their
        blood;
then, on the Pisan shore, while he was singing of the walls
    of the Arcadian people conquered by Florentine Mars,
long before the expected time, destroyed while still a youth,   135
    he left the battle, alas, which he had entered with such a
        stride.
So, Gabriele, stolen from us in the bloom of young manhood,
    you filled our stricken hearts with heavy sorrow;
still, the Muses have joined me to you, and patrilinear descent,
    and our house, derived from a single bloodline.   140
Fired by a great love of the Muses, you drove me
    to scale the heights of the mountains above Cirrha.
With you as my guide we reached the clear waters
    of the river Permessus, bathing our faces in its sacred pool.
But now if Apollo wishes to inspire his singer,   145
    so that I might tell the deeds of famous men,
if a greater sound shall thunder from the lips sublime
    of him who now sings rough songs to a slender lyre:
Cosimo and his remarkable offspring will perceive
    that I have never sunk below my ancestors.   150

: 25 :

De Xandra

Nunc virent silvae, nemus omne frondet,
ridet et tellus variisque frontem
floribus pingit, fugiuntque nubes
       montibus altis.
5   Naiades laetas agitant choreas
Gratiis passim Satyrisque mixtae
et comas flavas religant corona
       versicolore.
Concidunt venti, levis afflat aura;
10 parcit atque haedis lupus et capellis,
nostra dum celsas Faesulas frequentat
       candida Xandra.
Nunc suos tristis Philomena luctus,
immemor stupri simul et nepotis,
15 ponit et versus modulans sonoros
       cantat amores.
Gaudet et fructu segetis colonus
horreum quaerens ubi farra condat,
gaudet et Baccho nimium feraci
20   vinitor uvae.
Hos tamen montes mea si relinquat
Xandra, si Tuscae revocetur urbi,
arbores siccas videas et ipsa
       flumina sicca.

: 25 :

About Xandra

Now the forest grows green, now every grove is in leaf,
the earth laughs and paints its face
with many-colored flowers, the clouds take flight,
   from the high mountains.
The Naiads perform their happy dances   5
mingling everywhere with the Graces and Satyrs,
and they tie back their golden hair with
   parti-colored garlands.
Rough winds retire, light breezes blow;
the wolf spares both kids and goats,   10
as long as bright Xandra is visiting
   the heights of Fiesole.
Now the sad nightingale, heedless of her shame
and of her nephew, puts aside her grief,
and fashioning tuneful measures   15
   sings of love.
The farmer, seeking out a barn where he may store
his grain, delights in the fruits of his field,
and the vinedresser delights exceedingly in the
   strong wine from his grapes.   20
Still, if my Xandra should leave these hills,
if she is called back to the Tuscan city,
you would see the trees stand parched and
   the very streams run dry.

: 26 :

Ad Ginevram

Flavis crinibus aureisque pulchra
et nigri oculis, gena nitenti,
et tota facie nimis superba,
incedis tetrico, Ginevra, vultu.
5   Et nostras tibi cura nulla flammas
est restinguere, nec meo dolori
succurris, nimis ah nimisque saeva!
Sed fastus inimica saepe duros
opponis mihi saevior leaena,
10   quam caris catulis modo repertis
venator Libyca ferox harena
orbavit, paterisque me iacere
una pervigilem alterave nocte,
duro in limine, dum tuos recludi
15   postes auguror et tuum, Ginevra,
adventum nimio moror periclo.
At tu, si libuit venire tandem,
postquam septima iam hora praeterivit
accedis, neque postibus reclusis;
20   sed mecum bene tuta per fenestram
aeratam loqueris mihi, satisque
factum si semel auream papillam
et pectus niveum simul gulamque
pulchram tangere vel manu sinistra
25   magno contigerit labore credis,
aut si levibus osculum labellis
impressi tibi, tu cito reclamas.
Ah quanti sibi Gabriel beatas

: 26 :

To Ginevra

Lovely with your tawny-gold hair,
your dark eyes, and your glowing cheeks,
and over-proud of your whole appearance,
you walk, Ginevra, with a frowning face.
And you are utterly unconcerned   5
to quench my flames, nor to succor me
in my pain — ah, too, too cruel!
No, your hard arrogance blocks me often,
hostile, fiercer than a lioness
whom a savage hunter orphans of her cubs,   10
coming upon them in the Libyan desert;
and you suffer me to lie awake
one night after the next, awake
on your hard doorstep, while I take
the auguries for your doors to open,   15
and await your coming in reckless danger.
But if it has pleased you to come at last,
after the seventh hour has passed,
you arrive, and still the doors are latched;
but you speak to me in perfect safety   20
through a casement bound in bronze;
and if just once I could touch, what satisfaction!
your gleaming nipple and your snow-white breast
or your lovely throat, even with my left hand,
you think this would cost you a lot of effort;   25
if I kiss your soft lips, you quickly call out.
Ah, how costly are the kisses Gabriel
now buys for himself — those beatific kisses! —

istas nunc emat osculationes,
30 cui numquam digitum mihi minorem
attrectare semel fuit potestas!
Verum si tibi flavuli capilli,
auro qui similes modo refulgent,
in canos abeant, Ginevra, crines;
35 dentes si niveos eburneosque
liventes maculae nigraeque fuscent;
vel nunc qui roseis genis nitentes
vernant multiplici decore flores
perdat stridula conteratque bruma;
40 si testudineo peraequa collo
cervix cygnea fiat atque suci
plenas turgidulasve si papillas
nutricis similes geras papillis,
sulceturque frequentibus misellus
45 venter partubus utribusque fiat
rugosis similis malumque plenis;
totum denique si tibi maligna
quod nunc luxuriat suo nitore
corpus conficiat situ senectus,
50 heu quantis lacrimis quibusve, demens,
flebis spreta modis, amante nullo
iam te respiciente. Tunc equarum
te vexabit, anum, furens libido,
et circa iecur, usque saeviendo
55 flagrans crescet amor, tibique nullus
turpem subveniet timens senectam.
Demum tunc, posita ferocitate,
ultro nos, nimis ah nimisque supplex,
accedes placidaque voce quondam
60 noctes reddere mi voles negatas.

from her who never gave me once
the right to touch her little finger!   30
But if you still have shimmering hair
which still as yet gleams back like gold,
may it turn, Ginevra, to locks of grey;
if your snow-white, ivory teeth
darken with spots, discoloring and black,   35
if shrieking winter bruise and kill
the flowers that with manifold grace grow fresh
as they shimmer in your rosy cheeks;
if your swan-like neck becomes
like that of a tortoise, and if your breasts   40
should grow swollen and full of milk
just like those a wet-nurse has,
and if your poor little belly is stretched
by frequent childbirth and becomes
like a leather bag, wrinkled, full of evils;   45
if at last spiteful old age shall waste
with decay your whole body, which now
is flourishing in its splendor — alas!
with how many tears, foolish woman, shall you weep,
when no lover then even looks at you.   50
Then shall the lust of mares torment you,
an old woman, and burning love will grow,
raging all around your liver,
and to help you no one will come,
fearing the shame of your old age.   55
Then, at last, your ferocity laid aside,
very much the suppliant — oh yes! —
you will come to me of your own accord,
and with gentle voice say how you wish
to give back those nights you once denied me.   60

: 27 :

De reditu Xandrae

Corve quid dextrum crepitante rostro
mi latus stringis celerique penna
cur feris nostros humeros sinistrum
      garrula cornix?
5   Cernimus? Vel qui misere premuntur
semper a duro nimioque amore,
dum suis curis cupiunt mederi,
      somnia fingunt?
Cernimus certe: redit ecce nobis
10 rure materno, mea magna cura,
Xandra. Nunc omnis timor atque tristis
      luctus abito!

: 28 :

Ad Xandram

Maxima pars nostri, pulcherrima Xandra, doloris,
    qua sine nec Croesi regia tecta velim,
quando tuam faciem nullo prohibente licebit
    aspicere et coram mitia verba loqui?
5   Namque tuo postquam invitus sum, Xandra, revulsus
    aspectu, semper vita molesta fuit.
Nec mihi cura cibi, placidae nec cura quietis
    sed lacrimae tantum pocula nostra parant;
nec blandi comites durum lenire dolorem,

: 27 :

On Xandra's Return

Raven, why do you peck at my right side
with your rattling beak, and why do you
strike my left shoulder with your swift wing,
      talkative bird?
Do I see her? Or am I like those who are ever wretched   5
and oppressed by too much love and harsh,
who, wishing to be cured of all their cares,
      invent fantasies?
I see her for sure: Look! she's coming back to us
from her mother's country place, my one great care,   10
my Xandra. Away with you now, every fear
      and all gloomy sorrow!

: 28 :

To Xandra

Greatest part of my pain, most lovely Xandra,
   without whom I'd not want the palace of Croesus,
when shall I be allowed to look — no one gainsaying it —
   upon your face and speak soft words in your presence?
For after I was torn from your sight, all unwilling,   5
   life has ever been a burden to me, Xandra.
I have no desire for food, and none for tranquil calm,
   and my cups are filled with tears alone;
No charming companions can soothe my dire pain,

10   altera nec, quamvis pulchra, puella potest.
        Ah quotiens totas insomnes ducere noctes
           cogimur et curis invigilare tuis!
        Et nunc qui vultus, quae sit tibi gratia formae
           nunc memini, qualis rideat ore nitor,
15   sideribusque oculos similes et cygnea colla
           et niveum pectus, pectora nostra domans.
        Et memini cantum quo se pulcherrima victam
           non, modo sit verax, Calliopea neget;
        et memini in numerum soleant ut mollia crura
20   ludere et in girum molliter ire pedes.
        Omnia quae memori monitus dum mente retracto
           materiam, infelix, ignibus addo meis.
        Sic infelices nostros nutrimus amores,
           gaudia praeteriti dum meminisse iuvat,
25   inque dies crescunt flammae penitusque medullas
           exurunt: roseus deserit ora color.
        Pallentemque utinam faciem nunc cernere possis,
           quantaque mi macies squalida membra notet!
        Sed quamvis multae vexent mea pectora curae,
30   unum est quod doleam, candida Xandra, magis;
        vidi ego saepe: novis veteres tolluntur amantes,
           et longinqua minus flamma caloris habet.
        Non tamen hoc timeo tibi vel quia mobile pectus
           vel precibus vinci muneribusve putem;
35   namque hoc magna Venus novit, Venerisque Cupido,
           te nihil in casta sanctius esse fide.
        Nullus nec donis turpi te subdet amori,
           quin sis perpetua nota pudicitia.
        Auratis non te vincet Pactolus harenis,
40   divite non quicquid devehit amne Tagus.
        Sed tamen, heu fateor, timeo: licet ipsa timoris

nor can another girl, however lovely. 10
Ah, how often am I driven to pass whole nights
    awake, sleepless in my anxious care for you!
Now I recall your face, your grace of figure,
    now the glow that laughs upon your brow,
your eyes like stars, your swanlike neck, 15
    your snowy breast that masters my heart.
And I recall your song by which most lovely Calliope,
    if she were truthful, would admit herself bested;
and I remember how in the dance your supple legs
    played, and your feet moved smoothly round and round. 20
While I turn all this over in my remembering mind,
    wretch that I am, I add fuel to my flames.
Thus I feed my unfortunate love,
    and I enjoy recalling the pleasures of the past,
and day by day the growing flames burn down to my marrow 25
    and my rosy complexion has abandoned my face.
I wish that you could see my wan features now,
    and how gauntness marks my wasted limbs!
But although many cares harass my heart,
    there is one that grieves me more, bright Xandra; 30
I have often seen old lovers tossed away for new,
    and how a distant flame gives off less heat.
Still, I don't fear this from you, thinking your heart
    inconstant, or conquerable by gifts and prayers;
for Great Venus knows, and Cupid, Venus's son, 35
    that no one in chaste fidelity is more pure.
Let no one enthrall you to a base love with gifts;
    may you be distinguished by enduring modesty.
The Pactolus will not conquer you with its golden sands,
    nor anything the Tagus may carry down in its rich waters. 40
But still, alas, I must confess I fear: the cause,

vana sit, est tanti causa timoris amor.
Quod te per sanctum carae genitricis amorem
    et per germanam, quae tibi dulce caput,
45 perque meas lacrimas, lacrimis oculosque madentes,
    et tua per geminas lumina clara faces,
Xandra precor, nostri veniat non immemor hora,
    ulla tibi maneat non temerata fides,
Landinumque tuum memori sic mente reponas,
50   ne subeat pectus cura secunda tuum.

: 29 :

Ad Bernardum

Dum tu grandiloqui divina volumina Tulli
    pellegis et quicquid Quintilianus habet,
dumque genus causae dubium variosque colores
    et discis quae sint arma ferenda reis,
5 vel si quando iuvat mentis seponere curas —
    nam permixta licet seria ferre iocis —
ad Lisam properas: Lisa est tibi sola voluptas,
    dimidium vitae, candida Lisa, tuae.
Illa quidem nitidis placide te aspectat ocellis,
10   felicem risu te facit illa suo;
saepeque per rimam furtim tibi verbula dictat,
    tangendam furtim porrigit illa manum;
nos procul a nostra, dulcis Bernarde, puella
    cogimur insani discere iura fori.
15 At si quando vacat, cum turba molesta quievit,
    litibus et scissis omnia clausa silent,
protinus ad nostras avidus me confero Musas,

though baseless, is love, the cause of so much fear.
Because I beg you, Xandra, by the blest love
    of your dear mother, by your sister, whose life
is dear to you, by my tears, my eyes wet with tears,   45
    and by those twin fires, your bright eyes,
may the hour never come when you forget me,
    may your faithfulness remain unblemished,
and may you so keep your Landino in your memory
    that no lesser love may steal into your heart.   50

: 29 :

To Bernardo

While you are poring over the heavenly tomes
    of the orotund Cicero and Quintilian's riches,
and are learning ambiguous cases and specious pleas
    and what arms may be borne against the accused,
if you ever find pleasure in setting aside your worries —   5
    for it is permissible to mingle serious things with fun —
hurry off to Lisa: Lisa is your only pleasure,
    fair Lisa is one half your life.
For she looks at you calmly with her shining little eyes,
    she makes you happy with her smile;   10
often through a narrow cleft she stealthily chats with you
    and stealthily stretches out her hand to be touched;
while my girl compels *me* from afar, sweet Bernardo,
    to learn the laws of the lunatic forum.
But if ever I am free and the noisome crowd grows quiet,   15
    and all the documents of divisive lawsuits fall mute,
immediately I betake myself hungrily to my Muses,

quarum immortali pulsus amore feror.
Tum me Parnasi stupidum per devia montis
20   raptat honorati turba canora lacus,
et levibus contexta modis mihi carmina dictat,
    atque iubet sumpta ponere moesta lyra.
His nos Xandrinum studiis solamur amorem,
    his desiderium, Xandra, rependo tuum.
25 Tristibus atque elegis insanos ludimus ignes,
    et resonat Xandram pagina tota mihi.
Illam me Phoebus prima sub luce canentem
    invenit et seras cum subit udus aquas.
Nec tantum Eurydices discessu fleverat Orpheus
30   cum peteret Stygios icta dracone lacus,
quantum ego nunc a te spatio diductus iniquo,
    Xandra; sed hic magno grandius ore sonat.
Quippe ferunt vires Musae spiratque furorem
    divinum nato Calliopea suo;
35 et dat carminibus saevos mollire leones,
    Pangaeoque feros ducere monte lupos.
At me Castalio dignata est nulla sororum
    fonte, nec Aonium tangere passa nemus.
Ergo sic rauco dicemus pectore laudes,
40   Xandra, tuas, doctum quae meruere Linum.
Dicemus tamen: et quod nobis invida non dat
    natura, ingenium, tu mea Xandra dabis.

: 30 :

Ad Iohannem Antonium

Prime nostrorum comitum, Iohannes,
sive tu collem fluvio imminentem

and by immortal love of them I am driven and borne.
Then the tuneful throng of the celebrated pool carries me off,
    stunned, through the byways of the Parnassian mount   20
and repeats to me songs woven of effortless rhythms,
    and bids me put aside gloomy subjects, taking up the lyre.
With these studies I find solace for my love of Xandra,
    Xandra, with these I requite my longing for you,
With sad elegiacs I deceive my raging fires,   25
    and my every page echoes back my Xandra to me.
Phoebus finds me singing of her as the day first dawns
    and when he slips dewily beneath the evening sea.
Orpheus did not weep so much at Eurydice's departure
    when, struck by a snake, she sought the Stygian pool,   30
as I now do, separated from you by unjust distance;
    — though *he* sings of larger things with ampler voice.
Indeed, the Muses bring *him* strength and Calliope
    breathes divine frenzy into her son;
and she gives *him* power to gentle lions with his song,   35
    and to lead wild wolves through the mountains of Thrace.
But none of the sisters has deemed me worthy
    of the Castalian spring nor let me reach the Aonian grove.
So thus I sing your praises from my untutored heart,
    Xandra, you who deserve the learned Linus as your bard.   40
Still, I sing them: and the inspiration which envious nature
    will not gives me, you, my Xandra, shall.

: 30 :

To Giovanni Antonio

Giovanni, first among my companions,
whether you are visiting Poppi's hill which looms

Puppii, dulcem patriam, frequentas
    laetaque rura,
deque vinetis volucres propinquis
5   retibus pingues recipis dolosis,
et cani suades leporum fugacem
    vincere cursum,
sive te magnus remoratur urbis
ardor Etruscae, comitumque laetus
10   detinet sermo, faciesque pulchra
    dulcis Horectae;
oro, si nostri manet ulla cura,
si tuus non me fugit omnis ardor,
redde me certum, valeasne nostri
15   numquid amici.

: 31 :

Ad Leandram

Misisti mentam, credo, hac ratione Leandra,
    ut caperes nostra tu quoque dona manu.
Ast ego muneribus vincam te, namque virenti
    nunc tibi pro menta mentula nostra venit.
5   Nam mage ruta licet quam rutula cara puellae est,
    mentula quam menta carior esse solet.

: 32 :

Ad Anastasium

Dicis, Anastasi, nostros te optare libellos,
    et mea vis posita carmina adesse mora.

over the river, our precious native town,
    and the rich countryside,
and are catching fat birds from the neighboring   5
vineyards in cunning snares,
and encouraging your dog to surpass
    the swift flight of the hare,
or whether your great love of the Tuscan city
detains you, and the happy talk of comrades   10
holds you back, and the lovely face
    of sweet Oretta,
I beg you, if any regard for me is left,
if all your affection has not abandoned me,
please let me know — are you not well,   15
    my friend?

: 31 :

To Leandra

You sent me mint, Leandra, for this reason, I believe,
    that you might also take gifts from my hand.
But I shall surpass you in gifts, and in exchange
    for your fresh mint, my prick will come to you.
For though girls like a big rue-plant more than a small one   5
    they usually like the little mint more than the big one.

: 32 :

To Anastasio

You tell me, Anastasio, that you want my little books,
    and you'd like my poems to come to you without delay.

Dispeream versus cupiam ni mittere: at illi
    iam nequeunt claudi taedia ferre viae;
5 tristia praeterea tam sancti iudicis ora
    cum sint lascivi se tolerare negant.

⁚ 33 ⁚

Ad librum

Si nec Pierides, nec te defendit Apollo
    et vestire piper, claude libelle, times,
certa salus restat: cautus sic ampla subintres
    atria, nec Medicos egrediare Lares.
5 Namque illic tutus, tanta et securus in arce
    ridebis vulgi scommata dura levis.
Sic te de sacro nullus deducet asylo,
    nec feret audaces in tua terga manus.
Quod si Maecenas te noverit atque severus,
10 heu, dignum tanto non putet hospitio,
tunc demum claudo Veneris sua sacra marito
    confice: Vulcano vindice tutus eris.

Damn me if I don't want to send my verses, but right now
    their lameness makes them weary of the journey.
Besides, they say they can't bear such severe looks   5
    from so holy a judge, as they themselves are naughty.

: 33 :

To His Book

If neither the Muses, nor Apollo should defend you
    and you are afraid, lame little book, of wrapping pepper,
one sure refuge remains: steal into the great courtyard
    and do not leave the household gods of the Medici.
For safe and secure there in so great a citadel   5
    you will laugh at the rough jeers of the fickle crowd.
Thus no one will drag you from that blessed asylum
    nor lay presumptuous hands upon your back.
But if Maecenas recognizes you (and he's severe),
    he may not think you worthy, alas, of such a home;   10
then at last perform the rites for Venus' lame husband:
    with Vulcan as your protector you'll be safe from harm.

LIBER SECUNDUS

Ad Petrum Medicem

Nostri certa salus, Medices, quo sospite numquam
    defuerunt sacris praemia virginibus,
quo duce Tyrrhenis deductum montibus Arnum
    praeferet Aoniis turba canora iugis;
5   publica si quando cessant tibi munera et audes
    instaurare brevi seria longa ioco,
ne pudeat nostros percurrere, Petre, libellos,
    et nugas hilari fronte probare meas.
Magnos magna decent, fateor: tamen haec quoque fessos
10   quae reparent animos, ne fugienda putes.
Scipio nam quantus, cessit cui Punica virtus,
    fortia cum Libyci contudit arma ducis;
hunc tamen in placido viderunt otia ludo
    ostrea Campano spargere lecta salo.
15   Tristius in terris quam Stoica dicta Catonis,
    nil Danai, Latii nil meminere viri;
hic tamen ad multam convivia ducere noctem,
    et solitus curas saepe levare mero.
Sic tu, quo magni populi flectuntur habenae,
20   dum legis haec, sanctum pone supercilium.
Saepe tibi reditus, Petre, ad maiora dabuntur,
    si reparas mentem, qua geris illa, iocis.

BOOK II

To Piero de' Medici

O Medici, our sure salvation, through whose saving power
    rewards for the holy virgin Muses never fail,
through your guidance that melodious band prefers the Arno,
    flowing down from the Apennines, to Helicon's heights;
if ever your public duties cease and you should have a mind   5
    to refresh long, serious tasks with a brief bit of fun,
please don't be embarrassed, Piero, to peruse my little books,
    and to approve my trifles with a cheerful face.
Great things befit great men, I know, but don't also think
    you must flee the things that restore exhausted spirits.   10
For how great was Scipio, to whom Punic power bowed,
    when he crushed the brave arms of the African leader?
Still, his moments of leisure saw him play a gentle game,
    skipping oyster shells picked up by the Campanian sea;
The men of Greece and Latium keep nothing in their minds   15
    more severe than Cato's Stoic sayings;
Yet this man was wont to banquet late into the night,
    and to lighten his cares often with unmixed wine.
So you, who hold the reins that regulate a mighty people,
    while you read this, put aside high-minded disdain.   20
You'll be able often, Piero, to return to greater matters,
    if you refresh with lighter fare the mind that conducts
        them.

: 2 :

Ad Petrum Medicem

Carminibus nostris veniet tibi si qua voluptas,
    ut releves animum, carmina nostra leges.
Quod si nec salibus poterunt ullove lepore
    te retinere, Petre, tu tamen illa leges.
5   Sic rex Peliacus quamvis non docta poetae
    suscepit laeta carmina fronte tamen,
et magis officium studiosi hunc movit amici
    quam tardum vatis laeserat ingenium.
Ergo non munus, sed dantis munera mentem
10   inspice! Sicque libens carmina nostra leges.
Nam tam magnificus non est qui maxima donat,
    quam qui parva libens sumere dona potest.

: 3 :

Contra Avaros

Divitiae vobis variis quaerantur, avari,
    artibus, ut multas arca recondat opes.
Atque alius terras primo sub sole calentes
    et petat Eoo litora iuncta salo.
5   Alter ad extremas Hispani gurgitis urbes
    merce gravem Tusco solvat ab amne ratem,
adversasque hiemes durus fluctusque marinos
    substineat navi saepe labante miser.
Ast hic militiae saevos tolerare labores

: 2 :

To Piero de' Medici

If you'll get any pleasure from my poems, Piero,
    to relieve your spirit, then read my poems.
But if neither their wit nor charm can hold your interest,
    go ahead and read them anyway.
Thus the king of Pelion was happy to receive poems   5
    even from an uneducated poet,
and the service of a zealous friend moved him more
    than the dull mind of the poet gave offense.
So, look not on the gift, but on the gift-giver's thought!
    And in that spirit you'll read my poems gladly.   10
For the magnificent man is not he who gives great gifts,
    but he who can receive small gifts with gladness.

: 3 :

Against the Covetous

Greedy men, go seek riches by your various cunning arts,
    let your coffers fill with wealth unlimited,
Let one seek out the baking lands beneath the orient sun
    and the shores that run along the eastern sea.
Let another discharge his boat, loaded with Arno's goods,   5
    by the farthest cities of the Spanish seas,
and let the hardy fellow endure cold winters and sea waves
    often, and in a foundering ship, the wretch.
Let this one learn to bear the cruel work of soldiering,

10 discat et ad sonitum castra movere tubae,
  saepeque brumales horrenti sub Iove noctes
   exigat aut pluvio sidere currat iter.
  Quid tamen hinc pretii post tanta pericula vitae
   proveniet, semper ut miser esse velim?
15 An tanti est digitos nitidis ornare lapillis,
   vel Tyrio bibulam murice ferre togam?
  Verum agite, o cupidi: sed quantum crescet acervus
   nummorum, tantum crescet avara sitis.
  Sollicita assiduis involvite pectora curis,
20 nec veniat vobis laetior ulla dies.
  Me nec pauperies, nec tristior ulla cupido
   impellet patrio longius ire solo.
  Quod mihi si Musis fieri contingat amicum,
   illarumque meo si sonet ore furor,
25 tunc ego Persarum ditissima limina regum
   ridebo, aut siquid pulchrius Indus habet.
  Tunc dignum nostra carmen cantare puella
   dulce erit, et dominae sic placuisse meae;
  tunc tua forma meis nitide depicta libellis
30 diffugiet nigros, aurea Xandra, rogos.
  Verum agite, o Musae, mihi maxima numina, Musae,
   iam liceat vestro pellere fonte sitim!
  Me vestrum ventura aetas cognoscat alumnum,
   eductum vestris sentiat esse iugis.
35 Quod si me indignum vos tanto munere, divae,
   ducitis et nostri gratia nulla movet,
  hoc saltem tali libeat praestare puellae:
   non mihi, sed dominae carmina vestra peto.
  Quae si forte suo sic defraudetur honore,

to break camp at the trumpet's sound,   10
and to suffer often wintry nights and a shivering sky,
  or to march double-time, the heavens pouring rain.
What good will come of this, after all these threats to life,
  that I should want always to be wretched?
Is it worth that much to adorn your fingers with shiny gems   15
  or wear a toga soaked deep with Tyrian purple?
Speak the truth, greedy fellows: but as the pile of money
  grows, so much does the thirst for having money grow.
Wrap your anxious hearts in unrelenting worries
  and may a day more joyful never dawn for you.   20
As for me, neither poverty nor any unhappier lust
  shall drive me any distance from my native soil.
But if I am allowed to become the Muses' friend,
  and if their blessed madness should find utterance through
      my mouth,
then I shall laugh at the richest doors of Persia's kings,   25
  and anything lovelier still that India may hold.
Then it will be sweet to sing a song worthy of my girl,
  and so to have given pleasure to my mistress's ears.
Then your beauty, golden Xandra, painted radiantly
  in my little books, will escape black funeral pyres.   30
But come now, O Muses, my chief deities, my Muses,
  now let me at your fountain slake my thirst,
Let the age to come know me as your own nursling,
  and feel that I was nurtured on your mountain heights.
But if you consider me unworthy of this gift,   35
  and no charm of mine can move you, goddesses,
may at least it please you to bestow it for her sake:
  I ask your poetry, not for me, but for my mistress's sake.
If by chance she be thus robbed of the glory that she's due,

40   invidia nemo vos caruisse putet.
     Castior haec Helene est; fuerat nec pulchrior illa,
        Smyrnaeam potuit quae meruisse tubam.

: 4 :

Ad Xandram

     Callimachus roseam Graia testudine nympham
        et dominae lusit cygnea colla suae.
     Dicere sed Latio voluit te, Cynthia, plectro
        hic, cuius nota est Asis ob ingenium.
5   At Petrarca tuas versu cantavit Etrusco,
        Laura, comas: doctus carmina docta facit.
     Lauram cantavit, qua se sua Gallia iactet
        et nuribus Tuscis cedere velle neget.
     Ast ego nec Graia cithara nec posse Latina
10   sat videor: Tusce carmina nulla cano.
     Et tamen imperium dominae sua colla volentis
        dicier in versus surgere saepe iubet.
     Quid faciam? Pudor est indictum linquere crinem,
        possit Apollineas qui superare comas,
15   nec narrare manus longas et lumina nigra,
        labraque Paestanis non imitanda rosis.
     Verum Scipiadae gracili tam grandia facta
        ausus erat priscus ore poeta loqui,
     facta Sophocleo dignissima syrmate condi
20   exiguo versu dicere non puduit.

let no one think that you are without envy.   40
For she's more chaste than Helen, nor was Helen lovelier,
   Helen who won due praise from the trumpet of Smyrna.

: 4 :

To Xandra

Callimachus sang of his rosy nymph on the lyre of Greece
   and of the swan-like neck of his lady love.
He whose genius gave fame to the town of Assisi,
   chose to sing to you, Cynthia, on a Latin lute.
And Petrarch sang of your tresses, Laura, in Tuscan verses,   5
   a learned man who fashioned learned poetry.
He sang of Laura — she of whom her native France brags
   and claims she'd not yield place to young Tuscan wives.
But I seem to lack much skill on both Greek and Latin harps
   and I sing no songs at all in the Tuscan tongue.   10
Still my lady's imperious command to describe her neck in
     verse
   bids me often rise to the occasion.
What should I do? It's a shame to leave her tresses all unsung,
   locks which might well surpass Apollo's,
or not to tell of her dark eyes and elongated fingers,   15
   and lips which Paestum's roses must not match.
True, an ancient poet once dared with a reedy voice
   to tell of the lofty deeds of Scipio and his sons,
nor was he ashamed to describe in modest verse
   deeds most worthy to be cloaked in Sophocles' mantle.   20

Teque ego, Xandra, canam. Proh sors indigna duorum!
    Huc se debuerat Mantua docta dare.
Ille duces vicit Latio Romaeque tremendos,
    te virtute prior nulla puella fuit.
25 Nam neque tam moveor taurinis captus ocellis,
    ista satis quamvis causa furoris erat,
quam quod nec mores desunt in cuncta venusti,
    libera nec quicquid nosse puella velit.
Sive illam videas tractantem seria, dices
30   Pallada nequicquam posse decere magis;
sive iocos, sed quos laudet censura priorum,
    credas tunc Iulos illius ore loqui.
Cantat ut invidia possit torquere sorores
    Aonias, Phoebi vel superare lyram.
35 Cedite iam Charites, nam vobis doctior una est,
    quae movet ad numerum, nostra puella, pedes.
Huic pudor in faciem ducit persaepe colorem,
    qualem purpureas cernis habere rosas;
sed pudor ingenuus subtingens ora genasque,
40   quem nimis amota rusticitate decet.
Quando gravis cuiquam, quando non cuncta modeste,
    quando loquax visa est, aut taciturna nimis?
Haec possunt silices, haec ferrea pectora, tigres,
    flectere et hirsutas cogere amare feras;
45 nedum me, facilis molli quem pectore finxit
    natura atque Erato mollia corda facit?

So shall I sing of you, Xandra. Ah, two unmerited fates!
    Learned Mantua should have dedicated herself to this.
Her poet overcame the fearsome leaders of Rome and Latium,
    and you no maiden ever passed in virtue.
For I am not moved when caught by your doe-like eyes,   25
    — though that might be cause enough for passion —
so much as by your charming ways, complete in everything,
    and by your liberal longing to leave nothing unknown.
If you should see her discussing serious matters, you would
        say
    that Athena could not have spoken more fitly in any way;   30
or if frivolous ones (but ones which antique censors would
        approve),
    you'd think that then the Iulii were speaking through her
        mouth.
Her singing extorts envy from the Aonian sisters
    and surpasses even Phoebus Apollo's lyre.
Give way now, Graces, she's more expert than you are,   35
    all by herself, my girl, in dancing to the measure.
Her modesty brings often that color to her face
    which you see that crimson roses do possess,
but a noble modesty, suffusing her cheeks and brow,
    that befits a woman far removed from rustic ways.   40
When has she seemed severe to someone, when not modest,
    when has she been too talkative or too reserved?
Such qualities could move rocks, move iron hearts, or tigers,
    and drive shaggy beasts together in mutual love,
let alone me, whom deft nature has made with melting heart,   45
    and whose tender breast Erato has formed.

: 5 :

Ad Xandram

Ergo sic nostrae transibunt dura iuventae
    tempora? nec fiet mitior illa mihi?
Hocne fides meruit, qua me, saevissima, numquam
    notior in terris ullus amator erit?
5   Sed te non lacrimae, non verba precantia flectunt,
    non animum mollit nostra querela tuum;
cedam ego: nam furor est tali servire puellae,
    ferrea quae duro pectore corda gerit.
Iam tibi, iam liceat, miser o Landine, catenas
10   frangere et a duro demere colla iugo:
sed nimis, heu, sero datur haec medicina furenti!
    Iam mea sanari vulnera nulla queunt.
Tunc potui, recta rectus dum mente vigebat
    sensus et intacto pectore liber eram;
15   nunc qua ducit amor, qua me rapit, usque sequendus:
    heu nimium nobis imperiosus amor!
Ille quidem felix divusque beatior ipsis,
    qui fugit imperium, saeve Cupido, tuum.
Hem, quibus annexi vinclis urgemur amantes,
20   hem quibus addictos legibus esse iuvat!
Est puer, est caecus, cui nos parere necesse est;
    sed puer et caecus nocte dieque premit.
At verum fatear: nostra est haec culpa. Quis illum
    arguat? Invitus non iubet ille puer.
25   Nostra nimis nobis nocet indulgentia; pectus
    otia ni teneant, nullus adibit amor.
Haec possunt dulci venas complere veneno,

: 5 :

To Xandra

Shall the pitiless moments of my youth then pass thus?
    Will she never behave more gently towards me?
Has my loyalty deserved this, cruellest one, a loyalty
    that has made no lover anywhere more notorious than I?
But my tears and pleading words never alter you,   5
    my song of sorrow doesn't soften your soul;
I give up: it's mad to dance attendance on a girl like you,
    who keeps an iron heart in her stony breast.
Now — now! — you can break your chains, miserable Landino,
    and liberate your neck from that harsh yoke.   10
But this medicine comes too late, alas, to one who has gone
    mad!
    Now no medicine can heal a single one of my wounds.
Once I might have done it, while rectitude flourished
    in my upright mind, when free and whole of heart;
now wherever love leads me, wherever it drags me,   15
    it must be followed all the way — ah, too imperious love!
He is happy indeed, more blest than the gods themselves
    who flees your empire, pitiless Cupid.
Look at the chains we lovers are forced to wear!
    Look at the laws we love to be enslaved by!   20
He's a boy, he's blind, the one we necessarily obey;
    but that blind boy drives me day and night.
Still I must confess: this is my fault. Who can blame him?
    That boy does not unwillingly give orders.
My self-indulgence harms me overmuch; if no leisure   25
    occupied my heart, no love would try to enter.
Leisure can fill your veins with a sweet-tasting poison,

ignibus haec praebent semina magna malis.
Immo potens deus ille puer, cui caetera cedunt
30   numina; quem summus Iuppiter ipse timet.
Es pharetra et certa trepidandus, Phoebe, sagitta,
      qua tumidae Niobes pignora multa iacent;
non tamen his armis stimulos arcere molestos,
      nec potes ardentes pellere corde faces.
35   Mille quidem iactet Mars se obtruncasse Gigantes,
      terrigenum timuit cum fera bella polus;
hic tamen et faculis pueri, puerique pharetris
      cessit et, heu, superis fabula nota fuit.
Quid Venerem matrem, quid te Neptune, quid illum
40   nunc referam, falsi quem iuba texit equi?
Cuncta Cupidineae possunt vincire catenae:
      stultus erit qui te deneget esse deum.
At mihi si liceat vinclis impune solutis
      nunc animi certo vivere consilio,
45   non tamen ipse meam cupiam fugisse puellam;
      libertas tanti non erit ulla mihi.
An ego tam demens, tales ut linquere ocellos
      atque tua forma, Xandra, carere velim?
Sis, licet, et Daphne penitus crudelior ipsa,
50   aut quae Mercurio clausit amoris iter;
immitis nobis fastus obpone superbos,
      inque meum exerce tristia iura caput.
Haec satius multo tibi me tolerasse putabo
      alterius firmam quam coluisse fidem.
55   Quod me si primis properas extinguere in annis,
      nil ego de fatis quod querar inveniam.
Nam Paris atque Hector, magnae pars optima Troiae,

it supplies large seeds for feeding the fires of evil.
That boy's a powerful god indeed, to whom other gods give
      way,
  and even highest Jupiter is afraid of him.   30
You are fearsome for your quiver and that sure arrow,
      Phoebus,
  which felled the many children of prideful Niobe;
Still, with these weapons you can't ward off his troublesome
      darts,
  nor drive away his burning torches from your heart.
Mars indeed will boast that he's beheaded a thousand giants,   35
  when heaven feared the wild wars of the earthborn ones;
still he yielded to the boy's flames and his quiver and became
  a notorious story, alas, among the gods above.
Why now mention Venus, his mother, and why you, Neptune,
  why him whom the false mane of a horse concealed?   40
The chains of Cupid can indeed bind everything;
  the man's a fool who should deny that you're a god.
Yet even should I get away with loosening Cupid's bonds,
  and live henceforth with wisdom and fixed purpose,
still, for myself I wouldn't want to run away from my girl;   45
  no freedom will be ever worth so much to me.
Am I so mad that I would wish to leave behind such eyes
  and to find myself without your beauty, Xandra?
Go ahead: be more cruel than even Daphne herself,
  or she who shut the path of love to Mercury;   50
pitiless one, shut me out in your arrogance and pride,
  and exercise your woeful rights over my life.
Yet shall I think I'd rather have borne such attitudes from you
  than courted the steadfast devotion of another.
Still, if you hasten to snuff me out in my earliest years,   55
  I'll find nothing in my fate to make complaint of.
For Paris and Hector, the cream of Troy's nobility,

et Grai ad Troiam tot cecidere duces;
    semina tam dirae cladis tribuisse Lacaena
60   fertur, nec Xandra pulchrior illa fuit.

: 6 :

Ad Petrum Medicem
De suis et Maecenatis laudibus

Purpureis semper vernent tibi busta rosetis,
    inque tuum tellus sit levis usque caput,
ulla nec Elysios passim celebrata per agros
    quam tua, Maecenas, rideat umbra magis,
5   Maecenas, inopes quondam miserate poetas,
    Maecenas Phoebi Pieridumque decus!
Te duce grandisonans consurgit in arma virumque,
    olim qui denas vix cecinisset oves.
Alter erat tenuis pauper praeconis alumnus,
10   cuius erat Lalagen dicere posse labor;
hic ubi Campanos a te deductus in agros
    pauperiem verso sensit abire pede,
protinus heroum Lesboo carmine laudes
    et superum cecinit dulcia furta deum:
15 nec mirum, tristi pulsis e pectore curis
    libera si tantum mens agitabat opus.
Sed nunc Maecenas Tyrrhenis alter in oris
    conspicitur, claris qui favet ingeniis.
Vos modo sublimi, vates, consurgite versu,
20   qui cupitis sacra cingere fronde caput,
sive Sophocleis libet haec cantare cothurnis,

84

and ever so many Greek commanders fell at Troy;
Helen is said to have sown the seeds of this dreadful slaughter,
   but she was not more beautiful than Xandra.   60

: 6 :

To Piero de'Medici:
On His Praises and Those of Maecenas

May your tomb be ever vernal among gardens of red roses,
   and may the earth rest ever lightly on your head,
may no other shade that frequents the Elysian fields
   hither and yon, smile more than yours, Maecenas.
Maecenas, who once took pity on impoverished poets,   5
   Maecenas, the pride of Apollo and the Muses!
By your leading, he who once had sung of scarce ten sheep,
   rose in organ tones to sing of arms and the man.
The other was the pauper child of a crier of slender means,
   whose task it was to learn to sing of Lalage;   10
when you brought him down into the Campanian fields
   he felt his poverty slip away and his measure changed;
and straightway he sang the praises, in the meters of Lesbos,
   of heroes and the sweet deceits of gods above;
it's no wonder, with all those sad cares driven from his heart,   15
   if his liberated spirit was stirred to undertake great works.
But now a new Maecenas has appeared on Tuscan shores,
   one who looks with favor on distinguished minds.
Now, you poets, now rise up in lofty verse together,
   you who long to bind the holy laurel to your brows,   20
whether you like to chant your rhymes in Sophocles's buskin,

seu iuvat Aonii ludere more senis.
Nam Medicum Fesulis stabunt dum fulta columnis
   atria magnanimis concelebrata viris,
25   nec vos materies nec merces carminis unquam
   deseret: hoc virtus praestat utrumque Petri.
Ille colit Musas, doctos colit ille poetas,
   unquam nec merita laude carere sinit.
Nam novit quaecumque armis, quaecumque togata
30   pace gerant clari nobilitate viri,
ni fuerint magno Musarum fulta favore,
   tendere in aeternum non reditura situm.
Ergo colit doctos, doctorum et carmine vatum
   quae sint digna cani, maxima facta gerit.
35   Nusquam magnanimo genitus fortique parente
   inceptis gravibus degener ipse fuit.
Nam tantum emicuit iuvenili in pectore quondam
   consilium, quantum vix solet esse seni.
Inque dies crevit virtus crescentibus annis,
40   seque tulit gradibus accumulata novis.
Unde et maturo gravior cum accesserat aetas,
   nam cuncta ex usu mens meliora facit,
quid mage iam sanctum vel quid divinius unquam
   Lydius Etrusca vidit in urbe leo?
45   Ergo agite, o vates, sublimi insurgite versu,
   seu libeat natum dicere sive patrem;
iam canite altisono Medicum pia carmine facta,
   quis servata salus saepe fuit patriae.
Et si vos patriae pietas tenet ulla, parentes
50   iam patriae versu concelebrate novo.

or write songs with lighter themes in the old Aonian's
    manner.
For while the halls of the Medici stand upon their columns
    of Fiesolan marble, thronged with high-souled men,
you'll never lack for either the means or the matter of poetry,   25
    as Piero's steadfast virtue gives us both.
He cultivates the Muses, he fosters learned poets,
    he never lets them go without the praise they are due.
For he knows that whatever men have done in peace or war,
    however famous they might be for their noble deeds,   30
if those deeds find no champion or prop among the Muses,
    they slip into eternal dust, never to return.
Hence he fosters the learned and performs the greatest deeds,
    things worthy to be sung in verse by learned seers.
Born of a magnanimous and courageous father,   35
    he himself was no less worthy of grave endeavors.
The wise counsel that flashed from his youthful heart
    was greater than you'll often find in elderly men.
Day by day his virtue grew with ever-increasing years,
    and as it piled up it bore him ever to new heights.   40
Hence in riper years, when graver age approached—
    for the mind does all things better with experience—
what has the Lydian lion in her Etruscan city
    ever seen more more blameless or more divine?
So bestir yourselves, poets, rise up in lofty verse,   45
    whether you would tell of father or of son;
sing now in echoing song of the Medici's godly deeds
    by whom our country's safety has so often been preserved.
And if any love for your homeland binds you, celebrate
    the fathers of your country now in fresh poetry.   50

: 7 :

Ad Xandram

Quarta nimis misero mihi iam devolvitur aestas
    ex qua, Xandra, tuus me male vexat amor;
talis amor qualem nec mater sensit Amoris,
    cum stupuit vultus, pulcher Adoni, tuos;
5   Pontica nec qualem sensit male sana puella,
    Aesonidae timuit cum iuga saeva suo.
Ardebant ambae misere, penitusque medullas
    exurens ibat tosta per ossa calor.
At mea si spectes quantae praecordia flammae
10   involvant, quantis ignibus urat amor,
ultima iam nostri poterit scintilla caloris
    Colchidos et Veneris exuperare faces.
Me miserum! Non ora cibus, non lumina somnus
    intrat et in toto corpore nulla quies.
15   Multaque iam fractum quassant suspiria pectus:
    sic miser in luctu tempora nostra tero.
Ah quotiens totas gelido sub sidere noctes
    egimus ante tuas, dura puella, fores,
tristiaque in iunctos torquens convicia postes
20   lugebam misero limina clausa mihi!
Heu, modo vernali suspendi flore coronas,
    intexens rubris lilia cana rosis,
et modo per rimam tenui sub voce querelas
    immisi et tenui verba notata sono.
25   At cecini surdae; nam cum tibi carmina dicto,
    protinus aspideis auribus ista caves.
Sed iam tam saevo subducere lintea vento
    tempus adest; portum fessa carina petat!

:   7   :

To Xandra

The fourth summer has now come to me in my wretchedness,
    Xandra, since your love began to cause me bitter grief;
not even the mother of Love herself felt such a love
    when she gazed in wonder at your face, fair Adonis;
the girl from Pontus, unstable thing, did not feel such a love   5
    when she feared the cruel yoke for the child of Aeson.
Both burned pitifully and consumed their inward marrow,
    and heat shot through their desiccated frames.
But if you should see the fire that wraps around my vitals
    the intensity of flame with which my love burns,   10
the smallest spark of my heat could easily surpass
    the flames of Venus and the maid of Colchis' too.
How wretched I am! I can neither eat nor sleep,
    and no repose comes to my entire body.
Many a sigh shakes my already broken heart;   15
    and wretched thus, I wear away my hours in grief.
Ah, how often have I passed whole nights away
    under the chill stars before your doors, hard girl,
and, hurling sad reproaches at your fast-barred gates,
    wept at the entrance closed to my wretchedness!   20
At times, alas, I've hung there garlands of spring flowers,
    twining blushing roses with lilies white as snow,
at others, I've insinuated, whispering through a slit,
    my plaints and words expressed with a slight, subtle sound.
But I've sung to the deaf; for when I chant my songs to you,   25
    immediately you shun them with an adder's ears.
But now in this fierce wind it's time to drop my sails
    and let my tired bark at last seek port.

Tempus adest requiem tanto praestare labori,
30   nostraque disrupto solvere colla jugo;
seu iuvat aeterno pectus damnare furore,
      altera mi dabitur, quae velit esse mea.
Tu, quamvis tibi sim marcenti vilior herba,
      nec nostrae tangant pectora dura preces,
35   amissum frustra quondam revocabis amicum;
      ista tibi penitus verba superba cadent.
Novi ego: poscentes semper lusistis amantes,
      irrisos cupitis sponte subire viros.
Oenone Paridem nimium patienter amavit,
40   dum putat igne suo posse perire Parim.
Ast ubi Tyndaridos iuvenis succensus amore
      Iliacas movit per freta longa rates,
tum primum damnasse suos, male saucia, fastus
      dicitur et flammis incaluisse novis.
45   Tum primum penitus non indulsisse furori
      et doluit lentae damna subisse morae.
Ah quotiens patris recubans resupina sub antro
      torsit in absentem talia verba Parim:
Men refugis tanto, crudelis, flumine natam,
50   qua sine iurabas posse placere nihil?
Illa ego, si nescis, sum quam laudare solebas,
      praeferre et cunctis, perfide, Naiadibus.
Nunc aliam sequeris, pro qua Troiana iuventus
      occidat et Priami Pergama celsa ruant.
55   Talibus implebat iuga proxima saepe querelis,
      et gemitum audierat iam nemus omne suum.
Quin etiam lacrimis fluvios auxisse paternos
      fama fuit: tantus sensibus ardor erat.

The time is come to grant myself rest after toil,
 and to shake my neck free of your shattered yoke;   30
or if it helps to condemn my heart to endless insanity,
 I'll get another girl, one who wants to be mine.
Though I'm cheaper to you even than the rotting grass,
 and my prayers may not touch your stony heart,
someday you'll call back in vain the friend that you've lost;   35
 and those proud words of yours will be humbled utterly.
I know you women: you always tease your pleading lovers;
  still,
 you want the men you've mocked to endure it willingly.
Oenone loved Paris with far too much indifference,
 while she thought that Paris might die for love of her.   40
But when that youth, enamoured of Tyndareus' daughter,
 sailed the Trojan fleet through the rolling waves,
then, deeply wounded, it is said, she cursed her pride
 and grew red hot with unprecedented passion.
It was then she first felt sorry that she'd not indulged her ardor   45
 and had endured sad losses through prolonged delay.
Ah, how often, lying back, down in her father's cave,
 did she fling these words at the absent Paris:
"Cruel one, will you flee from me, born of a mighty river,
 without whom, you used to swear, you could have no   50
  pleasure?
I am she (if you don't know) whom you used to praise
 and prefer to all the Naiads, O faithless one.
Now you're after someone else, for whom Trojan youth
 may be slain, and Priam's lofty citadel fall to ruin."
With such complaints she used to fill the mountains round   55
  about,
 and every grove by now had heard her groans.
Indeed, the story goes, she even swelled her father's waters
 with her tears, so fierce were her emotions.

Non tamen his lacrimis Phrygiam retinere carinam,
60   nec Paridos potuit sistere vela sui.
Ergo si sapient, fastus fugisse decebit
      pulchras: pulchra licet, nulla superba placet.
Quod si iam nobis advertis mitius aures
      et flectis precibus pectora, Xandra, meis,
65   quod mihi cumque olim dabitur, pulcherrima, vitae —
      scribam sic — nobis nostra puella dedit.

: 8 :

Descriptio Montis Asinarii
Ad Laurentium Crescium

Est mons aeternum tribuit cui nomen asellus,
      quem Tusca octavus signat ab urbe lapis.
Hinc densis tegitur silvis et mollibus umbris,
      floribus hinc rident prata decora novis.
5   Nec non et varii passim per gramina rivi
      scabra inter rauco murmure saxa fluunt,
et purum innumerae circum sua rura volantes
      effundunt liquido gutture carmen aves.
Verticis at summo reginae Virginis aram
10   indigenae prisca relligione colunt;
namque ibi miranda constructum ex arte sacellum
      sancta sacerdotum pullaque turba tenet.
Huc nos, dum rapidi ferventia terga Leonis
      altior et flavas urit Apollo iubas,
15   Laurenti dulcis, saevos ex urbe calores
      fugimus; hic placido nos fovet aura gelu.

Yet even with tears like these she never could hold back
    the Phrygian keel, or stay her Paris's sail.   60
Therefore, if they're wise, it would beseem the beautiful
    to shun pride; loveliness may please, but not conceit.
But if you now turn your ear more gently to me, Xandra,
    and accommodate your heart to my prayers,
whatever life will be allowed me, loveliest one —   65
    thus I'll write — my girl gave it to me.

: 8 :

A Description of Monte Asinario
for Lorenzo Cresci

There is a mount to which an ass has given a lasting name,
    and which the eighth milestone from Florence marks.
On this side it is covered with thick trees and gentle shade,
    on that the meadows laugh, bright with new flowers.
Here and there, too, among the grasses numberless streams   5
    flow among the jagged rocks with a rushing sound,
and flying all around their country dwellings innumerable
    birds
    pour out pure song from their liquid throats.
At its peak the country folk, with piety as of old,
    have built an altar to the Virgin Queen;   10
for there a saintly, dark-robed band of priests has charge
    of a chapel built with marvelous skill.
Hither, sweet Lorenzo, we escape the blasting heat
    of the city, while at his peak Apollo burns
the glowing back and tawny mane of scorching Leo;   15
    here the breeze comforts us with its gentle chill.

At te cui patriae celebres debentur honores,
    fas erit urbanae taedia ferre togae,
sollicitumque piis pectus componere curis,
20   civibus unde queas consuluisse tuis.
At me, quem magnis sors adversissima rebus
    inferiore dedit, saeva, iacere gradu,
sit satis umbroso viridis sub tegmine quercus
    ludere Pierio carmina grata choro.
25 Quod si Castalios nequeam libare liquores
    nec folia ex lauro carpere, Phoebe, tua,
quis vetet imbellesque capras leporesque fugaces
    urgere alipede per iuga summa cane,
aut pingui incautas volucres innectere visco,
30   aut gregis insidias fallere casse, lupos?
Ipsaque iam nantes liventi calce supinum
    pisciculos nobis flumina parva dabunt,
nuper et emuncto poscenti villica lacte
    occurret multa rusticitate decens.
35 O te felicem, quisquis civilia temnens
    munera, florentis otia ruris amas!
Nulla hic mulorum poterit tibi rumpere somnos
    turma, nec aerato calce recussa silex,
nec faber ardenti nocturnum forcipe versans
40   ferrum, nec querula stridula plaustra rota.
Et procul hinc aberit (iuvat hoc quoque) nec mihi fastus
    opponet totiens Xandra superba suos;
non erit ad surdae cantandum limen amicae:
    crudelis dominae iurgia nulla feram.
45 Totum praeteriit (sed quae sunt praemia?) lustrum,
    ex quo, Xandra, tuus me male vexat amor;
et tamen interea mitis quandoque fuisti,

For you, to whom are due the frequent honors of your
        country,
    it's right to endure the urban toga's tedium
and to calm your heart made anxious by the cares of duty,
    for thus may you care for your fellow-citizens.   20
For me to whom a cruel fate, hostile to great endeavors,
    has given to remain at a lower rank,
let it be enough to please the Muses' choir with song
    under the shady covering of a green oak tree.
But if I may not drink from the Castalian waters   25
    nor pluck leaves from your laurel tree, O Phoebus,
who forbids me driving peaceful goats and fleeting hares
    over the mountaintops with a swift-footed dog,
or snaring careless birds with some sticky bird-lime,
    or tricking wolves, ensnarers of the flock, with a trap?   30
Soon the very brooks themselves will make a gift to us
    of little fishes swimming upstream over mottled rocks,
and not long ago a farmer's wife, with country grace,
    came to me with strained milk when I asked for it.
Happy all, O you who scorn the city's tasks,   35
    and love leisure in the flowering countryside!
Here no pack of mules can ever trouble your sleep,
    nor stone streets echoing to bronze-clad hoofs,
nor smith shaping iron by night with his glowing pincers,
    nor creaking wagon with its grating wheels.   40
And happily, too, proud Xandra will be far away from here
    and she won't be in my path so much with her haughty
        ways;
I'll not have to sing my songs at a deaf girl's door,
    and I'll endure no insults from my cruel lady-love.
A full lustrum has gone by (but with what reward?)   45
    in which your love has tortured me, Xandra;
still, there have been times when you've been gentle — though

multa sed, heu, minimo tossica melle bibi.
Nunc quoniam penitus nostro adversaris amori
50   inque dies minus est iam tibi cura mei,
concedam: sed tu, ni me Venus impia ridet,
flebis adhuc fido verba dedisse viro.

: 9 :

Conqueritur de amore

Fallitur, heu, si quis caecum iam credat amorem:
    lumina tot capiti non ferus Argus habet.
Nam quae me tenebrae, quae me loca devia possunt
    illius tutum surripere ex oculis?
5   Sunt ripae et ripas praetercurrentia curvas
    flumina, sunt testes frondea rura mihi,
in quibus indignas cupiens deponere flammas,
    nequicquam dominae iurgia saeva queror.
Me vos in vestris vidistis montibus olim
10   errantem frustra saepe latere, ferae.
Nam quid profeci? Sequitur deus ille nec usquam
    improbus a nostro pectore flectit iter.
An tibi, saeve puer, mortalia caetera desunt,
    quae possis faculis urere corda tuis?
15   An desunt superi? Iuncto seu foedere mavis
    otia cum superis tutus habere deis?
Scilicet et solus quo tela cruenta fatiges
    nunc resto; solum me tuus arcus habet.
Verum age, quandoquidem ternae, fera numina, Parcae
20   tam duras nobis imposuere colos,

alas, I've drunk much poison with the tiniest bit of honey.
Now, since you've become a total enemy to my love,
    and day by day you care ever less for me,   50
I'll give up; but unless wicked Venus is laughing at me,
    you'll yet weep that you've deceived a faithful man.

:   9   :

He Rails about Love

If anyone believes that Love is blind, he's deceived;
    alas, not even wild Argos has so many eyes.
For where are the shadows, where the secluded places
    that can steal me safely from his sight?
I call to witness the banks and the streams curving through   5
    them,
    I call to witness the leafy spots that heard my bootless cries
as I complained of my mistress's cruel abuse,
    as I longed to lay aside my guiltless love.
Once, you wild beasts, you used to see me wandering
    over your hills to hide myself, but to no avail.   10
For what did it profit me? That wicked god follows me
    and never steers his course away from my heart.
Don't you have some other mortals, savage boy,
    whose hearts you could set aflame with your little torches?
Aren't there any gods? Or have you made a treaty,   15
    and prefer to have your leisure safe from the gods above?
Plainly, I alone am left on whom you may tire out
    your bloody spears; I'm your bow's one target.
Well then, since the three Fates, those fierce goddesses,
    have prescribed so hard a destiny for me,   20

non ego iam nostrove modum finemve furori
    deprecor. In magno est nullus amore modus.
Sed tua quid possit saltem mea Xandra pharetra
    heu noscat, noscat quid sit amare malum!
25   Tunc, quamvis tigresque truces Siculosque gigantes
    atque ipsam possit vincere duritiem,
non tamen haec oculis cernet mea vulnera siccis.
    Dura puella quidem est: non tamen illa silex.

: 10 :

Ad Musam

Nunc, age, sub densa ventis leve flantibus umbra
    incipe versiculos, nostra Thalia, novos.
Incipe: vicinus crepitanti murmure labens
    Bellerophonteae sit vice rivus aquae.
5   Et nemora haec blandis non sunt incognita nymphis:
    texerunt multas proxima lustra deas.
Saepe sub hac longas Dryades duxere choreas
    arbore, nativum nec sibi numen abest.
Adde quod hic locus est unde omnis Etruria nostris
10   optima vel pars est subdita luminibus.
Hinc Apennini tergum collesque Mugelli
    cernimus et plani pinguia rura soli,
hinc Florentinas et summa palatia turres,
    Christiferaeque patent candida templa deae.

I shall not beg to end or to moderate my passion.
    For in great love there is no moderation.
But let my Xandra learn at least what your arrows can do—
    alas!—let her learn how bad it is to be in love!
Then, although she could defeat grim tigers and Sicilian   25
    giants, and even her own hardness,
Still, she will not look on my wounds with tearless eyes:
    she's a hard girl, indeed, but she's not made of stone.

: 10 :

To His Muse

Come now, my Thalia, under this thick-leaved shade
    with a breeze gently blowing, let new verses flow.
Let this nearby stream, gliding by with a whispering rush,
    serve in the place of Bellerophon's waters.
These groves, too, are not unknown to lovely nymphs,   5
    and the neighboring wood many a goddess has concealed.
Often under this very tree the Dryads have drawn out
    their long dances, and the native god is near.
Besides, this is a place from which all of Tuscany,
    or its best part, lies spread out before our eyes.   10
We see the Apennine ridge and Mugello's hills from here
    and the fertile countryside with its level fields;
from here there lie before us Florence's towers and great
      houses
    and the bright temples of the Christ-bearing goddess.

∴ II ∴

De insomnio

Tristia mi misero turbant insomnia pectus,
    nec secura venit sensibus ulla quies.
Cur nostram totiens iratam, somne, puellam
    obiectas oculis, visa tremenda, meis?
5   Hanc modo rivalis facis accepisse tabellas,
    me coram et placido reddere verba sono;
nunc illum nostra nimis exultare repulsa
    fingis et e lacrimis gaudia ferre meis.
Non ipsis satis, ah, fuerat mea damna diebus
10   sentire et quantum Xandra superba furit,
nunc etiam noctes nostro accessere dolori:
    sic lacrimis nullo tempore liber ero.
Improbe, tu dulci mortalia corda sopore
    lenire et curas demere, somne, soles;
15   nunc tua me horrendis vexant simulacra figuris
    et magis est ipso nox vigilanda die.
Felix Endymion, viridi quem mollis in herba
    pressit et evinxit lumina fessa sopor.
Ah quotiens illi gelida sub rupe iacenti
20   incubuit tepido Cynthia pulchra sinu,
et modo formosis puerum complexa lacertis
    carpebat niveis oscula grata genis,
et modo dissimili pingebat tempora flore
    Puniceis nectens lilia cana rosis.
25   His me, vel falsis, potuisses, perfide somne, —
    nam quoque falsa iuvant— ludere imaginibus.
Verum alter tibi sum— sensi— Palinurus et in me
    non mare sed dominae tristia bella cies.

: II :

About a Nightmare

Dreadful dreams disturb my wretched heart,
    and no untroubled peace comes to my senses.
Why, God of Sleep, do you thrust before my eyes
    so often that terrible vision — my girl enraged?
Now you show her taking up the tablets of a rival   5
    and answering him indulgently in front of me;
then you conjure him taking all too much delight
    in my rejection, and rejoicing in my tears.
It wasn't enough for me to feel my losses in the daytime,
    and to recognize how much proud Xandra rages;   10
now the nights also must be added to my sorrow,
    for thus shall I be never free from weeping.
Wicked Sleep, you customarily soothe human hearts
    with slumber sweet, and take away our cares;
now your phantoms vex me with their frightful shapes   15
    and night keeps me more awake than day itself.
Happy Endymion, he whom gentle sleep subdued
    among green grasses, conquering his tired eyes.
Ah, how often under an icy cliff did lovely Cynthia
    keep watch as he lay against her warming breast,   20
embracing now the boy with her beautiful limbs,
    stealing delicious kisses from his snowy cheeks,
and now, twining scarlet roses round with white lilies,
    she would paint his temples with contrasting flowers.
You might have teased me with such images, faithless Sleep,   25
    even were they false, for false things also give delight.
But to you (I know) I'm another Palinurus, and against me
    you rouse, not the sea, but my lady's bitter wars.

Helisabetha moriens
ad Bernardum fratrem

Quid iuvat in cassum tantas, germane, querelas
    fundere? Num precibus fata movere paras?
Desine: nam quicquid nostrae de stamine vitae
    restabat, rupit de tribus una soror.
5   Nec puduit primae miseram me aetate iuventae
    perdere, nec plenas dilacerare colos.
Crudeles divae, nostro quae funere nostram
    incestare domum gloria tanta venit?
Non lacrimae fratris, non vos pia vota parentum,
10   non dulcis movit multa precata soror.
Ecce caput Stygiis iam iam moritura tenebris
    mergor et ad Ditis limina fusca trahor.
Sed tamen, hoc superi norunt mihi dulce futurum:
    ibo per Elysias, umbra pudica, domos.
15   Nam scelus admisi nullum, quo nostra doleret
    mater, et in nobis militat ipse pudor.
Nec miserae novi Veneris mala gaudia, nec mi
    turbavit facibus corda Cupido malis.
Ergo libens, quamquam nimis immatura, sub umbras
20   descendam: Manes et data fata sequar.
Impia nam fugiam nunc Tartara nec mihi saevas
    incutient Dirae, lumina nigra, faces.
Non me Dictaei terrebunt iura tyranni,
    iura umbris numquam diffugienda piis,

: 12 :

The Dying Elisabetta
to Her Brother Bernardo

What's the good of pouring out so many laments in vain,
    brother dear? Do you plan to move the Fates by prayer?
Stop: for one of those three sisters has now snapped
    what remained of the slender thread of my life.
Sad as I am, I am unashamed to die in early youth,   5
    and not to wind full distaffs down to nothing.
Cruel goddesses, does so much glory come to you
    from polluting our house with my funeral rites?
Neither a brother's tears, nor parents' holy vows,
    nor a sweet sister's many pleas can move you.   10
See, on the point of death, my head now sinks to Stygian
    shades,
    and I'm drawn to the somber door of Dis.
But still, the gods above knew that my future would be sweet;
    I shall go, a chaste shade, among Elysian dwellings.
For I have allowed no wickedness to grieve our mother,   15
    and modesty herself has fought her fight in me.
I have not known the evil joys of the Venus who brings pain
    nor has Cupid roiled my heart with his wicked flames.
Hence I'll go down gladly, though too young, beneath the
    shades:
    I shall follow the Manes and the Fates that are my lot.   20
For now I shall escape accursed Tartarus, and the Furies
    will not strike me with their black fire and cruel torches.
The judgments of the Dictaean king will not frighten me,
    judgments that pious shades never should flee;

25   non rimosa nigris implenda paludibus urna,
        non erit inter aquas dira timenda sitis.
    Horrescant aliae falcatos comminus ungues
        et vetita extremum tangere saxa iugum,
    horrescant volucresque, rotas, scopulosque minaces,
30   flammiferumque caput, saeva Chimaera, tuum.
    Nam nos Elysios campos et amoena colemus
        flumina et umbriferum fronde virente nemus.
    Vos cari, nobis iustissima cura, parentes,
        Bernarde ante alios, frater amate, vale!
35   Atque vale atque meo memor haec duo carmina busto
        imprime, quae nomen sint habitura meum:
    Iunior hoc parvo iacet Helisabetha sepulchro,
        delitiae fratris delitiaeque domus.

ː 13 ː

De Bindo lusco

Quid mirum, uxorem luscus si non potes uno
    servare a moechis lumine, Marce, tuam?
Centum oculos habuit quondam Iunonius Argus,
    nec servata tamen credita nympha diu est.

I shall not be made to fill cracked urns from pitch-black   25
    swamps,
  I shall not fear dreadful thirst in the midst of water.
Other shades may dread hooked talons flying close at hand,
  and rocks that are forbidden to reach the mountaintop;
they may dread the threatening cliffs, the vulture and the
    wheel,
  and your flame-bearing crest, O savage Chimera.   30
But I shall come to dwell among the fields of Elysium,
  its pleasing waters, and its green and shady groves.
To you, dear parents, who are my most rightful concern,
  and you, Bernardo, my loved, my favorite brother, farewell!
Farewell once more, and, mindful of me, carve upon my tomb   35
  these two verses that will keep my good name:
In this little tomb lies Elisabetta, who died too young,
  her brother's darling and her home's delight.

:   13   :

About Bindo the One-eyed

Is it any wonder, Marco, if, having but one eye,
  you can't keep adulterers away from your wife?
Once upon a time Junonian Argos had a hundred,
  but still the nymph he guarded wasn't guarded for long.

: 14 :

De eodem

Una quod siccat vigesima pocula cena,
    non vitium Bindi est, sed iubet ipsa sitis.

: 15 :

Epitaphium Philippi architecti

Suspicis aeternum vasta testudine templum:
    Etrusci mirum est hoc opus ingenii.
Sed nomen fabri quaeris iam nosse: Philippo
    nomen erat, cuius hic lapis ossa tegit.

: 16 :

Aliud pro eodem

Qui venis externis fama commotus ab oris,
    Virginis ut cernas splendida templa Deae,
me quoque tam vasta celebrem testudine fabrum
    hoc tumulo clausum nosce: Philippus eram.

: 14 :

On the Same Man

That he drains twenty goblets at one dinner
    isn't Bindo's fault; thirst herself commands it.

: 15 :

Epitaph for the Architect Filippo

You gaze upon an immortal church with a mighty dome:
    this is a wondrous work of Tuscan genius.
Still, you want to know what the name of its builder is?
    Filippo was his name, whose bones this tombstone hides.

: 16 :

Another Poem for the Same Man

You who come from far-off places, stirred by its fame,
    to see the glorious temple of the Virgin Goddess,
know that I, the famous builder of so vast a dome,
    am enclosed in this tomb: I was Filippo once.

: 17 :

Ad Francia

Iunior ut cupido quam sis videaris amanti,
    non nisi cum vetulis, Francia, carpis iter.
Procerasque fugis, cum sit breve corpus, amicas;
    et nisi parva, tibi femina nulla comes.
5   Sic senior teneram mentiris saepe puellam,
    mentiris grandem, pumilione minor.
Nunc rogo, qua possis luteum occultare colorem,
    ora tibi cum sint pallidiora croco?
Haec via sola patet, si vis formosa videri,
10   ut sedeas nigris mixta cadaveribus.

: 18 :

Ad Xandram

Nescio quid maius nostro, crudelis, amori,
    improba ni fueris, poscere, Xandra, queas.
An me non macies totos tenuavit in artus,
    ut iam contracta vix tegat ossa cutis?
5   An mihi non mediis flammas errare medullis
    vidisti, et saevas dura per ossa faces?
Vidisti, heu, totiens: sed tu ni sanguine fuso,
    ni moriar, nunquam me sat amare putas.
Ah dura et Siculis nunquam cessura tyrannis,
10   ipsam quae possis vincere duritiem,
quae tibi — fac animam fato me perdere iniquo —

: 17 :

To Francia

To seem to an eager lover rather younger than you are,
    you always pick the path with older women on it, Francia.
You avoid tall friends, since your body is so short;
    and you'll have no woman by you unless she's small.
Thus, though older, you often counterfeit a young girl,   5
    you counterfeit height, though smaller than a midget.
Now, I ask you, how can you conceal your sallow skin
    since your face is yellower than saffron?
This is the only way, if you want to look comely:
    sit down and mingle with black cadavers.   10

: 18 :

To Xandra

Assuming you weren't unreasonable, merciless Xandra,
    could you ask for anything greater than my love?
Hasn't starvation made me gaunt in every limb,
    so now my shriveled skin scarcely covers my bones?
And haven't you watched flames travel all throughout my vitals 5
    and fierce fire penetrate my solid bones?
Alas, you've seen it often, but unless I haemorrhage blood
    and die, you may never think I love you enough.
Ah, hard girl, who'd never give in to even a Sicilian tyrant,
    who could overcome even hardness itself,   10
suppose I lose my life at last through an unjust fate:

morte mea tandem, quae tibi palma venit?
I nunc atque animum tali submitte puellae
et miserum dominae sub iuga subde caput.

15 Quid tamen inde tibi post milia multa laborum
continget pretii, praemia quanta feres?
Mille vigil noctes circum durabis amatae
limen; erit gelidus saepe cubile lapis:
at vix illa duo toto tibi dicet in anno

20 verbula, tangendam vix dabit illa manum.
Haec me non fugiunt, novi. Sed nosse misello
quid iuvat, invitum si rapit asper amor?
Heu nimis infelix duro et sub sidere natus,
quem nectunt laquei, saeve Cupido tui!

25 Spiritus huic uni propria de sede revulsus
in dominae maerens clauditur usque sinu,
exul ubi infelix, alieno in corpore degens,
arbitrio servus nil agit ipse suo.
Nunc aquilae obductum plumis te, maxime divum,

30 Asteriae credam concubuisse tuae.
Te credam nivei formam sumpsisse iuvenci,
cum mare per longum vecta rapina tibi est.
Ipse aries factus flavam Bisalpida novit
Neptunus: flammis nec valet omne mare.

35 Quis nescit curvumque pedum simasque capellas,
Phoebe, tuas, cum tu flumina pastor amas.
Liber at Erigonem falsa decepit in uva:
hos te inire dolos ipse iubebat amor.
Ergo si variis superos se condere monstris

40 invitos totiens, saeve Cupido, iubes,
quid mirum si me tali exurente puella
cogis in extrema vivere nequitia?

how does my death bring victory's palm to you?
So go! abase your spirit to a girl like this
   and put your wretched life beneath your mistress's yoke.
What then will your reward be after many thousand toils,   15
   how much recompense will you receive from this?
You'll suffer a thousand nights awake at your beloved's door,
   a freezing stone will often be your bed,
but she'll speak hardly two little words to you in a whole year,
   she'll barely give you one of her hands to touch.   20
I'm no fool, I know this, but does it help a wretch to know,
   if harsh love seizes him without his consent?
Alas, too unhappy I, and born under a cruel star,
   whom your fetters, savage Cupid, bind up tight!
As for me, my grieving soul, torn from its proper place,   25
   is imprisoned in the bosom of my lady-love,
where, dwelling in another's body, a sad exile,
   like a slave it does nothing by its own will.
Greatest of gods, now I shouldn't doubt that you have lain
   with your Asteria, covered with eagle plumes;   30
Now I shouldn't doubt you took a snowy bullock's form
   when you carried off your plunder across the wide sea.
To make love to golden Theophane Neptune became a ram,
   and the whole sea could not drown the flames of his
      passion.
Who doesn't know of your curving crook and ugly goats,   35
   Phoebus,
   when posing as a shepherd you made love to streams.
Bacchus deceived Erigone, disguised as a bunch of grapes;
   Love himself bade you to embark on these deceits.
Thus, if you, fierce Cupid, bid the unwilling gods
   to conceal themselves so often in so many strange shapes,   40
it's no surprise if you drive me, aflame for a girl like this,
   to live my life in the depths of vile servility.

III

Sed tu nostrorum pars optima, Xandra, laborum
   sola potes lacrimis consuluisse meis.
45   Et potes, et furor est, talem si perdis amantem.
   Quid furis? Heu, damno stant mea fata tuo.
Credo equidem: invenies qui circum candida flavas
   colla comas docto grandius ore canat;
invenies maiora tibi qui munera mittat—
50   flectere te quamquam munera nulla queant—
at mage me certus— cupiat quod sana puella—
   nullus erit, nulli maior in ore fides.
Te potui prima misere periisse iuventa,
   te potero cana, Xandra, perire coma.
55   Quin mea cum durae truncarint fila sorores
   meque feret Stygia navita tristis aqua,
idem amor haerebit, nec me ulla oblivia tangent,
   non si Lethaei flumina tota bibam.

: 19 :

Ad Bindum

Cur nisi purpureas ornat cui fusca lacernas
   martora, nulla tibi, Binde, puella placet?
Cur tantum sequeris, cui pulchra monilia collo
   pendent, cui digitis plurima gemma nitet?
5   Nempe aut in Veneris furto es stomachosus adulter,
   aurea seu potius quaerere furta iuvat.

But you, Xandra, are the best part of my suffering,
 You alone can have taken thought to dry my tears.
You can, and it's raging madness to lose such a lover.   45
 And why do you rage? Alas, my doom will be your loss.
So I believe: you'll find one, surely, skilled in how to sing
 gloriously of your golden hair against your snowy neck;
you'll find one who might be able to send you bigger gifts —
 not that any gifts seem able to influence you —   50
but you can't find anyone who's truer or surer than I,
 and that is what a healthy girl should wish for.
I could have died piteously for you in early youth,
 Xandra, I can die for you when my hair is white.
Indeed, when the sisters grim shall snap my life-thread   55
 and the stern sailor carries me across the Stygian stream,
the same love will cling to me, no oblivion shall touch me,
 not even if I drink all the waters of Lethe.

: 19 :

To Bindo

Bindo, why is it that you don't like a girl,
 unless dark marten-fur adorns her purple cloaks?
Why do you only chase them when they hang around their
  necks
 pretty necklaces, or when their fingers flash with jewels?
Surely, in the theft of Venus you're either a finicky rake   5
 or else you just really like looking for gold to steal.

: 20 :

Ad Franciam

Septima iam gelidae noctis devolvitur hora:
    nunc optata diu dulcia furta feram.
O nox purpureis nunquam cessura diebus,
    sis mihi perpetua, sis sine luce, precor!
5   Quos ego nunc referam, mea nox, te teste triumphos,
    tu modo secreta contege cuncta fide.
Sed fluit, heu, tempus: satis est, mea Francia, surge!
    Surge, suam foribus, Francia, pelle seram.
En iam purpureum prono labentia cursu
10   Oceano mergent sidera pulchra caput,
ipsaque lux aderit Veneris contraria furtis.
    Surge, suam foribus, Francia, pelle seram.
Me miserum! Quotiens miseri falluntur amantes!
    His quotiens ridens fregit amica fidem!
15   En iam stridenti borea mihi membra rigescunt,
    iam vitream fecit cana pruina togam,
dum promissa mihi reserari limina demens
    auguror, at molli nunc iacet illa toro.
Immemor et nostri geminas obdormit in aures,
20   aut in nos fictos ridet, amara, dolos.
Sed satis atque super lusisti, Francia, surge!
    Surge, suam foribus, Francia, pelle seram.
O mihi si magicae parerent carmina vocis,
    salvaque Medeae gramina nota forent,
25   his ego te invitam duxissem, perfida, sacris,

: 20 :

To Francia

The seventh hour of a freezing night is now past:
  now I shall carry out sweet thefts I've long desired.
O night, may you never yield to enpurpling day,
  I beg you, everlastingly stay lightless for my sake!
With you as witness, night of mine, what triumphs shall I   5
    score;
  just please conceal my every secret loyally.
But, alas, the time has flown: enough, my Francia, rise!
  Arise, Francia, and lift the bar from off the double doors.
For now the lovely stars, gliding downward in their courses,
  sink their glittering heads in the Ocean Sea,   10
and Venus' light, itself opposed to thieving, will be here.
  Arise, Francia, and lift the bar from off the double doors.
How wretched am I! How often are we miserable lovers
    cheated!
  How often has a smiling girlfriend broken faith with us!
Even now my limbs stiffen in the cold north wind,   15
  and white frost has made my toga stiff as glass,
and while in my folly I surmise that the promised doors
  stand unbarred for me, she now lies on her soft couch.
Either she's forgotten me and sleeps without a care,
  or, harsh girl, she's laughing at the trick she's played on me.   20
But you've teased me enough and more, now, Francia, get up!
  Arise, Francia, and lift the bar from off the double doors.
O, if only magic spells would answer my command!
  O, if only I knew Medea's health-giving herbs!
By these holy means I'd draw you out against your will,   25

quandoquidem sana mente venire negas.
Sed satis atque super lusisti, Francia, surge!
  Surge, suam foribus, Francia, pelle seram.
At tu crudeli domina iam durior ipsa
30   ianua debueras sponte patere mihi.
Quam fuit exiguum verso me admittere furtim
  cardine: sic falli nostra puella cupit.
Illa quidem per se nostro indulgere furori
  denegat, invitam se cupit usque rapi.
35 Vah minimo poteras binos obstringere amantes
  ipsa tibi obsequio, sed nihil ipsa sapis.
Hem cui frondentes volui legisse coronas,
  hem cui tot demens florea serta tuli!
Sed peream, si me posthac, ingrata, videbis
40   ad tua purpureas limina ferre rosas.
Te caries rodat, tibi Di... sed dum queror, ecce
  rimula perfulgens lumen aperta dedit.
Nonne pedum strepitum? Falsa vel imagine ducor?
  O me felicem, Francia nostra venit!

⁝ 21 ⁝

Ad Leandram

Anulus en, dicis, quo pignore nocte futura
  te mihi venturam, vana Leandra, putem?
Nec venis et rides et me sic ludere credis;
  verum ego sic abs te ludier usque velim.
5 Nam modicum malo, quod continet anulus, aurum,
  quam te, cui turpi pallet in ore color.

faithless one, since you won't come in your right mind.
But you've teased me enough and more, now, Francia, get up!
    Arise, Francia, and lift the bar from off the double doors.
And you, doors, harder even than your own cruel mistress,
    you should have opened to me of your own accord.   30
How slight a thing it were to admit me on the sly,
    just turn a hinge: my girl wants to be deceived this way.
Indeed, on her own she won't give in to my passion,
    she wants herself to be carried off against her will.
Bah! with the tiniest consideration you could have put   35
    two lovers in your debt, but you're an utter fool.
And for you, alas, I wanted to pick leafy coronets,
    for you, like a fool, I brought so many floral garlands!
But damn me if you'll see me after this, ungrateful doors,
    bringing blood-red roses to decorate your doorstep!   40
May you rot in hell . . . but look! in mid-complaint,
    a ribbon of light is gleaming through the open crack!
And isn't that the sound of feet? Or am I imagining things?
    O happy, happy me, my Francia is coming!

: 21 :

To Leandra

Look at the ring, which, you say, unreliable Leandra,
    I should think a pledge of your coming to me some night.
You don't come and you laugh and you think you toy with me
        this way;
    But in fact I want to be toyed with in this way.
For I prefer the bit of gold which this ring contains   5
    to you, who offer a yellow skin in an ugly face.

Detinet ergo auri— dices— te magna cupido:
  immo, Leandra, tui nulla cupido tenet.

: 22 :

Epitaphium Pauli
in ipso concubitu defuncti

Hic iacet ignotum Paulus de plebe cadaver,
  morte sed insolita nobilitatus erit.
Nam dum scortilli clunemque femurque fatigat,
  deposuit vitam pene vomente suam.

: 23 :

Ad Urbem Florentiam

Hactenus egregiam niveo candore puellam
  et dominae lusi lumina nigra meae.
Nunc tua maiori, praestans Florentia, versu—
  dent modo fata viam— fortia facta canam.
5   Quid iuvat antiquas heroum dicere laudes,
  aut quid Thebanos, bella nefanda, duces?
Nil mihi cum Priamo, nil tecum, fortis Achilles;
  tu Paris atque Helene, fabula nota, vale!
Haec Grai, haec Latii quondam cecinere poetae,
10   tritaque sunt nostris auribus ista satis.

My great lust for gold—you say—keeps you away from me:
    Oh no, Leandra, it's my lack of lust for you.

: 22 :

Epitaph for Paolo
Who Died While Having Sex

Here lies Paolo, an unknown corpse from the common herd,
    but who shall be renowned for his unusual mode of death.
For while he was working a little harlot's hindquarters and
      thighs,
    he laid down his life just as his penis spurted.

: 23 :

To the City of Florence

Thus far have I amused myself, singing of my special girl
    with her snow-white radiance and her jet-black eyes.
Now in loftier verse I shall sing of you, great Florence,
    and your mighty deeds, provided fate shall grant a way.
What's the point of talking about heroes praised of old,   5
    why tell of Theban generals and dreadful wars?
Priam is nothing to me, nor are you, bold Achilles;
    and goodbye, Paris and Helen, with your well-known tale!
The Greek and Latin poets once used to sing of all that,
    and all that now sounds rather trite to our ears.   10

Dicam ego Romanae florentes urbis alumnos
    a patribus nunquam degenerasse suis.
Et referam versasque acies et moenia celsi
    Boniti plano iussa iacere solo.
15   Et vos, o Pisae, cantabimus, altera nobis
    Carthago, tandem nostra tulisse iuga.
Nec semel adverso iam fractos Marte Senenses
    atque Lupam turpi terga dedisse fugae.
Quid Volaterranis sublimi monte superbis
20   profuit in summis moenia habere locis,
dispositasque suis muris armare cohortes,
    volvereque in nostros saxa superna viros?
Scanduntur rupes, tum denso milite porta
    frangitur et medio ponimus arma foro.
25   Ah quam felici, praeclarae mater alumnae
    Roma, Fluentina moenia condis ave!
Hinc manibus nostri procero corpore Casca
    Foresi moriens sanguine tingit humum.
Casca unus solitus Regias sistere turmas
30   non tulit Etrusci fortia tela ducis.
Sed nimis heu gracili tam grandia proelia versu
    ludo: meos humeros non onus omne decet.
Est furor, est cymba vasto me credere ponto
    exigua; fluvios nostra phaselus amet.
35   Sitque satis dominam miseris urgere querelis,
    mulcere et gracili pectora dura lyra,
imparibusque modis teneros disponere amores:
    haec tibi materies, parve libelle, datur.
Nec tamen exiguum talem dixisse puellam
40   duxeris: haec laudis gloria magna mea est.
Gloria magna quidem talem dixisse puellam,

Let me tell of the flourishing children born to the city of
    Rome
    who never have degenerated from their ancestors.
Let me recount the siegeworks around high Poggibonsi
    and how her walls were made to move to the plain below.
And I will sing how you, Pisa, to us another Carthage,   15
    had in the end to endure our yoke,
how the Sienese were shattered, and not once, by hostile Mars
    and how the She-wolf turned her back in shameful flight.
What did it profit the proud Volterrans on their lofty mount
    to build their bastions in the high places,   20
to arm squadrons, stationing them along their walls,
    and from above to roll stones down upon our men?
The cliffs are scaled, the gate is broken down by a rush of
    men,
    and we lay down our arms in the middle of their forum.
Ah, how happy an omen, Roma, mother to a famous child,   25
    led you first to lay down the ramparts of Fluentia!
Hence gigantic Casca with his blood stained the ground,
    dying at the hands of the Florentine Foresi,
Casca, who used all by himself to brace the troops of Reggio,
    could not withstand the mighty shots of the Tuscan leader.   30
But, alas, I mock great battles with these lines, all too slight;
    my shoulders are not suited to every kind of weight.
It's madness indeed to trust my skiff to the vasty deep;
    my pleasure-craft adores the river's waters.
Let it be enough to press my lady with sad laments,   35
    and to soften her hard heart with the tender lyre,
and to describe soft love-making in elegiac lines:
    this is the matter granted you, my little little book.
Yet it's no small thing to have sung of such a girl,
    my greatest glory lies in praising her.   40
And the glory is great indeed to have sung of such a girl

cui similis quondam nulla puella fuit.
Nam niveos vidi flores vidique rubentes
    virgineo mixtos molle decere sinu,
45   at dominae faciem si contemplabere nostrae,
    pulchrius in Xandra est fusus uterque color.
Quale ebur aequabit dentes, quae rubra labellum
    purpura? Quae vincent cygnea colla nives?
Fulgeat, ut libuit, tersum perfulgeat aurum;
50   non tamen has superet, candida Xandra, comas.
Ipsa tuis oculis cedet Venus, ipsa deorum
    regina incessus optet habere tuos.
Una Fluentinis nata es tu gloria nymphis,
    in te congessit, quicquid habebat amor.
55   Sis modo — iusta peto — nostro non saeva furori:
    hinc laus est formae tota futura tuae.
Laudamus, fateor, flavos in virgine crines,
    candidulam frontem candidulamque genam;
sed mage laudamus mores in cuncta venustos,
60   aut si quam precibus flectere possit amans.
Contra autem fastus qui non odere superbos?
    Quamvis pulchra, tamen nulla superba placet.
Oderunt superi crudelia pectora divi
    et trucibus nymphis multa dedere mala.
65   Heu, poteras Phoebo, Daphne, gaudere marito
    et conjux talem scandere laeta torum.
Sed dum illum dure refugis, vah stulta puella,
    qui, modo sana fores, ultro rogandus erat,
candida frondenti tibi sunt circumdata lauro
70   pectora et in ramos brachia versa novos.
Sic hominis veterem penitus mutata figuram
    flumina, nunc arbor facta, paterna colis.

to whom no girl of old could ever be compared.
For I have seen white flowers and I have seen red
    mingling together to adorn a maid's soft breast,
but if you will contemplate the face of my mistress,   45
    both colors are poured out more delightfully in Xandra.
What ivory equals her teeth, what deep red her lips?
    What snows can ever match her swan-white neck?
Let polished gold shine, let it gleam as it pleases,
    still it can't surpass these locks, resplendant Xandra.   50
Venus herself will be vanquished by your eyes;
    the god's own queen could wish for your carriage.
You've been born the one glory of the Florentine nymphs;
    Love's every resource has been amassed in you.
If only you won't be cruel to my passion — a just request! —   55
    then henceforth all my praise will be of your loveliness.
I praise, I confess, a maiden's golden hair,
    her gleaming brow and her gleaming cheek;
but I praise even more her charming ways in everything,
    — if a lover's prayers can influence any girl.   60
On the other hand, who does not hate haughty self-conceit?
    No prideful girl gives pleasure, no matter how lovely.
The divinities above hate hearts that are cruel;
    they imposed many punishments on pitiless nymphs.
Ah! Daphne, you could have had Apollo as your husband   65
    and joyfully mounted so fine a marriage-bed.
But while you flee him obdurate, you stupid girl —
    whom, had you been sane, you would have sought of your
        own free will —
your gleaming breasts are encircled by a laurel growing leaves
    and your arms are transformed into unfamiliar branches.   70
Thus entirely changed from your former human shape,
    you tend your father's river, for you've now been made a
        tree.

Sic Arethusa, sui nimium dum saeva querelas
    Alphei et placidas spernit, amata, preces—
75 vel dictu miserum— vitreas mutatur in undas.
    I nunc, te Alpheo, dura Arethusa, nega!
Iphis Anaxaretis nimia feritate repulsus
    ante diem Stygiae flumina vidit aquae;
at Venus indignos fastus non passa puellae
80   in lapidem verti candida membra iubet.
Ergo si sapies externis docta periclis,
    Xandra, in me facilis mitia corda geres,
neve, heu, sit tanti lacrimas vidisse furentis,
    tristia cum falsus irrigat ora liquor,
85 ut tibi vel minimum iubeat nigrescere dentem,
    si quis adhuc miserans vindicat ista deus!

: 24 :

Ad Bindum

Ut moechos abigas, uxorem credis amato,
    Binde, sacerdoti: creditur agna lupo.

: 25 :

Ad Xandram

Quis malus, heu, rumor nostras pervenit ad aures?
    Me miserum, nobis Di meliora velint!
Vera sed haec fama est: abiit mea cara puella;

Thus belovèd Arethusa all too harshly spurns
    the plaints and gentle prayers of her Alpheus, and—
pitiable even to tell!—she is changed into glassy waters.   75
    Now, harsh Arethusa, deny yourself to Alpheus!
Iphis, driven off by Anaxarete, too untamed,
    saw the waters of the Styx before his time.
But Venus, who could not bear the girl's unmerited pride,
    ordered her lovely limbs to be turned into stone.   80
So, Xandra, if you're smart, you'll learn from these outlandish
        perils;
    you'll be ready then to show me a kindly heart.
And may it not be, alas! that some avenging god
    —if any still there be who pity the sight of a weeping
        madman—
while the poor deceived fellow wets his unhappy face,   85
    will order even your littlest tooth to change to black!

⁞   24   ⁞

To Bindo

To ward off those adulterers, Bindo, you entrust your wife,
    to a beloved priest: a lamb's entrusted to a wolf.

⁞   25   ⁞

To Xandra

Ah me, what evil tale has now come to my ears?
    Wretch that I am, may the gods will better for me!
But the story is true: my dear girl has gone away;

delitias nostras, invida Roma, rapis.
5   Heu, heu, quot nostrum rumpent suspiria pectus,
      quot lacrimae ex oculis, flumina quanta cadent!
    Vos eritis noctes testes et sidera nobis;
      audiet et gemitus candida luna meos
    et coeli medium peragrans miserabitur ignes
10   saepe meos; novit quid sit amare dea.
    Eoumque petens nonnumquam Aurora cubile
      narrabit Phrygio tempora nostra viro;
    saepeque dum cano feret oscula grata marito,
      cogetur nostris ingemuisse malis.
15   Hem cui desertus querar? Hem quae numina poscam?
      Si prodis partes, saeve Cupido, meas,
    nostrane perpetuis confides pectora telis,
      semper et e nostro corde cruentus eris?
    Illa tuus numquam quid possit sentiet arcus,
20   nec tantum pharetram cernet iniqua semel?
    Heu durum quotiens gelida sub nocte cubile
      vestibulum fecit mi, fera Xandra, tuum,
    vel quis carminibus tua limina saepe rogavi
      et foribus clausis oscula quanta dedi!
25   Hoc tenebrae norunt, hoc novit rimula, per quam
      ad te pervenit vocula saepe mea.
    Cantabam posti, borea mihi membra rigebant,
      albebat cana paenula nostra nive;
    seu pluviis poteram madidam vix tollere vestem
30   sive erat a glacie vitrea facta toga.
    Te tamen interea tepidus, te lectus habebat,
      auribus et surdis carmina nostra dabas.
    Tu nostro in gemitu tam molles carpere somnos,
      tu siccis oculis cernere nostra mala?
35   Nec satis hoc fuerat, nimis ah nimis aspera Xandra,

hateful Rome, you are carrying my darling off.
Alas, alas, how many sighs will now break my heart,   5
   how many tears, what a flood will fall from my eyes!
Stars of the night, you shall be my witnesses,
   and the bright moon, gliding through the middle heaven,
will hear my groans and oft take pity on my fires:
   that goddess has known what it is to love.   10
And sometimes, moving towards her chamber in the East,
   Aurora will describe my lot to her Phrygian spouse;
and often, giving welcome kisses to her white-haired husband,
   she will be compelled to bewail my sufferings.
To whom shall I complain? What deities shall I sue?   15
   If you won't take my part, fierce Cupid, will you still
keep giving my heart over to your ceaseless darts?
   Will you be always drenched with blood from my heart?
Will she never realize what your bow can do?
   Will she, wicked girl, never once see your quiver?   20
Alas, how often was your doorway my hard bed
   under the cold night sky, untamable Xandra.
O the verses I beseeched your threshold with so often!
   How many kisses have I given to your closed doors!
This the shadows knew, the little crack through which   25
   my whispering voice has often come to you.
I used to serenade your doors while the north wind froze my
      limbs;
   my cloak used to whiten with hoary snow;
either I could barely hold up under clothing wet with rain,
   or my toga would turn stiff as glass with ice.   30
You, however, all the while were lying warm in bed
   turning a deaf ear to my poetry.
While I groaned, how could you snatch such pleasant dreams,
   how could you view with dry eyes all my sufferings?
And if this were not enough, ah, too, too heartless Xandra,   35

nunc me, nunc patriam, saeva, relinquis humum.
Meque abitus comitem, crudelis, spernis amantem,
    ultima qui tecum Bactra aditurus eram.
Sed sic iussit iter. Credan? Te quis tamen egit
40   tam cito? Non abitus, sed fuga, Xandra, tua est.
Heu, mora parva mihi solatia magna fuissent,
    dum mea, me miserum, fata dolere docent.
Nunc reliquum in silvis, postquam me Xandra relinquis,
    tempus agam; silvas et iuga summa colam.
45 Est nive brumali mons horridus— hunc tamen aestas
    floribus et viridi candida fronde tegit—
unde per abruptos scopulos se spumeus Arnus
    deiicit et rapido flumine frangit aquas;
Arnus Etruscorum fluvium notissimus amnis,
50   qui radit patriae moenia parva meae.
His ego verticibus misero deceptus amore
    tentabo flammas pellere corde malas.
Namque ibi Naiades grata testudine nymphas
    mulcebo et Satyros; rustica sacra canam.
55 Et Dryades nobis aderunt, laetissima turba,
    quae montes et quae florea prata colunt.
Quarum aliae tensis aptabunt carmina nervis,
    et modulis capient pectora nostra novis;
pars variis numeris suspendet in aëra saltus,
60   ad citharam tremulos ducere docta choros.
Nullaque non, nostros placide solata dolores,
    mi caput in gremio ponet amica suum,
nec fastus totiens nobis iactabit amaros,
    ut tu blanditiis facta superba meis.
65 Certatim interea sparsae per rura volucres

now you're leaving me and our native soil behind.
You scorn my loving company, cruel one, on your journey
    hence,
  me who would have gone with you to farthest Bactria.
"But the journey was coerced." Really? But who has made you
    go
  so quickly? Yours is not departure, Xandra, but flight.   40
Alas, even a small delay would have been a great solace,
  while fate teaches me how to grieve in my wretchedness.
After you leave me, Xandra, I shall spend my remaining time
  dwelling in the woods and on high mountain tops.
There is a mountain shivering with wintry snow — although   45
  bright summer covers it with flowers and verdant leaves —
from whose steep cliffs the foaming Arno hurtles down
  and shatters its waters in a rapid-flowing stream;
the Arno, the most famous of all the Tuscan rivers,
  which skirts the low ramparts of my fatherland.   50
On those cliffs, deluded by my wretched love, I'll try
  to expel its evil flames from my heart.
For there upon my pleasing lyre I shall charm the nymphs,
  the Naiads and the Satyrs; I shall sing of rustic rites.
And there I shall find Dryads in their light-hearted throngs,   55
  dwelling among the flowery meadows on the mountainsides.
Some will adapt poetry to their tightened strings,
  and will captivate my heart with their novel rhythms;
some will leap in the air in varied numbers, having learned
  to lead flickering dances to the zither's sound.   60
And I'll not lack a girlfriend to give solace to my sorrows,
  who'll put her head placidly upon my lap,
and she won't throw her peevish pride at me so many times
  as you did, once my flattery had made you proud.
Meanwhile the birds, spread throughout the country, will   65
    compete

129

diffundent varios per nemus omne sonos.
Quas inter flammas Terei Philomena nefandas
    dicet et ut pennas sumpserit ales Itys,
et cur puniceis spargat sua pectora signis
70   Prognes, cur natum raptet iniqua parens.
His ego, Xandra, tuos, nimis crudelis, amores
    pensabo studiis— sic ego rura colam—
seu canibus timidas agitabo ad retia capras,
    et leporem imbellem per iuga summa sequar.
75 Vos cari comites et tu, Florentia, celsis
    aedibus et templis facta beata, vale!
Iamque iuvat gravidas humeris aptare pharetras,
    et caeca hirsutas fallere casse feras.
Sed quid ago infelix? Quo me furor impius urget?
80   Nil prodest nostris haec medicina malis.
Nullus amor, nulli pectus sanare labores
    mi possunt: medio pectore Xandra sedet.
Illa mihi quondam teneram furata iuventam
    prima dedit leges imposuitque iugum.
85 Illi igitur seram fas sit servire senectam:
    principium fuerat, sic quoque finis erit.

: 26 :

Ad Xandram

Quo ruis hinc? Ne Xandra dolos neu perfida fraudes
    necte! Licet fugias: te tamen usque sequar.
Te sequar extremae properantem ad litora Thyles,
    aut qua decurrit Indus in Oceanum,

to pour out their varied songs through every grove.
Among them, Philomena will tell of Tereus' wicked passion,
    and how Itys took upon himself a bird's wings,
and Procne, why she sprays her breast with purple marks,
    and why that wicked parent dragged her child off violently.   70
With these pursuits, cruel Xandra, I shall offset your love —
    and thus shall I dwell in the countryside —
either my hounds will drive the shy she-goats to my nets
    or I shall chase the gentle hare over the high ridges.
Dear comrades, farewell, and farewell to you, Florence,   75
    blessed in your lofty palaces and temples!
Now it suits me to hang a heavy quiver on my shoulder,
    and to trick hairy beasts with a hidden snare.
But what am I doing? Where does impious madness lead?
    This medicine does not help your hurt, unhappy man.   80
No love, no toils and hardships can ever heal my heart,
    for Xandra resides in my very heart's core.
Long ago she stole away my early youth from me,
    laying down her laws and imposing her yoke.
Therefore it is right that my sere old age serve her: 85
    she was my beginning, thus she'll also be my end.

: 26 :

To Xandra

Where are you going, faithless Xandra? No more tricks and
    lies!
    You may flee, but I'll pursue you all the way.
I'll follow if you rush to the shores of Ultima Thule,
    or to where the Indus sinks into the Ocean Sea,

5   nedum Romanos cupias si visere colles
      et Vaticani limina sacra Petri.
    Arne Fluentinis pergratum flumen alumnis,
      tuque mihi in primis, urbs memoranda, vale!
    Te invitus linquo, fateor. Sed nigra puellae
10   lumina, sed dominae cygnea colla trahunt.
    Hac ego non horam possem spirare relicta,
      hac sine nec Darii ditia regna velim.
    Hoc seu fata mihi dederint Parcaeque malignae
      nascenti, seu nunc sic trahat asper amor,
15 heu, latet. At quaecumque fuit, vis maxima certe est,
      quam contra vires nil valuere meae.
    Ergo sequar! Sed vos, quis nondum perdita vitae
      libertas proprio pectore tuta sedet,
    expertus moneo: venturo obstate furori!
20   Capta semel nunquam corda furore vacant.

∶ 27 ∶

Quod Roma Xandram admiretur

Dives erat quondam formosis Roma puellis,
    quarum nunc cineres ossaque cana tegit.
Errantemque suis vidit te, Cynthia, laeta
    porticibus flavis spargere colla comis;
5 vidit et, egregium cum Lesbia pulchra Catullum
    ureret, et dixit: Lesbia pulchra mea est.
Vidit et arrisit, facies cum blanda Corinnae

let alone if you merely wish to see the hills of Rome 5
    and the holy portal of St. Peter at the Vatican.
Farewell Arno, river delightful to your Florentine children,
    and you, city, you that stand first in my memory!
I confess I leave unwilling. But the dark eyes of my girl
    and my lady's swan-white neck pulls me after her. 10
If she left, I could not breathe even a single hour;
    without her, I'd not want even Darius' wealthy realms.
Whether the Fates and the malevolent Parcae gave me this at
    birth
    or whether it's harsh Love that drags me about this way
    today —
that, alas is hidden; but whichever one it is, 15
    it's an overwhelming force that I cannot fight at all.
Therefore I shall follow! But I'll give you this advice,
    you who keep your liberty safe within your breast
and haven't yet lost your life: resist passion when it comes!
    For hearts once caught by passion are never free again. 20

: 27 :

The Way Rome Marvels at Xandra

Once upon a time Rome was rich in comely girls,
    whose ashes and whose whitened bones she now conceals.
She saw you, Cynthia, wandering happy through her
    colonnades,
    with your golden hair scattered all along your neck;
she witnessed, too, the lovely Lesbia kindling the fires of love 5
    in famous Catullus, and said: lovely Lesbia is mine.
She saw and smiled, when Corinna's charming face

sub iuga Nasonem cogeret ire suum,
atque oculos Nemesis figentes corda Tibulli
10   vidit: erat vatis carmine nota sui.
At nuper Xandrae vidit cum lumina nostrae,
   iuravit nihil hac posse decere magis.

: 28 :

Ad Iohannem Antonium
de carminibus Burchi

Plurima mitto tibi tonsoris carmina Burchi;
   haec lege. Sed quid tum? Legeris inde nihil.

: 29 :

Ad Musam
Quod Florentiam ad Iohannem Antonium pergat

Curre sed extemplo Tuscum visura leonem
   atque Fluentinas, candida Musa, domos.
Verum ubi sublimem turrim portamque Senensem
   intraris, recta perge subinde via,
5 et Veterem transi Pontem, quem mollibus undis
   suffluit et placidis irrigat Arnus aquis.
Exhinc sericeas intervectere tabernas,
   et Mercatorum compita pulchra Fori.

brought Ovid to submit and go beneath love's yoke.
She saw the eyes of Nemesis nailed into Tibullus' heart:
    that girl became notorious through the poem of her bard.   10
And just now, when Roma saw the eyes of my girl,
    she swore there could be nothing more splendid than
        Xandra.

: 28 :

To Giovanni Antonio
on the Poems of Burchiello

I am sending you lots of poems by the barber Burchiello.
    Read them. Then what? You'll get nothing out of them.

: 29 :

To His Muse
to Hurry to Giovanni Antonio in Florence

Run right away, bright Muse, to see the Tuscan lion
    and the dwelling-places of the Florentines.
And when you enter the Sienese Gate with its high tower,
    immediately take the street straight ahead,
and cross the Ponte Vecchio, under which the Arno flows   5
    with a gentle motion, and with moisturing, tranquil waters.
Then make your way from there between the silk-maker's
        shops,
    and the lovely crossroads of the Merchants' Forum.

Neve Malum post haec Callem transire timebis,
10   namque habet hic falsi nomina vana metus;
neve iter inflectes, quamvis sit propter eundum
     Lustra Lupae: fugit hanc nulla matrona viam.
Hinc trivium a Paleis dictum et Laurentia velox
     templa petes, opibus nobilitata novis.
15   Non tamen hic vastis moles miranda columnis
     inque dies surgens te remoretur opus,
nec latus in dextrum, dum magna palatia magni
     suspectas Cosmi, pes tibi lentus eat.
Sed breve quod spatium superest, decurre, Camena;
20   sic demum in Gallam, Musa, ferere viam,
dulcis ubi aediculas carique subibis amici,
     in cuius primum fessa quiesce sinu.
Exhinc quam multam memori refer ore salutem
     Iohannemque meum longa valere iube.
25   At te quid Romae faciam si forte rogarit,
     dicito me veterum discere relliquias,
quas oculis si quis poterit iam cernere siccis,
     hunc hominis pectus non habuisse putem.

: 30 :

De Roma fere diruta

Et cunctis rebus instant sua fata creatis,
     et, quod Roma doces, omnia tempus edit.
Roma doces olim tectis miranda superbis,
     at nunc sub tanta diruta mole iaces.
5   Heu, quid tam Magno, praeter sua nomina, Circo

After this don't be afraid to cross the Evil Lane,
 for this way has an empty name that gives a false alarm;   10
Don't swerve from the route, though it may be going
 near the hookers' dens: no matron fears this street.
From there, swiftly seek the crossroads named for Pales,
 and find the church of San Lorenzo, famous for its new
   riches.
Don't let this marvelous structure with its massive colonnades,   15
 rising higher each day, keep you back from your task,
nor, on the right, gazing at the mighty palace
 of Cosimo the Great, let your foot be slow.
But since the distance left is short, hurry, my Camena;
 and so at last, dear Muse, you'll come to Via San Gallo;   20
there you'll enter the little house of my dear, sweet friend,
 and first, rest your tired body at his breast.
After that, remember to wish the best of health
 to my Giovanni, and bid him to fare well for long.
But if he happens to ask you what I'm doing in Rome,   25
 say that I am studying the ancient ruins,
and if anyone can look at them without moist eyes,
 I should not think he has the heart of a man.

: 30 :

On the Near Ruin That Is Rome

What you teach, Rome, is this: that its own ruin looms
 over every created thing, and Time devours all.
You teach, Rome, once admired for your proud buildings;
 now you lie demolished under ruins vast.
Alas, what is left of the Great Circus but its name,   5

restat, ubi Exquilias sola capella colit?
Nec sua Tarpeium servarunt numina montem,
    nec Capitolinas Iuppiter ipse domos.
Quid Mario Caesar deiecta trophaea reponis,
10   si quod Sylla fuit, hoc sibi tempus erit?
Alta quid ad coelum, Tite, surrigis amphitheatra?
    Ista olim in calcem marmora pulchra ruent.
Nauta Palatini Phoebi cantaverat aedes,
    dic tua, dic Phoebe, nunc ubi templa manent?
15 Heu, puduit statuas Scopae spectare refractas,
    haec caput, ista pedes, perdidit illa manus.
Nec te, Praxiteles, potuit defendere nomen,
    quominus ah, putris herma, tegaris humo;
hanc nec Phidiaca vivos ostendere vultus
20   arte iuvat: doctus Mentor ubique perit.
Quin etiam Augusto Stygias remeare paludes
    si licet et vita rursus in orbe frui,
inquirens totam quamvis percursitet urbem,
    nulla videre sui iam monumenta queat.

where a single she-goat dwells on the Esquiline?
Her own divinities did not save the Tarpeian rock,
   nor Jupiter himself his Capitoline dwelling.
Why give Marius back his toppled trophies, Caesar?
   If Sulla was something, will there come a time for him?   10
Why build your lofty Colosseum to the heavens, Titus?
   Those lovely marbles one day shall turn to lime.
Nauta once hymned the fane of Apollo Palatinus;
   tell us, Phoebus, where does your temple stand now?
Alas, I blushed to look on Scopas' shattered statues: 15
   this one had lost his head, another feet, another hands.
Nor was your name, Praxiteles, able to defend you
   from a covering of earth, a decaying herm, alas.
Nor did its lively features help this statue last, though carven
   with Phidian art: wise Mentor has perished everywhere.   20
And even if Augustus were allowed to cross once more
   the Stygian swamp and have life in this world again,
although he might pass through the entire city in his search,
   he could not see any of his monuments now.

LIBER TERTIUS

Ad Petrum Medicem

Qui dominae varios nuper lusistis amores,
    quae iocunda mihi, tristia quaeque forent,
nunc elegi tempus graviori insurgere plectro,
    exiguum vestro munere crescat opus.
5   Sunt acris nunc acta viri celebranda; sed illi
    hoc date, Castalia quas lavat unda, deae.
Namque favet Musis Medices: vos numina, Musae,
    vestra meo — meruit — conciliate Petro.
Non hic armorum sonitus, non vestra movebunt
10   pectora crudeli proelia gesta manu;
nam neque torquetur validis hastile lacertis,
    nec celeri cursu fessus anhelat equus,
non galeae cristas, non exhorrebitis ensis
    mucronem et dirae tela parata neci;
15   sed ducis egregii virtus memoranda togati;
    huius enim cedunt fortia castra togae.
Novimus invicti divinas pectoris artes,
    tradita cum denis publica cura viris.
Tunc stupuit Cosmus iuvenili in pectore nati
20   consilium, quantum vix solet esse seni,
ingeniumque videns illi per cuncta paternum,
    maxima sub tacita gaudia mente tulit.
Ah quanta in dubiis patuit prudentia, quantus
    tunc patriae vigilem sollicitavit amor!
25   Auctor erat pacis: sed quae sine fraude tueri

BOOK III

To Piero de' Medici

You amused yourselves just now with my lady's mutable loves,
   things that made me happy and that made me sad;
now, elegiacs, it's time to rise up with weightier pen:
   by your kindly favor let my modest work expand.
Now I must celebrate a strenuous man's deeds;   5
   grant this to him, goddesses of the Castalian spring.
Because Medici shows favor to the Muses, do you, Muses,
   commend your powers divine to my deserving Piero.
Neither clashing arms nor battles waged with brutal hand
   shall here stir inspiration in your breasts;   10
for no long spears will be hurled by powerful arms,
   and no exhausted horse will pant from galloping hard,
you'll not take fright at helmet plumes or sharpened swords,
   or weapons primed to deal out dreadful death;
but what I must record is a famous statesman's virtue,   15
   for the bravery of the camp here yields to the toga.
I experienced the godlike skills of his invincible heart,
   when public business was committed to the Ten of War;
then Cosimo was amazed at the wisdom his son had
   in his youthful breast, such as old men scarcely have,   20
and seeing that he had his father's gifts in all things,
   Cosimo, in his silent thought, felt the greatest joy.
Ah, how much discretion he showed in uncertain things,
   how much love of country filled his waking thoughts!
He was author of a peace which might preserve the city's   25
      power,

imperium posset, quae sine labe decus.
Sed quoniam excierat, nobis ut bella moverent,
    improba regnandi saepe cupido duces,
censuit invicto surgendum pectore contra,
30   cum sit turpe gravi frangere corda metu.
Vos hunc insomnes vidistis ducere noctes,
    collegae, et curis invigilare piis.
Ergo sic casusque graves, sic saeva pericla
    vitavit monitis Curia nostra suis.
35 Sic patriam Calabro tutam iubet esse tyranno,
    cum Florentinos ureret hostis agros,
neve opera solum magnoque ex pectore curis,
    sed populum multo sublevat aere suum.
Verum quid Medicum non praestat maxima virtus?
40   Quot bona iam nobis contulit una domus!
Haec Ligurum populos, nobis saevissima regna,
    sub iuga iam socii compulit ire ducis.
Novit Sfortiades, qui quamvis Caesar in armis
    viribus et valida mente superbus eat,
45 hac sine Bebriaci tamen expugnare tyranni
    sceptra olim comite se potuisse negat.
Aere igitur Medicum, Medicum virtute fideque
    publica res summo constabilita loco est.
Nam neque qui multus Tuscis exercitus oris,
50   Insubribus nec qui castra locabat agris,
censu hunc Syllanus populus nutrisset Etrusco,
    ni Cosmus Medicas accumulasset opes.
Ergo et pace bonos, quorum et prudentia bello
    cuncta gerat, Medicum protulit alta domus.
55 Nec tantum iuvit Fabius natusque paterque

but without deceit, and her honor without stain.
But since a wicked urge to conquer often spurs commanders,
    so that they begin to stir up wars against us,
he resolved with his invincible heart to rise against them,
    since it's base to break hearts with the weight of fear.   30
You, his colleagues, saw him pass those sleepless nights,
    and keep watchful surrounded by the cares of office.
Thus, thanks to his counsel, our Senate fended off
    terrifying dangers and disasters grave.
Hence he bade his country be saved from the Calabrian   35
      tyrant,
    when that enemy was burning the fields of Florence;
his efforts and great heart not only lighten his people's cares,
    but he supports them also with his ample wealth.
But what does the infinite virtue of the Medici not provide?
    How many good things has that one house given us!   40
It has made the Genoese realm, most hostile to us,
    submit to the yoke of a captain, our ally.
Sforza's son acknowledged it, who, although like a Caesar,
    proud of his power in arms and his strength of mind,
still said that, without Medici virtue as his partner,   45
    he could not have overcome the Lombard tyrant's scepter.
By Medicean wealth, by their loyalty and strength,
    the state has been stabilized in a place supreme.
For without Cosimo and his accumulated riches,
    the people of Sulla lacked the substance to sustain   50
the man who kept on Tuscan shores his numerous army
    the man who pitched camp in the fields of Lombardy.
Thus the lofty house of Medici, by whose prudence in war
    all actions are performed, provides good men too in peace.
Fabius did not do as much, nor the son and father   55

oppositus Poeno, consul uterque, duci,
quantum nunc Medices proceres natusque paterque
   fregerunt lenta cum fera castra mora.

: 2 :

Ad Petrum Medicem Maecenatem suum

Musa Fluentini, claudo licet anxia gressu,
   i, Maecenatis splendida tecta subi.
Dic modo qui misere poterat vix stridulus anser
   exiguum rauco carmen hiare sono,
5   iam liquidum niveis sublatus ad aethera plumis
   sperat olorinos edere posse modos.
Nam quod Gorgonei non praebuit unda liquoris
   olim nec Clarii laurea silva dei,
hoc ego nunc hausi Tyrrheno e fonte profectus,
10   qui fluit e Medica lucida lympha petra.

: 3 :

Ad Antonium Canisianum
De primordiis urbis Florentiae

Has omnes lautis opibus quas suspicis aedes,
   seu sacra te stupidum sive profana tenent,
nullas Syllanus miles conspexerat olim,
   cum Fesulos primum forte teneret agros.

who opposed the Punic leader, though consuls both,
as now the Medici leaders have done, the son and the father,
who broke the enemy encampments by slow delay.

: 2 :

To Piero de' Medici, His Maecenas

Go, Muse, go, though with anxious, halting step,
enter the splendid palace of the Florentine Maecenas.
Say that he who, like a hissing goose, was scarcely able
pitifully to utter his meager song in a hoarse voice,
now, lifted up on snowy wings to the clear sky,   5
hopes that he might send forth the sounds of a swan.
For that which the spring of Hippocrene never offered
nor the laurel woods of Clarian Apollo,
I now have drunk, flowing from the Tyrrhenian fountain,
whose clear waters flow from the Medicean rock.   10

: 3 :

To Antonio Canigiani
on the Beginnings of the City of Florence

All the buildings you look upon which hold your spellbound
gaze,
wealthy and sumptuous, whether sacred or profane:
None of them were seen by Sulla's soldier long ago,
when he first chanced to occupy the lands near Fiesole.

5 Sed quae nunc multo splendent exculta labore,
  limoso turpis texerat alga lacu;
 namque retardatus spumantis vertice saxi
  in stagnum pigras verterat Arnus aquas.
 Nec pedibus tellus habilis, nec lintribus unda
10 nec fluvius pisci nec fuit herba bovi.
 Nondum quaternos admirans advena pontes
  transibat sicco flumina recta pede.
 Nondum sublimi in nostram defluxerat urbem
  fornice longinquis unda petita locis;
15 excelsam sed nunc ubi tollit Curia turrim,
  piscator nulla fecerat arte casam,
 et Baptisteri sacras ubi condimus undas,
  garrula ranarum voce lacuna fuit.
 Nam quis templa Crucis, quis saxis ducta superbis
20 viderat Albertum tunc monimenta virum,
 quis Florentini norat praetoria iuris
  aut quod te cingit, Curia celsa, forum?
 Omnia limosa squalebant arva palude,
  quae nunc erectis molibus astra petunt.
25 Syllanus primus fugiens asperrima montis
  purgavit nostros arte colonus agros,
 atque Arnum recta contractis undique lymphis
  obice disrupto compulit ire via,
 vicinumque libens primus descendit in aequor,
30 ut strueret pulchrum nobilis urbis opus.
 Hic Capitolinae primus non immemor arcis
  Romano nobis nomine tecta dedit,
 et fora disposuit Romano condita ritu,
  Romano ritu Curia prima fuit.
35 Quin et Gradivo longis suffulta columnis
  construxit vario marmore templa deo.

Lowly water-plants concealed a muddy lake,   5
    where now there gleams a landscape made with arduous
        toil;
for the Arno, foaming in its descent down the rocks,
    slowed and poured its sluggish waters into a swamp.
There was no earth fit for walking, no water fit for boats,
    no streams for fish, no pasturage for cattle.   10
Not yet could the traveler, marveling at four bridges,
    pass straight across the river with dry feet.
Not yet had water, brought to us from far-off places,
    flowed into our city on a lofty aqueduct;
but where the Signoria now raises its high tower,   15
    a fisherman had built his crude and artless hut,
and where we put the holy waters of the Baptistry,
    there was a pond noisy with the sound of frogs.
Who then had seen the temple of the Cross, who beheld
    the monument in proud stone to the Alberti clan,   20
who had experience of the Florentine courts of law
    or the forum which surrounds you, lofty Signoria?
All the fields were squalid, lying in a muddy marsh,
    which now reach in towering structures to the stars.
The Sullan settler, fleeing the bitter mountain air,   25
    was the first who skillfully drained off our fields,
and gathering Arno's waters together, bursting every block,
    he forced them to flow into a straight river-bed.
First it gladly made its way down to the nearby sea,
    so that a noble city might be built, a lovely labor.   30
Here, not unmindful of the Capitoline citadel,
    he first gave our dwellings a Roman name,
and laid out forums fashioned in the Roman style
    and, following Roman style, he built a Curia first.
But then he built as well a temple made of varied marble,   35
    supported with long columns, to the war-god Mars.

Et quae rupta iacent turpi vitiata senecta
   moenibus adiunxit alta theatra novis.
Alite felici sic prima exordia nostrae
40   urbi et praeclaro contulit auspicio.
Ipsaque paulatim saeclo deserta sequenti
   implevit nostras urbs Fesulana domos,
migrantesque viri montis de sede vetusta
   auxerunt opibus moenia nostra suis.
45 Quos inter stirpis generisque novissimus auctor
   affuit Antoni Canisiane tui;
hinc tibi, qua maneant patriae monumenta prioris,
   aerea in niveo marmore luna micat.
Lunam etenim Fesulus populus gestaverat olim,
50   index quae priscae nobilitatis erat,
lunam nunc Fesula tu qui descendis ab urbe,
   insigne antiquae nobilitatis habes.
Longa referre mora est, priscorum stirpis avorum
   si quot erunt nobis, enumerare velim.
55 At tibi quem simili, Medices, dignemur honore,
   nullum quod norim sanguis avitus habet.
Namque inter reliquos tantum domus ista decorum
   egregios cives exserit alta caput,
quantum Christifera gaudet quod virgine, templum
60   molibus exuperat cetera templa suis.
Hinc meritisque gravis multa et pietate verendus
   eloquioque potens Verius exoritur;
namque hic civiles rabie insurgente tumultus
   pressit et exortum seditione malum.
65 Nunquam alias maiore ruit plebs concita motu,
   portabatque atras iam fera turba faces;
tunc Medices praevectus equo, quique albus ubique
   signabat maculis candida terga nigris,
vixque erat aspectus populo, et iam nota furentis

He also added lofty theatres to new-built walls,
   which now lie broken, crumbling with ugly age.
Thus under blessed omens and the best of signs
   he brought into being the first beginnings of our city.   40
Bit by bit, the city of Fiesole, abandoned
   in the following age, peopled our homes,
and men, migrating down from their ancient hill,
   enriched our city with their wealth and resources.
Among them was the very earliest representative   45
   of your clan and kin, Antonio Canigiani;
hence, that some memory of your earlier land may live,
   a bronze moon glitters for you on snowy marble.
For the people of Fiesole used to bear a moon
   as their device, a mark of old nobility;   50
now you, who descend from the Fiesolan city,
   have a moon as the sign of your ancient nobility.
If I should wish to catalogue the number of your stock
   of old forefathers, the tale would be long to tell.
But you whom we deem worthy of like honor, Medici,   55
   have no ancestral blood that I might find out.
Indeed, that lofty house acquires its honored eminence
   only amongst the rest of it famous citizens,
as much as that temple exceeds all the rest in size
   that rejoices in the virgin Mother of the Christ.   60
Hence arose Vieri, powerful in eloquence,
   grave in merit and for deep piety revered;
he suppressed the civil tumult with its rising fury,
   the evil that sedition had caused to emerge.
Never had there ever been a plebs so aroused: 65
   blindly the mad mob ran, carrying deadly torches.
Then Medici, borne upon a snow-white horse,
   whose bright coat was marked all over with black spots,
scarcely had been seen by the people, when the man's

149

70   maiestas vulgi presserat ora sui.
        Utque fretum, hinc Sicula cohibet quod parte Pelorus,
            hinc claudent Latiae regia saxa plagae,
        nunc Scyllae illidit scopulis nunc atra Charybdis
            gurgitibus rapidis ima per antra vorat —
75   et vorat et rursus fluctus eiectat in auras,
            saxa tegunt spumae, litora curva fremunt —
        at si caeruleos magnarum rector aquarum
            illa Neptunus parte reflexit equos,
        tunc cadit omne maris murmur, rabidosque furentum
80   latratus cohibet Scylla maligna canum;
        excipiunt pelagi tunc muta silentia regem,
            ille volat paribus per freta summa rotis:
        sic rabies populi cecidit taciturnaque cunctis
            iam stupidum placuit ora tenere viris.
85   Verius at placidis commiscens aspera dictis
            pectora multisonae plebis acerba domat;
        nam notus pietate sui, qui publica semper
            duxit privatis anteferenda bonis.
        Insanos multa cum libertate furores
90   rettulit in veram Verius ipse viam.
        Haec igitur sumens exempla domestica magnus
            ante omnes Cosmus enumeratur avos.
        Dicite vos: veterem quisquis laudare senatum
            optarit, patriae quis bona tanta tulit?
95   Nemo prior vidit ventura pericula, nemo

majesty had chastened the raging crowd.   70
Like the strait, which on Sicily's shore Pelorus confines
    and which the royal rocks of the Latian shores enclose,
which strikes now the cliffs of Scylla, now black Charybdis
    swallows up in swirling whirlpools through its deepest
        caves,
swallows and disgorges its waters again into the air,   75
    mantling the rocks with foam, the curving shore roars;
but if Neptune, the ruler of the waters wide,
    should rein in his seablue horses in that place,
then the full noise of the sea subsides, and evil Scylla
    tempers the savage barking of her maddened dogs;   80
then utter silence welcomes the king of the sea,
    as he flies over the wavetops on steady wheels:
thus the fury of the people sank and now, amazed,
    it seemed good to every man to hold his tongue.
So Verius, mingling stinging words with calming ones,   85
    tames the hostile passions of the shouting populace.
For he was known for his sense of duty, he who always
        thought
    the public weal should be preferred to private goods.
Verius himself brought their maddened fury back
    into the right path, but with large liberty.   90
Hence great Cosimo, copying these family models,
    is reckoned far ahead of all his ancestors.
Tell me, whoever you are, who might wish to extol
    the old senate: who brought such good to his country?
No one saw the coming danger earlier, and no one,   95

succurrit visis promptius usque malis.
Alter Aristides, alter Cato, publica iusto
    munera magnanimus iure gerenda capit.
Dives erat quondam Crassus, sed dives avara
100   sollicitus vetitas arte parabat opes,
nec partem posuitve suis inopesve levavit
    cives, nec sacris stant pia tecta focis.
At diversa locis struxit quae Cosmus eodem
    si fundare solo ditia templa velis,
105   vix Capitolinae circumdent moenibus arcis
    Tarpeio quondam limina sacra Iovi.
Adde etiam excelsos, urbis decora alta, penates,
    quaeque tot hospitibus tecta benigna patent.
Rebus at in duris illo quid fortius unquam
110   cive tulit magnis urbs populosa viris?
Testis erit nobis armis opibusque superbus,
    qui sua rex Calabris castra refersit equis
et quicumque gravi Tyrrheni sceptra leonis
    ausus erat duro subdere Marte iugo.
115 Nam neque magnanimum fregerunt horrida pectus
    bella nec adverso proelia gesta deo.
Turris ut in summi fundata cacumine montis
    immotam scopulis se tenet alta suis,
et licet hinc Boreas, rapidis hinc flatibus Eurus
120   certent et pluvii flumina nigra Noti,
pedibus illa suis haeret tamen usque, nec ima
    parte nec in summo vertice pulsa tremit:
sic ille intrepida quaecumque pericula mente
    excipit et duris casibus antevenit.
125 Hinc igitur felix populus felixque senatus
    natis et Cosmo sospite noster erit.
Ille quidem magnos hoc consultore tumultus

having recognized the evil, was more prompt to help.
Like another Aristides, another Cato, this great-souled man
    with due right administers his public duties.
Crassus of old was rich, but in his riches, with greedy skill
    he anxiously kept piling up forbidden wealth,   100
and didn't share with his family or with needy citizens
    and built no sacred buildings with holy hearths.
But if you were to found in a single place
    the rich churches Cosimo built in different spots,
they would circle the precincts sacred to Tarpeian Jove   105
    by the walls of the citadel on the Capitoline.
Add to them the lofty home, a high glory of the city,
    whose kindly rooms lie open to so many guests.
But in hard times, has a city peopled with great men
    ever begotten someone stronger than this citizen?   110
Witness the king, proud in his wealth and arms,
    who filled his camps with horses of Calabria,
and anyone else who dared put the scepter of the lion
    of Tyrrhenia under the hard yoke of Mars.
For dreadful wars did not break his great-souled resolve   115
    nor battles waged under adverse omens.
Just as a tall tower on the crest of a mountain-top
    keeps itself motionless on its rocky base,
and though the North Wind on this side and the East on that
    and the black storms of the South contend with violent   120
        blasts,
still it holds fast to its foundations and never shakes,
    though stricken in its lowest part and on its highest peak:
so with fearless mind he took on every danger
    and anticipated every misfortune.
Hence happy will our people be and happy our senate   125
    so long as Cosimo and his sons are safe and sound.
Indeed, with him as guide, the state has fended off

reppulit et mitis ocia pacis habet.
Ille etiam Cosmi conductas aere catervas
130   instruit, et Cosmi militat aere leo.
Aspicite, o cives, quicquid micat urbe decorum,
    quae multis annis aedificata nitet!
Hoc decus ille novum populoque urbique paravit,
    ut vetus ingenti cresceret arte decus.
135   Vos ergo humano geniti de semine divi,
    quis nova templa pius Cosmus habere dedit,
tu Virgo ante alias, tibi iam si rite columnis
    suspendit Medices marmora pulchra Petrus,
hunc nobis servate senem, date candida Cosmo
140   vellera longaevis continuare colis,
ut natos, serum dum iam sub tempus habenas
    tractant, longaevus cernat utrosque senes.

∴ 4 ∴

Eulogium in fratrem suum

Ergo heu mi misero sine te — nec fata pudebit —
    perpetuus, frater, pectora luctus edet.
Te sine nunc, vitae frater pars maxima nostrae,
    cogar in aeterna vivere maestitia;
5   nam mihi te teneris durus Mars subripit annis,
    quinta nec, ah, licuit lustra videre tibi.
Ille etenim octava Saturno a sede malignum
    oppositus vitae contudit astra tuae,
unde et crudeles nimium te saevus in hostes
10   impulit irato sydere ferre pedem.

great tumults and has the leisure of gentle peace.
The state has also marshaled troops, hired by Cosimo's wealth
    and, through the wealth of Cosimo, the Lion wages war.   130
Look, O citizens, at the glory beaming on our city,
    look at the buildings that shine now for many years!
He has secured this new glory for people and city alike,
    so that its old glory may grow through the grandeur of its
        art.
You, therefore, you holy ones, sired by human seed,   135
    to whom the pious Cosimo has given temples new,
you, Virgin, before the rest, if for you Piero de' Medici
    has now raised up on columns lovely marbles in due form,
preserve for us this old man, grant that pure white wool
    run unbroken from long-lived distaffs for our Cosimo,   140
so that while his sons yet hold the reins beyond their time,
    the long-lived old man might see them both, too, grow old.

: 4 :

Eulogy for His Brother

Your loss then makes me wretched — no shame to the Fates —
    ah, endless grief, dear brother, will eat at my heart.
Without you now, my brother and best part of my life,
    I shall be forced to live in everlasting sorrow;
for pitiless Mars has snatched you from me in your youth   5
    and you were not allowed to see your twenty-fifth year, alas.
For Mars, opposed by Saturn from his eighth abode,
    in malice crushed the constellation of your life;
hence, himself too savage against the cruel foe,
    he drove you to walk beneath an angry star.   10

At tamen hunc Stygiae submersit unda paludis,
    bellica qui primus duxit in arma viros,
qui pacem subito potuit turbare tumultu,
    dum movet horrenti Martia castra tuba.
15   Hic adamanta tulit ferrato in pectore durum,
    durius aut siquid esse adamante potest,
Hic miseram nato privavit saepe parentem,
    et caruit sponso pacta puella viro.
Hic te subripuit, teque hic mihi, frater, ademit:
20   et vita atque oculis frater amabilior;
tam dilecte mihi, quantum nec Castora Pollux,
    unica nec quantum pignora mater amat.
Sed tamen haec durum mulcent solatia casum
    et faciunt tantis me superesse malis,
25   quod nihil indignum tam dirae mortis imago
    impulit audaci te subiisse viro,
nec Lusitani vidit te turma tyranni,
    nec Calabrum cunei terga dedisse fugae,
sed pedes adversos equitis iaculatus in armos
30   prendisti occurrens frena fugacis equi.
Nam vires aderant volucrisque celerrima plantae,
    quae posset fluvios exuperare fuga.
Sed frustra, heu miseri, si nobis fata repugnent
    nitimur impositas exuperare colos!
35   Iam Lusitanum victus porrexerat ensem
    hostis et in nexus brachia capta dabat,
ecce ferox Arago turmam provectus et acri
    auxilio comiti tela inimica quatit.
Et tibi, me miserum, frater dum vincula nectis
40   captivo et reditus ad tua signa paras,
improvisus adest et dextras vulnere costas
    transigit et medium pervolat hasta iecur.
Accurrit tum densa cohors cunctique manipli

Still, the waters of the Stygian swamp closed over him
    who first led men into warlike arms,
who with sudden tumult could overturn peace,
    moving Mars' camps to arms with trumpet blasts.
He bore adamantine steel in his ironclad heart,   15
    or, if it is possible, something harder than steel.
Many times he's robbed the grieving mother of her son,
    and the sweetheart of the man to whom she's betrothed.
He has stolen you, he's snatched you from me, brother:
    a brother more beloved than my life and my eyes;   20
so loved by me that Pollux did not love Castor more,
    or more than a mother loves her only child.
But still there are comforts to soothe my bitter loss
    and to let me to get beyond this great disaster.
Because the image even of so terrible a death   25
    drove you to nothing unbefitting the brave;
the squadrons of the Spanish tyrant and his Calabrian wedge
    never saw you offer your back in flight,
but a foot soldier, thrown against the armor of a knight,
    you ran up and seized the reins of his fleeing horse.   30
For a strength was yours, a swiftness of winged feet
    that was able to outrun a river in spate.
But, wretched ones, if fate fights against us, it's vain
    to struggle to defeat what the distaff demands!
For when the vanquished enemy gave up his Spanish sword   35
    and was offering his forearms to be bound,
lo, a fierce Aragonese, riding up with his troop,
    brandishes hostile weapons to help his comrade.
And while tying up your captive and preparing to return
    to your standards, he's rushing at you, brother, unawares,   40
O horrible! his spear pierces, wounding your right side,
    and slides into the center of your vitals.
Then a tight-knit cohort rushes up and all the soldiers,

et clipeo flentes saucia membra locant.
45   Ille ubi se certa vidit iam morte teneri,
        talia magnanimo pectore verba refert:
     "Sensimus hoc dudum, cum durum in viscera ferrum
        irruit, extremum lucis adesse diem.
     Verum communis veni cum Martis ad arma,
50   noram quas soleat sors variare vices,
     ut durae immineant quam saeva pericula pugnae
        et circa fatum militis arma volet,
     nec mihi tum certam statui sperare salutem,
        aut quod commune est posse carere malo.
55   Sive igitur, quodcumque meae de stamine vitae
        restitit, ante diem fors inimica tulit,
     seu potius certum nec devitabile fatum
        hoc tantum dederat quod superare nefas,
     intrepidus forti quamvis horrenda subibo,
60   quae natura parens ultima dona dedit.
     Nam qui militiae pulchro raptatur amore,
        exuat hic omni pectora mollitiae;
     vulgus enim et vilem demulcent prospera plebem,
        quae sua denervat corda cupidinibus;
65   terrores vero mortis trepidosque tumultus
        est animi proprium vincere fortis opus.
     Non ergo invitus cogar, sequor ecce volensque
        iam iam Lethaei pocula nigra bibam.
     Sed tamen heu cari miserum genitoris imago
70   sauciat atque domus maxima cura, soror.
     Politianeas nam me dum tristis in arces
        alitis adversae mitteret ominibus,
     egressum Laribus me ad portas usque secutus
        illacrimans fracta talia voce dabat:
75   Novi ego quae sedeat iuvenili in corde cupido
        laudis et egregiae gloria militiae,

weeping, place your wounded limbs upon a shield.
When he saw that he was now in the grip of certain death,   45
   my brother from his noble heart spoke these fine words:
"When the hard iron broke into my bowels, I knew
   that the final day of my life had finally come.
Truly, when I took up arms in our common battle,
   I understood the chances I was going to take,   50
how cruelly loom the dangers of a difficult fight
   and how fate hovers round a soldier's arms.
I decided then not to hope for certain safety,
   or that I could evade the evil common to us all.
So, if hostile chance has carried off before its time   55
   whatever is left of the thread of my life,
or rather, if a sure and ineluctable fate,
   has given only this much life, wrong to exceed,
fearless I shall bear the last gifts, though dreadful
   even to the brave, which parent Nature has given.   60
For he who is seized by the splendid love of war
   strips his breast of all that is soft or cowardly;
prosperity emasculates the crowd of common folk,
   whose hearts are enervated by false desires;
in truth, it is the proper task of the brave soul   65
   to overcome the terror and the tumult of death.
I'll not therefore be forced unwilling—see, I follow freely—
   now, even now, I drink from Lethe's black cups.
But still, alas, the sad image of my dear father
   and my sister, our house's greatest care, does wound me.   70
For sending me to the stronghold of Montepulciano,
   depressed and under a bird of ill-omen,
he followed me up to the gates as I left the house,
   and full of tears, with breaking voice he spoke these words:
'I knew what lust for praise lived in your youthful heart,   75
   how you loved the glory of military service,

quis furor in bello, quam nescia cedere virtus
    viribus inferior maxima saepe ciens.
Quod te per nostros annos lacrimasque seniles,
80   quae nunc ex oculis fluminis instar eunt,
si pia solliciti flectit te cura parentis
    atque suum pondus verba precantis habent,
parce precor, miseroque patri qui dura senectae
    incolumi nato taedia ferre potest.
85   Siquis at adversus casus — sed triste recusat
    omen inhorrescens lingua referre metu —
hoc prius, omnipotens, coeli qui templa frequentas,
    ad Styga terribili fulmine mitte caput,
ad Styga mitte caput prius hoc, quam dura superstes
90   ante diem nati funera conspiciam.
Haec tunc ille gemens, verum interrupta frequenti
    singultu, salsae flumina fudit aquae,
nec mihi nunc animum, sed mors iam degravat artus,
    deficit in medio frigida lingua sono."
95   Sic ille, at stridens crassum vomit ore cruorem
    vulnus, et e gelido sanguine vita fugit.
Proh dolor! At magno quis possit verba dolore,
    Musa licet faveat, digna referre satis?
Ille per obscuras fauces grave olentis Averni
100   ingreditur nigrum non rediturus iter.
Lurida rimosa iam tranat flumina cymba,
    cernit Echidnei guttura lata canis.
At soror interea — quanta ab caligine rerum
    obruimur! — totis noctibus urget opus
105 utque reversuro tenui velamina lino
    consuit, heu votis fisa puella piis,
nocturnum et vario cantu solata laborem
    ad breve, qui periit, tempus adesse putat.
At nobis fusco velatus somnus amictu

how warlike madness, how lesser power, not knowing
    how to yield to strength, often urges the greatest deeds.
By my aged years and by an old man's tears,
    which now like a river flow down from my eyes,   80
if dutiful concern for an anxious parent moves you,
    and the words of the one who begs you have any weight,
spare, I pray you, a miserable father who can bear
    the weariness of age only with his son safe.
But if any mischance should befall — though in fear   85
    my shuddering tongue rejects the gloomy omen —
O Almighty One who dwells in heaven's holy precincts,
    before it happens, strike me dead with your bolt.
Send my spirit to the Styx before then, before I see,
    alive still, the untimely, bitter funeral of my son.'   90
Lamenting thus, interrupted by repeated sobs,
    he poured forth a river of salted tears,
and now I have no spirit; death now weighs down my limbs,
    and my tongue, grown cold, fails me in mid-speech."
Speaking thus, his wound spits forth a thick bloody mass,   95
    hissing, and from that cold blood his life flees away.
O the pain! But, though the Muse look with favor,
    who could utter words worthy of so great a sorrow?
Through the dark jaws of foul, reeking Avernus
    he enters on a black road from which he'll not return.   100
Now he crosses the ghastly river in a leaking boat,
    and he makes out the gaping throats of Cerberus.
But meanwhile his sister — ah, the dark cloud of our ruin!
    all night long is carrying on her eager work;
against his return she stitches cloaks of fine linen,   105
    a maiden who trusted in her holy prayers, alas!
Solacing her nightlong work with various songs,
    she thinks that the dead man will soon be home.
But Sleep, veiled in her dusky robe, comes to us

110 heu nimium veris venit imaginibus.
Nam quam porta nigri Plutonis cornea misit,
nota mihi ante oculos affuit umbra tui.
Haec properans: nostrae, frater, persolvimus, inquit,
transfuga nec venio, munera militiae.
115 Nunc reditum in sedes mater me accersit avitas
laetus et ad patriae limina prisca paro.
Iamque vale dixit, simul et vestigia torquens
elapsa est visus umbra benigna meos.
O me infelicem! nox o mihi prima malorum
120 nuntia, quid potuit durius esse mihi?
Excitor infelix et iam praesaga futuri
mens mihi sollicito pectore concutitur.
At mox fama ruens somnique obscura recludit
atque prius dubium narrat aperta malum.
125 Ex illo binos sensi mea lumina fontes,
qui mihi perpetuis imbribus ora lavant,
ex illo curae maerentis cordis edaces
noctes atque dies pectora nostra premunt.
Nec possunt docti a luctu seducere amici,
130 multa licet vera de ratione ferant,
nec me longa dies, lacrimas quae siccat aniles
quaeque oblita mali mollia corda levat,
sed nec Pyerides, quo Manes coniugis Orpheus
demulsit, possunt me revocare sono.
135 At tu casta parens felix, quam praevia tanto
maerori eripuit de tribus una soror;
nam quos heu luctus, gemitus quos dulcis acerbo
viventi natus funere concuteret!
Tu tua sensisses, ah quanto victa dolore,
140 viscera barbarica dilaniata manu,

with images which are, alas, all too true.   110
For your familiar shade, which dark Pluto's gate of horn
    sent to me, appeared before my eyes.
In haste it says: "I come not as a deserter, brother,
    I've paid the debt of my military service.
Now mother calls me to return to our ancestral seats;   115
    happy I prepare for my homeland's ancient doors."
Then the kindly shade said, farewell! and turned its steps
    at the same moment, slipping from my sight.
Unhappy me! O night that first brought this evil news,
    what could ever have been crueler to me?   120
Sorrowfully I awake, and my mind, full of foreboding
    already is stricken in my anxious breast.
Soon rumor rushes in, making clear the dream's dark message
    and the evil that before was doubtful now stands plain to
        see.
At that, I felt my eyes turn into double fountains,   125
    that bathe with constant showers my countenance.
At that, the gnawing cares of a grieving heart
    press upon my spirit night and day.
Wise friends cannot extricate the grief from my heart,
    though they offer many arguments of true reason,   130
nor can passing time, which dries old women's tears
    and lightens tender hearts, forgetful of evil,
nor even the Muses, by whose song Orpheus soothed
    the spirit of his wife, could summon me back.
Happy you, chaste mother, who was saved from such grief   135
    by one of three sisters, going on before,
for what groans, what laments a sweet son, alas!
    stirs up in the living by his bitter death!
Overcome by so much pain, would you not have felt
    your vitals torn to pieces by a barbarian hand,   140

cumque tuo aeternis lacrimis damnata marito
    aerumnas praeter quid tibi vita daret?

∶ 5 ∶

Elegia in bello Aragonensi

Octavum nitidis implet iam cornibus orbem
    errans purpureis aurea luna rotis,
ex quo mordaci praefixus corda dolore
    vix cecini de te carmina Xandra decem.
5   Sed Musae testes et magni mater Amoris
    et qui me miserum tam male vexat Amor,
nulla tui nostram cepisse oblivia mentem:
    ultima si fallo lux eat ista mihi.
Sed mea mens tristi belli concussa tumultu
10   qui caneret dulcis proelia laeta deae?
An ego delitiis penitusque addictus amori
    mandabo imbelli carmina blanda lyrae?
Solus et a curis communi in peste solutus
    longa teram molli tempora desidia?
15   Interea nostris praeda ditatus ab agris
    et pecus et dominos Appulus hostis aget.
Magne Fluentinae Mavors primordia gentis,
    cur fuit heu nostri tam tibi cura levis?
An tibi Tyrrheni sordent sic facta leonis,
20   ut nos tam subito, dive, perisse velis?
Moenia tu Mavors Fesulis sub montibus olim
    numine iussisti surgere nostra tuo,
et dixti: Ominibus proh quam Florentia magnis
    crescet; erit Tuscis urbibus ista caput!

and with your husband damned to eternal tears
    what would life offer you but suffering and pain?

: 5 :

Elegy on the Aragonese War

Now the golden moon wandering on her dark wheels
    for the eighth time fills the circlet of her shining horns,
yet in that time, with my heart pierced by biting sorrow,
    I've scarcely written ten poems about you, Xandra.
But the Muses and the mother of great Love shall testify   5
    and Love himself who persecutes me, wretched as I am,
that no forgetfulness of you has ever seized my brain:
    may this day be my last if I'm deceiving you.
But with my mind stricken by the sad tumults of war,
    who may sing the happy contests of the sweet goddess?   10
Shall I be wholly pledged to the pleasures of love,
    and pluck charming songs on an unwarlike lyre?
Alone and free from worry about our common scourge,
    shall I wear away long hours in soft idleness?
Meanwhile the Apulian foe, enriched by his plunder,   15
    will drive off both cattle and their masters from our fields.
Mighty Mars, source of the Florentine people,
    why was your care for us so fickle, alas?
Or do you find the deeds of the Tyrrhenian lion so base,
    that you, holy one, would wish us dead so suddenly?   20
Once upon a time, O Mars, you bade our walls arise
    by your nod divine beneath Fiesole's hills;
how Florentia shall grow, you said, beneath our auspices!
    She shall be the chief among the Tuscan cities!

25   Nunc nostra, infandum, longa obsidione tenentur
        oppida, maiorum quae posuere manus.
    Quid faciat patriae spes et tutela, Senatus,
        quique decem curant bella gerenda viri?
    Stat Gallicanis exercitus alter in oris,
30   multaque de nostro pascitur aere cohors;
    nec facile est castris sumptus praebere duobus,
        nec contemnendus hostis utrimque premit.
    Hinc ruit Aragonum disrupto foedere princeps,
        nec satis est terra, ni paret arma mari;
35   hinc Venetae innumero complentur milite turmae,
        atque urbes socias Braccius urget eques.
    Sed vos, Syllanidae, si quid virtutis avorum
        restat adhuc animo pectoribusque sedet,
    ne gerite inceptum conducto milite bellum;
40   exempla a priscis iam repetantur avis.
    Audendum propriis manibus patriaeque vetustis
        legibus ; insultet per sua castra leo.
    Sitque ea vis animo, qua quondam saeva minantem
        impulit audacem vertere terga Lupam.
45   Si valuit quondam Regias sternere turmas
        hic populus patrio signa movente duce,
    si Campaldinae testantur funera pugnae,
        sanguine qua rubris fluxerat Arnus aquis,
    si Volaterrani nostro sub Marte domantur
50   nec iuvat excelsis moenia habere locis,
    cur Nolana cohors Calabri vel principis alae
        sic poterunt Fesulas nunc superare manus?
    Nondum adeo amisit vires Florentia priscas,
        ut sit Campanis praeda futura viris.

Now, dreadful to say, our towns, laid out by the hands   25
    of our forebears, are being gripped by a long siege.
What should the Senate do, the country's hope and guardian,
    and the decemvirs, whose charge is to wage war?
Another army stands on the borders of Lower Gaul,
    and many a cohort feeds itself off our resources;   30
it is not easy to supply the costs of two camps,
    and a fearsome foe presses hard on either side.
Hence the prince of Aragon, breaking pacts, rushes down,
    and readies arms on sea as well as land;
hence Venetian squadrons fill with countless troops   35
    and Braccian cavalry besets our allied cities.
But you, sons of Sulla, if any courage from your forebears
    remains and still resides in your minds and hearts,
do not wage the war that has begun with a hired army;
    now seek out examples from among your ancient fathers.   40
We must be daring with our own hands, by the old laws
    of our land: let the lion run rampant through his camp.
Let such strength be in his spirit, as when long ago,
    he forced the bold and menacing Wolf to turn his back.
If this people once could overthrow Rhegian squadrons   45
    when that country's leader was advancing beneath his flag,
if the deaths bear witness of the field of Campaldino,
    when the Arno's waters flowed scarlet with blood,
if the people of Volterra are tamed by our martial hand,
    and are not helped by having walls in lofty places,   50
why have troops of Nola or the horse of a Calabrian prince
    now been able to surpass the troops of Fiesole?
Florence has not yet lost so her ancient prowess
    that spoils of war will be won by men from Campania.

: 6 :

Ad Paulum ne timeat bellum Aragonense

Etsi praeclari sint haec pia munera civis,
　　ut sibi sit patriae maxima cura suae,
ut varios casus semper variosque reflexus
　　fortunae et varias cogitet usque vices,
5　　non tamen adversis te adeo diffidere rebus,
　　Paule, velim ut turpi sic quatiare metu.
Provida namque decet fidentem cautio civem,
　　sed timor a forti sit procul usque viro.
Sit satis, humanae quod possunt cernere mentes,
10　　consulere et culpa non maculare caput.
Cetera linque Deis: nam Di mortalia curant,
　　Di Florentinis saepe tulistis opem.
Saepeque maiores urbs haec experta tumultus,
　　saepeque maiori venit ab hoste metus.
15　　Quis turmas equitum nescit peditumque cohortes
　　Caesaris Herrici Teutonicasque minas?
Hic opibus magnique Augusti nomine fretus
　　sperarat Fesulam perdere posse domum.
Quin etiam ad Salvi posuit praetoria templum
20　　et tetigit castris moenia nostra suis;
mox tamen effugiens multa virtute ruentes
　　non tulit Etruscos in sua terga viros.
Nam quid Topori cladem mediaque receptas
　　morte acies socium vinclaque rupta canam?
25　　Urbi nempe mihi nostrae hoc dare fata videntur,
　　possit ut adversis spe meliore frui.
Testis tu nobis dum, Piccinine, Mugelli
　　per iuga terribilis Gallica signa rapis.

: 6 :

To Paolo, Not to Fear the Aragonese War

Even though it is the duty of a famous citizen
    to devote his greatest care to his country,
continually to take thought for its manifold mischances,
    and different turns of fortune and vicissitudes,
still, Paolo, I would not want you in adversity   5
    so to despair that you're shaken with shameful fear.
For a prudent caution suits well a confident citizen,
    but a brave man always keeps fear far away.
Let it be enough, as far as human minds can see,
    to take wise counsel and not stain one's life with blame.   10
Leave the rest to the gods, for mortal matters are their care;
    you, gods, have often brought good help to Florentines.
Often this city has experienced still greater tumult,
    and often a greater enemy has caused us fear.
Who does not know of the emperor Henry's horse,   15
    and of his infantry cohorts and the German threat?
He, relying on his wealth and the imperial name,
    had hoped he could destroy our Fiesolan home.
He even made his headquarters the church of San Salvi,
    and pitched his camps hard by our very walls;   20
soon he fled, however, from the charge of brave Tuscans
    and could not bear to have them at his back.
What shall I sing of the disaster at Montopoli,
    our allies' line broken, their chains and death?
Surely (it seems to me) the Fates gave this to our city: 25
    that it could in bad times enjoy a better hope.
You stood witness, Piccinino, when, terrifying all,
    you marched Milan's standard through Mugello's hills.

Quando alias meliore duce et melioribus armis
30   Bebriacus Lydum terruit imperium?
Quin Florentinus comitem se fecerat exul,
      cresceret ut nostra seditione malum.
Ergo hominum atque boum vastantur culta labore
      et ferro et flammis plurima tecta cadunt.
35 Heu memini, insolito trepidant dum Marte, colonos
      vicinas urbi deseruisse domos.
Hostibus adversis et Fullonaria cessit,
      quam removet nostra quintus ab urbe lapis.
At vos aeterni mortali e semine divi,
40   Syllanum quibus est maxima cura genus,
Insubris exuvias vos atque inversa Philippi
      iussistis vestro pendere signa tolo.
Tu tibi Romulidae spolium affectare leonis
      Piccinine tuis viribus ausus eras.
45 At secus evenit Liguremque Anglaria vallis
      Tyrrhenis vidit cedere militibus,
rebus et infractis vidit te turpe latentem
      turpeque mutata carpere veste fugam.
Ergo amissa tuo redierunt oppida bello;
50   nec tamen est nobis haec rediisse satis.
Namque Casentinas quicquid possederat olim
      regulus, antiquae stirps generosa domus,
omne Fluentino nova praeda adiungitur agro.
      Sic o sic, quisquis foedera rumpit eat!
55 Sic quondam, Catilina, tuae Pistoria cladis
      urbs memor in nostras ire coacta manus,
sic Pratense solum, sic pinguia culta Bisenti,
      et quae parvus aquis irrigat Umbro suis.
Nam quis Pisanas magno in certamine vires
60   aut quis Parrhasiae nesciat urbis opes?
Omnibus imperii certatum viribus hic est,

When did Bebriacus with a better captain and better arms
  terrify the empire of the Lydians?   30
Indeed, the exiled Florentine became their comrade
  that the danger might increase from our disharmony.
Thus the lands farmed by men and beasts are laid to waste
  and many a dwelling falls to his fire and sword.
I remember, alas, how the farmers, trembling at   35
  unfamiliar war, fled their homes near the city.
Fullonaria, which lies only five miles from our city,
  also yielded to the advancing enemy.
But you, divine beings, sprung from mortal seed,
  you who care the most for the Sullan race,   40
you bade the Insubrian spoils and Filippo's standards
  hang up-side-down from your temple dome.
You, Piccinino, dared with all your might to win
  the spoils of the sons of the Romulan lion.
But it turned out otherwise, and the vale of Anghiari   45
  saw the Ligurian yield to the troops of Tuscany.
It also saw you basely hiding, as things fell apart,
  and basely taking flight in disguise.
Then the towns lost in your war came back to us;
  still, for us it's not enough that they return.   50
For once a kinglet, noble offspring of an ancient house,
  had possessed a portion of the Casentino;
all this now is added to Florence's territory as spoils.
  Thus, O thus, let treaty-breakers take themselves off!
Thus Pistoia, long ago, mindful of your ruin,   55
  Catiline, was compelled to come into our hands.
Thus came the soil of Prato, thus Bisenzio's rich fields
  and those irrigated by little Ombrone's waters.
For who is not aware of Pisan strength in that great contest,
  or of the resources of the Parrhasian city?   60
Here there was a struggle with an empire's full strength,

cum populus nollet arcas habere pares.
Di reprimunt fastus et nulla superbia longa est,
    quique pares refugit, cogitur esse minor.
65   Ergo focos arasque deum sacra atque profana,
    quamvis ille ferox, sub iuga nostra dedit.
Denique si solers annales volvere priscos
    et studeas populi noscere facta tui,
per quos ah casus, per quanta pericula cernes
70   ex humili hunc summum iam tetigisse gradum.
Nam qui olim armati bello impendente timebat
    Empori promptas in sua damna manus,
Tyrrhenas inter nunc admirabilis urbes
    extat, et Etruscis quis neget esse caput?
75   Et credemus adhuc tanta ad fastigia rerum
    venisse ut Calabro sit nova praeda duci,
quin ultro iniusti contundet saeva tyranni
    arma? Pias causas numina sancta fovent.
Ergo agite et primis felicia castra movete
80   ominibus: vates omnia fausta canunt.
Et mihi Pierides iam prospera signa puellae
    ostendunt certa non caritura fide.
Iamque dies aderit cum Florentine fugatis
    hostibus exolves maxima vota deis.
85   Tunc ego captivos longa procedere pompa
    aspiciam et vinctos post sua terga duces,
victoresque sequi nostros; tum maxima sanctis
    ignibus et ture templa calere novo.
Spectatorque aderit populus plausuque frequenti
90   turba salutantum carmina festa canet.
Hunc ego, Paule, diem quamquam mihi vita iucunda est,
    natali potero praeposuisse meo.
Namque hinc Saturni consurgent aurea prisci
    saecula, florentis otia pacis erunt.

though the People would not wish to equal it in wealth.
The gods curb arrogance and no pride lasts for long,
    and he who flees equality is forced to be lesser.
Therefore our enemy, though fierce, put his homes,   65
    and altars, both sacred and profane, beneath our yoke.
Finally, if you have the skill of unrolling old records,
    and eagerness to find out the deeds of our people,
through what misfortunes, how many dangers, you will see,
    they've now reached the heights from their old humility.   70
For the people who once feared the arms at Empoli,
    the hands eager to destroy them in impending war,
now stand among the Tuscan cities, admired by all,
    and who can deny that she is Tuscany's chief city?
And shall we believe she has come to so great a height   75
    only to be fresh plunder for a Calabrian duke?
Won't she blunt, instead, the cruel arms of that unjust tyrant?
    The sacred divinities foster the cause of the pious.
Therefore, march forth and advance joyfully to good omens:
    of all things auspicious our inspired poets sing.   80
To me, too, the Pierian maidens now give favorable signs,
    certain signs that will prove worthy of our trust.
And soon the day will come when Florence's enemies will flee,
    and you'll offer massive votive offerings to the gods.
Then I shall watch the captives going by in a long train,   85
    their captains with their hands bound behind their backs,
and our victorious heroes following; then our largest churches
    will glow with holy fires and fresh incense.
The people will come to watch and with repeated applause
    the crowd will sing festive songs of salutation.   90
Though life is pleasant to me, Paolo, still I could prefer
    this victorious day to my own birthday.
For the golden age of old Saturn henceforth shall rise,
    and the leisure of flourishing peace will be ours.

95   Mos etenim Fesulo semper fuit ista leoni,
        victor ut in victis mitior usque foret;
    mos fuit adversos pro libertate tyrannos
        comprimere, at victis mollia iura dare.
    Nam bellum semper nos hac ratione movemus,
100   ut pacem praeter nil voluisse putes.

: 7 :

Eulogium in Carolum Arretinum

Ergo immaturo, nec te tua sancta iuvabit,
    Carle, fides, nobis funere raptus abis?
Sed vos dum vestri celebramus funera vatis,
    dicite Pierides carmina pauca mihi;
5   dicite, sed tanto sint quae dicenda poetae,
      efficite ut nostro crescat in ore sonus.
Occidit heu Latiae lumen splendorque Camenae,
    Carolus Etrusci gloria magna soli;
Carolus Aonio qui vos de monte vocabat,
10   viseret Etrusca vester ut antra chorus.
Ergo ut defunctum luxit Verona Catullum,
    utque tuum flevit Umbria, Nauta, rogum,
Lesbos ut Alcaeo simul et tibi, mascula Sappho,
    legitimas merito contulit inferias,
15   sic pia nunc doctum luget Florentia vatem
      et quaerit tumulo praemia digna suo.
At vos crudeles, o ferrea pectora, Parcae
    ante diem quid vos hunc rapuisse iuvat?
Non ego mortali immortalem sorte creatum
20   optabam aut cervi saecula longa seni,

Indeed, it was always the custom of the Fiesolan lion   95
    to be gentler to the vanquished in victory;
it was his custom, on behalf of freedom, to check tyrants
    and to grant gentle laws to those he had overcome.
Indeed, we always go to war on such a plan
    that you would think we wished for nothing else but peace.   100

: 7 :

Eulogy for Carlo Aretino

So, Carlo, are you leaving us, seized by untimely death?
    Will your holy faith be of no assistance to you?
But you, Muses, while we honor your poet's funeral rites,
    do put into words a few verses for me;
speak, but let my words be apt for this great poet;   5
    make the song grow more sonorous in my mouth.
Alas, the splendid sun of the Latian Muses sets,
    Carlo, chief glory of the Tuscan land;
Carlo, who called you from the Aonian mount
    that your chorus might visit the Tuscan glens.   10
Thus, as Verona mourned for dead Catullus,
    and Umbria wept at your pyre, Propertius,
as Lesbos for Alcaeus and for you, manly Sappho,
    once offered the sacrifice due your worth,
so now Florence piously mourns her poet-teacher   15
    and asks for worthy honors at his tomb.
But O you cruel Fates, O hearts of iron, why
    did you order him snatched away before his time?
I did not wish immortality for a mortal
    or the age-long life of an ancient stag,   20

sed veteris ternos Saturni evincere cursus
    humana potuit conditione dari.
Hoc fas, hoc fuerat ius: sed nunc publica cura,
    heu, iacet in gelido corpus inane toro,
25   purpureaque toga clarus Phoebique corona
    iam subit obscurum non rediturus iter.
Lucida praecedunt longa funalia pompa
    et signa a multis tradita principibus.
Namque sua antistes tibi dat vexilla Latinus,
30   ex illo hoc magni pignus amoris habes.
Aureaque hinc Galli succedunt lilia regis,
    illinc Bebriaci signa superba ducis.
Quarta Fluentini sequitur crux rubra leonis,
    nam sunt haec populi munera magna tui.
35 Nam quid ego Arreti, quod te patriaeque parentem
    quodque decus dicit, ultima dona loquar?
Ipsa tuum subeunt gymnasia nostra feretrum,
    doctaque turba pio fungitur officio.
Assunt quaterni quaterna e classe tribuni,
40   quique decem curant bella gerenda viri,
assunt custodes magnae bis quattuor urbis,
    quosque magistratus longa referre mora est.
At vos in primis, Guelphae quibus inclita sectae
    est aquila in viridi facta dracone potens,
45 nec non Syllani populariter inde Quirites
    certatim celebrant triste ministerium.
Omnia supremo possunt quae tempore reddi,
    reddita sunt tumulo, docte poeta, tuo;
nec tamen heu quisquam meritos impendere honores
50   sat putat. Huic vati quid satis esse potest?
Quis tenuit lacrimas? Quis non crudelia dixit
    astra? Quid in tota non fuit urbe dolens?
Sed quod praecipuum est, magni suspiria Cosmi

but that he could be given a chance to surpass
 three of old Saturn's circuits in human form.
This had been right and just; but now, alas, he lies,
 an empty corpse on a cold bier, a state concern,
and bright with scarlet toga and Apollo's crown,   25
 he now endures the dark journey, never to return.
Bright torches go before your long procession
 and banners handed down from many a prince.
For the Latin bishop presents you with his standard,
 and from him you have this pledge of his great regard. 30
And on this side come the golden lilies of the French King,
 on that the proud banners of the Duke of Milan.
Fourth follows the red cross of the Florentine lion,
 for these are the abundant gifts of your people.
What can I say of the last gifts of Arezzo,   35
 who calls you its glory and the father of your country?
Our gymnasia themselves follow after your bier
 and the learned throng carries out its pious duties.
Four tribunes are present from each of four classes,
 and the ten officials whose charge is to wage war, 40
the eight guardians of our great city are here,
 and magistrates it would take too long to list,
but you, first of all, who carry the famous eagle
 of the Guelf Party, strong in the Green Dragon,
and the People of Sulla thereafter, in a body,   45
 emulously throng to their melancholy duty.
All honors that at the final hour can be paid
 have been offered at your burial, learned poet;
yet no one thinks sufficient the honors that are paid,
 alas! What honor could be, for so great a seer?   50
Who held back his tears? Who did not blame the cruel stars?
 What was there in all the city that did not feel grief?
But most of all, we witnessed all the sighs and tears

et lacrimas tanto vidimus ire viro.
55   Quin et vicinos dicunt gemuisse leones,
      et triviis fidos exululasse canes.
    Ipsae per montes sacrataque flumina Nymphae
      solverunt moestas in sua colla comas;
    sed tamen ante alias pulcherrima sola sororum
60   ploravit natum Calliopea suum.
    Hanc aderant circum Phoebus doctaeque sorores,
      frigida Parnasi quae iuga summa tenent,
    nec liquido ut quondam mulcebant aera cantu,
      nec cythara in manibus nec coma culta fuit.
65   Squalebant atris in vestibus ipsaque laurus
      Castalii frondes vidit abire suas.
    Quin et Gorgonei quas eruit ungula monstri,
      Bellorophonteae delituistis aquae.
    Heu tunc fata pii damnans immitia nati
70   edidit hos questus Calliopea novos:
    "Quod scelus admisit vel quo vos crimine Parcae
      laeserat? An tristis vos quoque livor habet?
    Huic ego cum primae polleret flore iuventae
      versibus in lyricis aurea plectra dedi.
75   His iuvenum curas et mobile pectus amantum
      lusit et aligeri regna superba dei.
    His etiam laudes rectae et virtutis amorem,
      quem sequitur vera nobilitate decus.
    At matura gravem multis ubi fecerat aetas
80   artibus et poterat carmen hiare novum,
    me duce Cirrhaei vatis deductus in antrum,
      silva quod horrenti laurea fronde tegit,
    hic tantum a Phoebo suscepit mente furoris,
      Maeonius quantum ceperat ante senex.
85   Sic igitur maiora sonans iam pectore pleno

Cosimo the Great produced for this great man.
They say that even lions in the neighborhood groaned,   55
    and faithful dogs howled at the crossroads too.
Among the hills, among the hallowed streams the very
    Nymphs
    loosened their hair along their necks in mourning,
but yet, before the others, the loveliest of the sisters,
    Calliope wept all alone for her child.   60
Around her stood Apollo and her learned sisters,
    who dwell on Parnassus' chilly mountains heights,
nor did they, as before, charm the air with liquid song;
    no lyre was in their hands, their hair was unkempt.
They stood filthy in black garments, and even the laurel   65
    of Castalia saw its leaves fall from the stem.
Indeed, you are in hiding too, O waters of Bellerophon,
    whom the talons of the monstrous Gorgon unearthed.
Calliope, condemning the harsh fates of her pious son
    then brought forth these new lamentations: 70
"What crime has he committed, how has he injured you,
    Parcae? Or has bitter envy struck at you as well?
As he grew stronger in the flower of young manhood
    I taught him to pluck out verses on the golden lyre.
In these he sang of the cares of youth and lovers' fickle hearts   75
    and the proud monarchy of the wingèd god.
In these he sang the praises and love of upright virtue,
    and the honor that comes from true nobility.
But when ripe age had loaded him with many arts,
    and he was enabled to utter a new song,   80
then I led him up into the grotto of Apollo,
    which a laurel wood covers with its trembling leaves,
and Phoebus put into his mind as much inspiration
    as the old man of Maeonia had received of old.
Thus singing, then, of greater things with a full heart,   85

ausus sublimis spiritus alta loqui;
ausus quod vatum pauci de stirpe priorum,
    ausus quod veteres vix potuere patres,
ut quod Smyrnaeo cognoscunt carmine Grai,
90   hoc legerent Italo saecula nostra pede.
Spes hominum fallax, medio quae perfida cursu
    saepe cadens miseris irrita vota facit.
Nam quod iam multos frustra vigilaveris annos,
    cum minus heu credes, auferet una dies.
95   I nunc, Cecropiis vigilanti pectore chartis
    insuda, ut veterum dogmata prisca legas,
et nunc Socratici noscas praecepta Platonis,
    nunc quod Aristotelis pagina multa docet.
Tu mundi secreta paras atque abdita rerum
100   discere: quid coelum, quid mare, terra ferat,
unde genus nostrum, vel quo plantaria surgant
    sidere, num cuncta haec ignis et humor alat,
unde nives volitent, curque humida grando rigescat,
    qua vi de summo fulmina torta ruant,
105   quid natura petat, rectae quae munera vitae,
    et quae sint animi vera putanda bona.
Scilicet hoc memori divino pectore Carlus
    noctes atque dies advigilabat opus,
artibus ut post haec vates suffultus honestis
110   Moeonia posset digna referre tuba.
Iam Danaum morbos Phoebique furentia tela
    dixerat et densis funera nigra rogis,
Pelidaeque animos et verba minantis Atridae
    quique bonus fuerat Nestora consiliis,
115   sacraque navigiis ad Chrysam vecta Pelasgis,
    redditaque irato pignora cara patri.

   his lofty spirit dared to speak of matters sublime;
he dared what few of the ancient poets dared,
   he dared what our ancestors could scarcely dare,
so that what the Greeks learned from the Smyrnaean's song
   our age might finally read in Italic verse.   90
Ah, false human hope, which oft betrays in mid-course,
   and in her fall makes futile the vows of wretched men.
For what you once invigilated for many years in vain,
   though you'd scarce believe it, a single day destroys.
Come now, study the Cecropian page with vigilance of heart,   95
   so you may read the ancient teachings of the men of old,
and understand the teachings of Socratic Plato now,
   and now what Aristotle's many pages pass down.
You prepare to learn the hidden secrets of the cosmos:
   what the heavens, what the sea, what the earth brings forth,   100
whence comes our kind, or by what star plant cuttings grow,
   whether fire and wetness nourish all these things,
whence snows fly, and why liquids harden into hail,
   through what heavenly power twisting thunderbolts flash
      down;
what are nature's goals, what the gifts of an upright life,   105
   and what we should think are the true goods of the mind.
Plainly, Carlo, day and night, delved into this task,
   storing knowledge up in his memory divine,
so that later, buttressed by these honorable arts, the poet
   could match worthily the Homeric trumpet's sound.   110
For he described the Greeks' diseases and Apollo's furious
      darts
   and dire rites of death thick with funeral pyres,
the spirit of Achilles and the menaces of Agamemnon,
   and Nestor, the man renowned for his good counsel,
and the sacred cargo brought on Pelasgian boats to Chryse   115
   and the dear pledge returned to her wrathful father.

Tunc etenim culti torrentem sensimus oris
  qui foret et quantum surgeret ingenium,
quantum divini spirarent corda furoris,
120 cresceret et quanto splendida lingua sono.
Heu iam felici Carlus turgentia vento
  ausus erat vasto credere vela mari,
iam procul a terra scopulisque vadisque relictis
  currebat celeri per freta longa rate.
125 Ecce autem, infandum, subito nil tale timenti
  mutavit faciem fors inimica suam.
Nam subito fluctu vastaque impulsa procella
  mersa est in mediis naufraga puppis aquis,
quae si speratum tetigisset sospita portum
130 et pleno intrasset ostia tuta sinu,
nullo Arnus tantum sese iactasset alumno,
  egregios quamvis viderit ante senes."
Talia moesta parens flebat, sed plura parentem
  non tulit infandus addere verba dolor,
135 pluraque dicturae rumpunt suspiria pectus
  et flendo mediis deficit in lacrimis.
Te Florentini gymnasia docta leonis,
  natorum ut luget turba relicta patrem,
te rebus dubiis nunc publica cura Senatus
140 advigilans tanto cive carere dolet.
Intima tu magni noras praecordia Cosmi
  et quaecumque sacro pectore clausa tenet,
nec comitem rebus dubiis te respuit unquam,
  consuleret populo cum bonus ille suo.
145 Tu felix, tanti posses qui principis aures
  implere et tanto grata referre viro.
Namque tibi ingenium veloxque tenaxque reperti
  plurima quod posset condere mente fuit.

Then indeed we felt the torrent of words from his learned
        mouth
    and understood the scale of the talent that was rising,
how much his heart was filled with the madness divine,
    and how his brilliant tongue swelled with mighty sound.   120
Then, alas, Carlo dared to trust his swelling sails,
    driven by a favorable wind into the open sea,
then far from land, with cliffs and shallows left behind,
    he rushed on his swift bark through the long sea waves,
But lo, when he least expected it — and shocking it was —   125
    suddenly hostile chance took on a different face.
For in the midst of the waters his vessel was shipwrecked,
    sunken by a sudden billow and a mighty gale,
which, had it touched its longed-for harbor safe and sound,
    and entered its safe refuge with bellying sail,   130
Arno would have boasted of none of its offspring more,
    although it had had experience before of famous men."
Thus did his grieving mother mourn, but her ineffable grief
    did not allow his parent to add further words;
more sighs shatter her breast as she is about to speak,   135
    and as she wept she falters in the midst of her tears.
As a flock of orphaned children mourn for their father,
    so the learned schools of Florence mourn your loss;
The Senate's public eye, in doubtful matters ever watchful,
    grieves now to lose you, its great citizen.   140
You knew the inmost heart of Cosimo the Great
    and whatever he holds closed in his hallowed breast.
In doubtful matters you were always at his side,
    when that good man gave counsel to his people.
You were blest who could fill the ear of such a leader   145
    and express your thanks to so great a man.
For your mind, swift and holding fast to all it found,
    could store many things deep within its thought;

Adde tot egregias artes vitaeque magistrum
150   adde usum et longa multa notata die.
Legerat historias omnes et legerat omnes
   annales, priscum maxima facta virum.
Nemo quidem melius Romani aenigmata iuris
   solvit et ambiguis vincula caeca reis.
155   Nam quid ego aeterno labentia sidera cursu
   aut referam certis cognita signa locis?
Te maris undisoni, te quae gerit omnia terrae
   mensorem certa novimus esse fide.
His te purpureis sublimem ad sidera pennis
160   docta per ora virum Carule fama levat,
nec ventura tuas reticebunt saecula laudes,
   neve teget nomen qui tegit ossa lapis.
Dumque Fluentini vestigia magna leonis
   molibus ostendet Curia celsa suis,
165   dumque domos Medicum magnique palatia Cosmi
   suspiciet stupidis advena luminibus,
usque tui de te dictabunt maxima cives,
   livida nec poterit lingua nocere tibi.
Elysios igitur lucos umbrasque beatas,
170   nam sic fata iubent, docte poeta, petes.
Illic quos genitor produxit in omnia Nilus,
   quique artes primum perdocuere bonas,
quos genuit Persis, quos et Babylonia tellus,
   doctorum occurrent maxima turba tibi,
175   illic Cecropiae quot iam vidistis Athenae,
   et quisquis Latii claruit urbe Remi:
sed tu Tyrrhenae gentis contentus honore
   Etruscis cupies semper adesse tuis.
Sunt in secessu liquidi prope fluminis undam
180   quae rident herbis prata decora novis;
quot natura tulit, tot habent haec prata colores

Add so many famous skills and practical experience,
    the master of life, and the notes of many a day.   150
He'd read every history, had read every chronicle,
    the greatest deeds done by the men of old.
No one indeed better loosed the knots of Roman law
    and blind fetters from defendants doubtfully accused.
Why shall I tell of stars gliding in their timeless courses   155
    or the constellations known by their places fixed?
We knew by sure report that you had surveyed
    all things upon the earth and the sounding sea.
Fame through the learned lips of men lifts you high,
    Carlo, to the stars on these gleaming pinions,   160
and ages to come will not be silent in your praise,
    nor will the stone that covers you conceal your name.
And as long as our lofty senate house shows in its stones
    the great pawprints of the Florentine lion,
and the visitor gazes at the dwellings of the Medici   165
    and the palace of Great Cosimo with awestruck eyes,
your fellow citizens will always give you highest praise,
    and no envious tongue will be able to harm you.
Therefore, learned poet, you will seek the Elysian groves
    and its blessed shades, for so fate prescribes.   170
There, those whom Father Nile led on into all things,
    and who first imparted the liberal arts,
those whom Persia and the land of Babylon begat,
    that whole mass of learned men will be greeting you,
there, all the men of Athens whom you saw in this life,   175
    and whoever won fame in the city of Latian Remus;
but you, happy with the honor of the Tyrrhenian race,
    will always wish to be near your own Tuscan men.
They're in a quiet spot near a clear river's waters
    whose meadows laugh, bright with new grasses;   180
these meadows have as many colors as Nature has made,

pictaque diverso flore relucet humus.
Non illic Phrygiis suspensa theatra columnis
    nec sunt artifici plurima facta manu.
185   Sponte sua variis consurgit mixta rosetis
    buxus nativis sedibus unus honor;
desuper et platani castae Daphnaeaque laurus
    extendunt sacrum fronde virente nemus.
Flumen habet cycnos, at caetera turba volantum
190   permulcent liquidis ruris amoena modis.
Non illic rapidos accendit Sirius aestus,
    nec riget Arcturi sidere tristis hiems,
sed levibus Zephyris et lenis flatibus aurae
    aeterno ridens tempore vernat ager.
195   Hic Fesulae placuit sedem componere genti,
    huc veniens priscos dinumerabis avos.
Nam qui pulchra tuos cecinit, Proserpina, raptus,
    prima tenet vates primus in urbe sua.
Cui nec concedit qui terras sidera Manes,
200   quod stupeant omnes, evigilavit opus.
Hunc iuxta Gallam Tyrrheno carmine Lauram
    qui canit et Latio Punica bella pede.
Hic et Boccaci spectabis nobile nomen,
    qui pinxit varium doctus amoris opus.
205   Nec Leonardus abest, tibi qui Florentia tantum,
    quantum Romanis Livius ipse dedit.
Enumerare mora est variis quos artibus olim
    edidit illustres lenibus Arnus aquis.
Hic te certa manet sedes vitaeque laborum
210   hic bene transactae praemia, Carle, feres.
At nos aeterni sint quae monimenta decoris
    addemus tumulo carmina nostra tuo:

and the earth reflects the hues of various flowers.
There is no theatre there held up by Phrygian columns
    nor numerous works made by an artist's hand.
But of its own accord, mixed with many kinds of roses,   185
    the box-tree grows, the unique beauty of its native land;
and overhead chaste plane trees and the Daphnean laurel
    shade the blessed grove with their leafy green.
The river holds swans, but flocks of flying birds
    soothe the charming countryside with liquid song.   190
There the Dog Star does not kindle burning heat,
    nor gloomy winter freeze under Arcturus' star,
but with light zephyrs and with gentle breaths of air
    the smiling land stays springlike everlastingly.
Here the race of Fiesole delight to make their seat,   195
    and coming there, you will count your ancient forefathers.
For he who sang of your abduction, lovely Proserpina,
    holds the first place in his city as a poet.
Nor did he give place who sang of earth, stars and spirits,
    in that laborious work at which the whole world marvels.   200
Next to him stands the man who sang of Gallic Laura
    in Tuscan rhymes, and the Punic Wars in Latin verse.
Here too you will observe the noble name of Boccaccio,
    the learned man who painted various works on love.
Nor is Leonardo missing, who gave as much to you,   205
    Florence, as Livy himself gave to ancient Rome.
But it would take too long to list the famous men
    whose varied arts the Arno nourished with its gentle
        waters.
Here a sure abode is yours and here you'll win the prizes,
    Carlo, of your life and labors so well done.   210
For our part, we shall only add to your tomb these lines
    to be a monument to your everlasting glory:

Urbs tulit Arreti Carlum, Florentia lauro
  cinxit, at ingenium Calliopea dedit.
215 Luserat hic lyricos; mox dum traducit Homerum,
  occidit heu patriae gloria magna suae.

: 7a :

Aliud Epitaphium Caruli Arretini

Ampla tenent quicquid radiantis moenia mundi,
  non est humanae noscere mentis opus.
Et tamen haec Carlus norat; sed condere versu
  dum parat et nato Calliopea favet,
5 heu, ternae invidia motae vetuere sorores:
  sic cecidit nostri gloria quanta soli.

: 7b :

Aliud

Quid sumus heu miseri! Terras en sidera Manes
  qui norat, tenuis pulvis et umbra iacet.
At lauro non hunc cinxit Florentia Carlum,
  sed docuit, sacris quem pia turba colit.

Arezzo gave birth to Carlo, Florence crowned him with the
    laurel,
  but Calliope herself gave him poetic genius.
He played first with lyrics; then, while translating Homer,   215
  he died, alas, the great glory of his native land.

: 7a :

Another Epitaph for Carlo Aretino

It is not needful for the human mind to know
  all the vast walls of the shining cosmos hold.
Yet Carlo knew these things; but while putting them down
  in verse, while Calliope shows favor to her son,
alas, the triple sisters, moved by envy, forbade it: 5
  what great glory of our native soil died this way.

: 7b :

Another

Alas, how wretched are we! Behold how he who knew the
    earth,
  the stars and spirits lies here, a bit of dust and shade.
But Florence has not crowned this Carlo with the laurel,
  but taught him whom the pious mob worship with holy
    rites.

: 8 :

Epitaphium Dantis Poetae

Noras qui terras, clari qui sidera mundi
    dixit et infernos tertia regna lacus:
ille ego sum Dantes; Tusco me carmine vatem
    ornavit lauro pulcher Apollo sua.

: 9 :

Aliud

Mantua Virgilium, Smyrnae mirantur Homerum,
    quippe decus Latiis hic venit, ille suis.
Nunc paribus celebret mater Florentia Dantem
    laudibus: Etruscae nam decus omne lyrae est.

: 10 :

Epitaphium Francisci Petrarcae poetae

Quantum Pindarico vix debet Graecia plectro
    et quantum Latia vix tibi Flacce lyra,
tantum Etrusca pio concessit Musa Petrarcae,
    quo celebri fama Laura pudica viret.

: 8 :

Epitaph for the Poet Dante

You knew the man who spoke of earth, of stars in heaven
    bright,
  and of the infernal lake in the third kingdom below:
I am that Dante, to whom fair Phoebus gave his laurel,
  a seer who wrote poetry in the Tuscan tongue.

: 9 :

Another

Mantua reveres Vergil, and Smyrna her Homer,
  the one a glory to Latin folk, the other to his own.
Now let our mother Florence honor Dante with like praise;
  for he is the whole glory of the Tuscan lyre.

: 10 :

Epitaph for Francesco Petrarca, the Poet

Greece scarcely owes to Pindaric poetry
  and the lyre of Latium to you, dear Flaccus,
as much as the Tuscan Muse grants to pious Petrarca
  through whom still pure Laura lives in renown.

⁝ 11 ⁝

Aliud

Cantasti patrio Tyrrhena poemata versu,
  cantasti Latio Punica bella pede:
hinc te fronde sua Phoebus, Petrarca, coronat,
  hinc, vates, Fesula doctus in urbe vires.

⁝ 12 ⁝

De Sibylla

Bis quinas toto nosti, reor, orbe Sibyllas,
  quas inter palmam tu mihi iure dabis.
Namque ego venturum mundi in nova gaudia Christum
  Cumano cecini vaticinata solo.

⁝ 13 ⁝

De Farinata Uberto

Guelpha meo, fateor, superavimus agmina ductu,
  sanguine cum rubris Arbia fluxit aquis;
sed tamen ut priscas teneas, Florentia, sedes,
  sola Farinatae mens tibi magna dedit.

: 11 :

Another

You chanted Tuscan poems in the language of your homeland,
    you described the Punic Wars in Latin meter;
hence Apollo crowns you, Petrarch, with his wreath,
    hence, learned seer, in Florence your memory is green.

: 12 :

The Cumaean Sibyl

You know, I think, that there are twice five Sibyls in the
       world,
    among whom you must give me, rightly, the victor's palm.
For, prophesying on Cumaean soil, I sang
    that Christ would come to bring new joy into the world.

: 13 :

About Farinata degli Uberti

I was captain when we bested the Guelf army, I confess,
    when the waters of the Arbia ran red with blood;
still, only the great soul of Farinata gave you, Florence,
    the chance to go on living in your primeval site.

: 14 :

Tamyris Scytharum regina

Bis centena tuo, Tamyris, sub milite Cyrus
    Massagetum vidit milia caesa iugis.
Sanguinis et cupidum, nato placitura sepulto,
    mersisti in pleno sanguinis utre caput.

: 15 :

Ad Iohannem Salvettum
De laudibus magni Cosmi

Quid tu me totiens, Salvetti, impellere tentas,
    ut referam grandi tristia bella pede?
Quid veterum pugnas regum clarosque triumphos,
    et quae sint terra, quae bene gesta mari?
5   Nescis heu tenuis nostro ut de pectore surgat
    spiritus, ut surdum buccina nostra gemat?
Magnos magna decent Salvetti proelia vates;
    mi sat erit tenues ludere posse iocos,
nequitiasque meae tenui describere Xandrae
10   carmine et insidias, magne Cupido, tuas.
Quod si Pierio quondam licuisset in antro
    percipere Aonii numina sancta chori,
aut si me Phoebus tanto dignatus honore
    frondibus ornasset tempora nostra suis;
15   non ego magnanimi cantarem Caesaris arma,
    non ego Scipiadas, fulmina bina, duces,

: 14 :

Tamyris, Queen of the Scythians

Cyrus saw two hundred thousand slaughtered by your army,
    Tamyris, on the ridges of the Massagetae.
To placate your buried son, lusting for bloodshed,
    you plunged Cyrus' head into a bag full of blood.

: 15 :

To Giovanni Salvetti
on the Praises of Cosimo the Great

Why, Salvetti, do you keep urging me so often
    to tell of dreadful wars in a broad, ample style?
Why record the battles and brave triumphs of old kings
    and deeds well done on land or on the sea?
Don't you know, alas, how thin my spirit breathes within me   5
    so that my trumpet blows with but the faintest of sounds?
Great battles befit only great poets, Salvetti;
    for me it is enough to play my thin little jokes,
and to describe the naughtinesses of my dear Xandra
    and your snares, great Cupid, in a thin little poem.   10
For if I had been allowed once in the Pierian cave
    to behold the sacred deities of the Aonian band,
or if Apollo had deemed me to merit such an honor,
    and had adorned my temples with his leafy crown,
I should not sing of the arms of great-souled Caesar,   15
    nor those twin thunderbolts of the stock of Scipio,

non celerem cursum properataque castra Neronis,
    Hasdrubalis victrix cum tulit hasta caput;
denique non Latiae quaecumque egere secures,
20   consulis imperio cedere regna gravi:
sed Florentinae canerem primordia gentis,
    nobile Syllanum tempus in omne genus;
Syllanumque genus, Romana a stirpe colonos,
    a patribus nunquam degenerasse suis.
25 Ah, quos ista viros tellus tulit, et quibus olim
    viribus Etruscum nomen in astra tulit!
Quos magnus tantum Cosmus supereminet omnes,
    Eoum quantum signa minora iubar:
nostra igitur magnum cantabit pagina Cosmum,
30   inceptis gravibus tu modo Musa fave.
Musa fave coeptis: non hic fera monstra Gigantum,
    nec quicquid mendax Graecia finxit, inest.
Vera canam et verae referam virtutis honores,
    et quae sint Medica praemia digna domo.
35 Testis erit populus, testis mihi, Cosme, senatus,
    urbe tua uno te clarius esse nihil.
Verum unde initium, quae prima aut ultima ponam?
    Nos inopes rerum copia tanta facit.
Hinc patriae pietas, illinc prudentia, rebus
40   hinc se offert miseris, Cosme, benigna manus.
Nam qui te patriae non dicat iure parentem,
    hunc hominis pectus non habuisse putem.
Magnus erat Caesar, sed magnus Caesar in armis;
    at tu Cosme tua maior in urbe toga es.
45 Ille armis patriam saevaque tyrannide pressit,
    Te libertatis unica cura tenet;
illum hostem vidit desertae Curia Romae,
    hostes e patria tu procul urbe fugas.
Egregia haec virtus magna et constantia civis,

nor the rapid marches and hasty camps of victorious Nero,
  when he carried on his spear the head of Hasdrubal;
nor, finally, of whatever kingdoms Latian axes forced
  to yield to the consul's solemn command.   20
But I should hymn the beginnings of the Florentine race,
  the descendents of Sulla, noble for all time,
the Sullan race, settlers of ancient Roman stock,
  never degenerating from their ancestors.
Ah, the men this earth brought forth, ah, the energy   25
  that once did lift the Tuscan name up to the stars!
All of whom great Cosimo overtops as much
  as the dawn's radiance exceeds the lesser stars.
Therefore, our poems will sing of Cosimo the Great:
  favor me, O Muse, in this grave endeavor now.   30
O Muse, my venture favor; here are no savage giants
  nor whatever monsters lying Greece has devised.
I shall sing the truth and tell the glory of true virtue,
  and the prizes merited by the house of Medici.
Both the people and the Senate, Cosimo, will stand witness, 35
  that nothing in your city is more famous than you.
But where to begin, what to put first or last?
  Such rich material leaves us destitute.
Here patriotism, there wisdom, and here your kindly hand,
  Cosimo, that offers help to those in misery.   40
Indeed, he who wouldn't call you "father of your country"
  does not have a human heart, in my opinion.
Caesar was great, but his greatness was in arms alone;
  your greatness, Cosimo, lies in the urban toga.
He oppressed his land with arms and savage tyranny,   45
  but you a special care for liberty informs.
The senate of a deserted Rome saw him as their enemy;
  you drive the foe in flight far from your city and your land.
This is conspicuous virtue and great civic constancy,

50   humanis et quae rara sit ingeniis:
        quos opibus post te, quos et virtute relinquas,
           hos tibi consimiles, inclite Cosme, pati.
        Nam qui magnarum rerum dum tractat habenas
           privati potuit civis habere modum,
55   hunc ego non homini, quamvis in cuncta modesto,
           sed similem superis esse putabo deis.
        Heu maiora meis video me viribus urgent,
           nec sunt ista quidem carminis huius opus.
        Hic ego, quo Phrygii dixisti facta parentis,
60   nunc Publi cuperem carmen habere tuum.
        Nam cur sit Cosmus tali indignandus honore,
           aut mereat tantam cur magis ille tubam?
        Aeneas Troiae flagrantia tecta reliquit
           et duce vix potuit carpere matre fugam;
65   bellorum at contra diversa incendia Cosmus
           civibus extinxit, portus et aura suis.
        Nec victa Aeneam patrios ex urbe Penates
           atque viae comites eripuisse negem;
        sed magis est patria templis in sede dicatis
70   munera tanta piis exhibuisse sacris.
        Hoc et Laurenti sublimibus alta columnis
           templa docent opibus facta superba tuis,
        templa docent Marci mira et testudine dives
           porticus et sacra fronde virente nemus,
75   et quae vicinus semper mirabitur Arnus,
           addita Christiferae plurima tecta Cruci.
        Aeneam laudant humeros tardante senecta —
           quis neget esse pium? — supposuisse patri;
        sed quisquis vidit quo funere utrumque parentem
80   extulerit Cosmus, esse putabit idem.
        Quod si ille Ascanium, spes esset ut altera Romae,
           edidit, unde domus Iulia nomen habet,

a quality rarely found in the human mind.   50
Those whom you surpass in either wealth or in virtue
    you tolerate, famous Cosimo, as similar to yourself.
For he who, while he holds the reins of weighty affairs,
    can keep to the measure of a private citizen,
him I must consider (although he's modest in all things)   55
    not like a man, but like a higher deity.
Alas, I see things press me greater than my strength,
    and they are not, in truth, the business of this poem.
Here I would wish to have composed your poem, Publius,
    that in which you told of our Trojan father's deeds.   60
For why should Cosimo be unworthy of such honor?
    Why does Aeneas deserve so fine a trumpet more?
Aeneas left behind the burning houses of Troy
    and could barely get away, though his mother led him.
By contrast, Cosimo put out various fires of war,   65
    and proved a haven and fair wind for his countrymen.
I would not deny Aeneas snatched his household gods
    from the conquered city, and comrades for his quest,
but it is a greater thing to furnish holy rites,
    and dedicate temples in one's native land.   70
The lofty church of San Lorenzo with its high columns,
    made splendid by your wealth, illustrates the point;
the marvelous San Marco shows this, and the portico,
    rich with its vault, and its flourishing holy wood,
and the building added to the church of Santa Croce,   75
    which constantly amazes the Arno nearby.
They praise Aeneas for carrying on his shoulders a father
    whom age had slowed — and who will deny his piety?
But anyone who saw the funeral rites of both his parents
    will think Cosimo his equal in dutiful respect.   80
If Aeneas begat Ascanius to be the second hope of Rome,
    he from whom the Julian house takes its name,

hic geminam eduxit patriae duo lumina prolem,
    esset ut haec Medicum gloria magna domus.
85   Quorum qui maior quantum, ah Florentia, nomen,
    dum redit e Venetis rettulit ille tibi!
Huic leo Tyrrhenus nec non et Gallicus anguis
    et belli et pacis ius simul omne dedit;
nunc dignum tantae ferret qui pondera molis
90   exitus exacti foederis esse probat.
Sed quid ago ah, demens? An grandi digna cothurno
    versibus exiguis ludere facta paro?
Di tibi dent alios, insignis Cosme, poetas,
    qui tua facta suis versibus aequiparent:
95   incautum nam me tantarum gloria rerum
    dum rapit, in medio deficit ore sonus.

: 16 :

Ad Iacobum Azarolum
De laudibus magni Cosmi et domus Azarolae

Saepe meas supra vires me cogis, amice
Azarole, novis heroum in proelia surgam
versibus et spretis elegis horrenda canoro
bella sono referam. Vel si civilia malo
5   consilia et multa claros virtute togatos
ad coelum meritis extollere laudibus, oras,
Iacobe, magnanimi referamus ut inclita Cosmi
facta, Sophocleo non dedignanda cothurno.
Quid faciam? Pudor est tibi si parere negabo:
10   sed nimium gracilis rauco de pectore surgit
spiritus et primo desit mihi versus in ore.

our Cosimo has raised two sons, twin lights of their country,
    that the glory might be great of the house of Medici.
He who was elder of these — ah, what renown, Florence,   85
    did he carry back to you when he returned from Venice!
To him, both the Tuscan lion and the Lombard serpent
    gave full authority in war and in peace.
Now the outcome of the treaty that was signed proves him
    worthy to bear the weight of so great a burden.   90
But I'm mad: what am I doing? Getting ready to play
    in my slight verse with deeds worthy of an epic?
May the gods give you other poets, illustrious Cosimo,
    who may match your deeds with their poetry:
for while the glory of great affairs enthralls me despite myself,   95
    the sounds that might express them fail me in mid-voice.

: 16 :

To Jacopo Acciaiuoli in Praise of Cosimo the Great and of the House of Acciaiuoli

You often push me past my strength, Acciaioli, my friend,
to rise to a new strain and tell of heroes' battles,
and, scorning elegiacs, to narrate sonorously dreadful wars;
or, Jacopo, if I prefer, to exalt to the skies
civic deliberations and statesmen famed for their virtue,   5
giving them the praise they deserve. And you beg me
to record the famous deeds of high-souled Cosimo,
which would not disgrace the Sophoclean buskin.
What shall I do? Say I won't obey you? Shameful!
But too thin an inspiration comes from my hoarse throat   10
and verses fail me whenever I begin to speak.

At vos si quondam tanto me munere dignum,
quae iuga Gorgonei fontis rorata liquore
incolitis, Phoebo gratissima numina Musae
15   feceritis, si vestra mihi nemora alta patebunt,
tunc ego non humilis ventura in saecula vates
cantabo magnum sublimi carmine Cosmum.
Cosmum qui tanti mensuram nominis implet,
Cosmum Tyrrheni moderantem frena leonis.
20   Cosmum qui Latios privatus transvolat omnes
virtute atque opibus reges, ducibusque togatus
praevalet in rebus dubiis. Nam pectore fido
consilia expromit, quibus et Campana fugemus
finibus Etruscis, Etrusco milite, castra,
25   et quibus ad Sanum revocentur stulta Lupai
coepta, Fluentinam rumpentia saepe quietem.
Ergo an pace prius Cosmum miremur an armis,
incertum: sed pace simul mirandus et armis,
Cosmus erit, Cosmo resonabit pagina. Sed tu
30   post magnum Cosmum venies mihi cura secunda,
Azarola domus, multis ditata trophaeis.
Nam tibi Cecropiae parent Tritonidis arces,
tu regis anguigenas Mavortia moenia Thebas,
tu quicquid veteres olim tenuere Pelasgi
35   imperio cohibes; tibi dives Apulia magni
tutelam regni et summum mandavit honorem.
Adde et tot merita in patriam, tot maxima facta,
adde et templa deum multo constructa decoro.
Verum praecipuos inter numerandus alumnos
40   Angelus, egregia nulli virtute secundus,
emicat. Hic duris rebus, mandante Senatu,
eloquioque potens prudenti et pectore fretus
Gallorum nobis adiunxit foedere regem,

But if, O Muses, you should ever find me deserving
of such a gift, you who dwell on mountains dewy
with waters from Pegasus' spring, deities most pleasing
to Apollo, if your high groves will lie open to me,   15
then I, no humble poet, will sing of great Cosimo
in a lofty song that will live throughout the ages.
Cosimo, who fulfills the measure of that great name,
Cosimo, holding the reins of the Tyrrhenian lion,
Cosimo, who, though a private citizen, soars past   20
all Romans in virtue and all kings in wealth,
who, though a statesman, in doubtful things prevails
over captains. For he gives advice from a loyal heart:
how we may drive from Tuscany with Tuscan soldiery
Campanian armies, how Siena's schemes may be reversed,   25
foolish schemes which often spoil Florentine repose.
Hence, whether to admire him more in war or peace
I don't know; but he *will* be admired in war and peace
alike, and my page will echo with "Cosimo!"
But after Great Cosimo, you are my next concern,   30
House of Acciaiuoli, enriched by many victories.
For the Cecropian citadel of Athena now obeys you;
you rule Thebes, born of dragons, and the walls of Mars;
The lands the ancient Greeks once held answer your nod,
and rich Apulia trusted you to keep a great realm safe   35
and assigned to you a place of the very highest honor.
Add your many services to country and great deeds,
add too the elegant temples to the gods you built.
But among its most distinguished offspring must be counted
Angelo, who shines out second to none in famous virtue.   40
On the Senate's orders, in dire circumstances,
powerful in eloquence and with wisdom in his heart,
he allied us by treaty to the King of the French,

Gallica perque Alpes eduxit castra nivales;
45 castra tibi auxilio, fortuna urgente, futura,
inclite Sfortiada. Gemino nam pressus ab hoste,
partitis tantae turmis te opponere moli
Braccia nec poteras solitis impellere signa
viribus. At postquam diversa e parte tumultus
50 Gallorum adventu Taurinaque bella quierunt,
tunc tua quid virtus invictaque dextera posset
nobilis experta est amisso Brixia campo,
et qui se infami vallo tutoque tenebant
aggere Marcicolae turpi formidine capti.
55 Bebriacis igitur sic venit terror ab armis,
sic sua Tyrrheno crevit reverenda leoni
maiestas, aequis sic conditionibus orta
otia, quae nostri nolint turbare nepotes.
Atque olim memores placida dum pace fruentur
60 auctorem tanti noscant te muneris omnes,
Angele, sicque tuum vivat per saecula nomen.

: 17 :

Ad Petrum Medicem de laudibus Poggi

Iam gelidum nigris subvecta per aëra bigis
    nox maris occiduas prona subibat aquas,
cum matutine Thetis statione relicta
    Oceanum rutilo Lucifer exit equo.

and caused the Gallic forces to pass through the snowy Alps —
forces that, when Fortune pressed, would come to your aid,   45
O famous Sforza. For assailed by doubled enemies,
and with divided forces, you faced a mass of might,
nor could you drive the Braccian pennons with your usual
     force.
But after the tumult of the French arrival from the rear,
the wars around Torino ceased their violence.   50
Then noble Brescia learned, having lost the lands about her,
what your virtue could accomplish and unconquerable right
     hand,
as did the Venetians who, though behind the safe trench
and ignominious palisade, were captured through shameful
     fear.
Thus terror came then from the weapons of the Milanese,   55
thus the majesty of the Tuscan lion gained respect;
thus peace came, which arose from equitable terms,
a peace that our children would not wish to disturb.
And one day, while they enjoy this tranquil peace,
they will all remember that this gift came from you,   60
Angelo, and thus your name will live on forever.

: 17 :

To Piero de' Medici in Praise of Poggio

Now Night, borne through the chilly air on her black chariot,
   was heading down beneath the waters of the Western
     Ocean,
when Lucifer, abandoning his post on the morning sea,
   rode out from Ocean on his horse of reddish gold.

5   Hic mihi Castalii nemoris regina nitentes
       venit Apollinea fronde revincta comas.
    Nulla tamen docto resonabant pollice fila,
       nec fuit in levi barbiton ulla manu,
    sed tamen ut moesto tristis dedit ore querelas
10   cognita mi voce est Calliopea sua;
    haec ita: "Proh vestri scelus atque infamia saecli,
       proh dolor, heu, Musis hiccine venit honos?
    Hiccine venit honor Musis, quis semper Etrusca
       supremus fuerat hactenus urbe locus?
15   Te propter Graios olim Florentia fontes
       et nemus et Clarii linquimus antra dei,
    nec piguit Fesulos montes nec claustra Mugelli
       neve Casentini visere saepe iuga.
    Quin et aquas placidi nobis sacravimus Arni,
20   seque suo castus lavit in amne chorus,
    ut nobis celebres vates celebresque venirent
       rhetores et quicquid floret in historia.
    Hinc Dantes terras et clari sidera coeli
       dixit et infernos tertia regna lacus;
25   hinc tu divino, Petrarca, incensus amore
       cantasti Laurae cygnea colla tuae.
    Cantasti patrio Tyrrhena poemata versu,
       cantasti Latio Punica bella pede.
    Nam quid Boccacci lusus, quid docta Colucci
30   dicta Salutati nunc numerare iuvat?
    At nuper Tuscae dedimus duo lumina genti,
       quales rara solent saecula ferre viros.
    Gesta Fluentinum descripserat alter et arma
       quaeque notanda domi quaeque notanda foris;
35   alter Cecropiis imbutus pectora chartis
       viribus ingenii subdidit artis opus.
    Nemo magis dubiis potuit cognoscere rebus

Presently, there came to me the queen of the Castalian grove,   5
    her shining hair bound back with Apollo's leafy crown.
Yet no strings vibrated to her well-versed thumb,
    nor was there any lyre in her nimble hand.
But still, as she uttered sad laments with grieving mouth,
    I came to recognize Calliope by her voice.   10
These were her words: "O the wicked infamy of your age!
    O the pain! Is this the honor that the Muses get?
Is this the honor the Muses get, who always, hitherto,
    occupied the foremost place in your Tuscan city?
Long ago on your account, O Florence, we left behind   15
    Hellenic groves and fountains and Apollo's cave,
nor were we displeased to haunt the hills of Fiesole,
    or the seclusion of Mugello or high Casentino.
Indeed we made the waters of the quiet Arno sacred
    to ourselves, and our chaste chorus bathed in its stream,   20
 to the end that famous poets and famous orators
    and whatever flowers in history might come to us.
Here Dante told of earth and of stars in heaven bright
    and of the third kingdom and the waters of Hell.
Here you, Petrarca, all aflame with heavenly love,   25
    sang of the swanlike neck of the Laura you loved.
You sang Tuscan poems in the tongue of your native land,
    and you sang of the Punic Wars in the verse of Latium.
What's the use of listing now Boccaccio's lighter works,
    or the learned utterances of Coluccio Salutati?   30
Only just now we gave twin luminaries to the Tuscan race,
    such men as only a few ages are wont to produce:
One described the deeds of Florence and her feats of arms,
    whatever was worthy to be known at home or abroad.
The other, having steeped his soul in the pages of the Greeks,   35
    produced a work of art by the power of his genius.
No one could better recognize the useful when in doubt;

utile nec docto promptius ore loqui.
Ille etiam nostri nemoris pius incola fonte
40   cum biberet tota proluit ora sacro;
hinc cecinit lyricos; mox dum traducit Homerum
      occidit heu patriae gloria magna suae.
His ego Daphnea populo plaudente corona
      ornavi propria tempora docta manu.
45   Nam duce me quondam magni secreta palati
      mandarat tantis Curia vestra viris.
Sic olim vestram semper celebravimus urbem,
      dum meruit magnus praemia digna labor.
Nunc ne defunctis dignus successor abesset,
50   instructum egregia misimus arte virum.
Hunc nos irriguis Parnasi eduximus arvis,
      Bellorophontei qua fluit unda feri,
et dedimus gravibus dictis placidoque lepore
      edere grandiloquo verba soluta sono.
55   Ergo quis docti divina volumina Poggi
      nesciat et libris cuncta referta suis?
Ah quam precipiti stultos conturbat avaros
      fulmine, quam veras imprimit ille notas,
quamque asper retegit qui summa in pelle decori,
60   dum lateant, alacres in scelus omne ruunt.
Hic nihil esse docet miseris mortalibus usquam
      humana maius conditione malum.
Atque docet varios fluxus variosque reflexus
      fortunae et iussu cuncta movenda suo,
65   quamque sit infelix cuiusvis principis aula,
      ipsa licet veri nescia turba neget.
Et recte addubitat senibus ducenda sit uxor,
      cum multum teneat utraque causa mali.
At te nobilitas generoso pectore veris

no one was ever readier or more learned in his speech.
A pious dweller in our wood, he drank also from our font,
    and cleansed his face fully in its sacred stream.   40
Hence he sang sweet lyrics; then, while translating Homer,
    he died, alas, the great glory of his native land.
For these merits, while the people clapped, with my own
      hands
    I adorned his learned brow with a laurel wreath.
For under my direction did your Senate once entrust   45
    the secrets of its palace to great men such as he.
Thus formerly we always sang the praises of your city,
    so long as great effort earned worthy rewards.
Now, lest there be no successor worthy of the dead,
    we have sent a man well-versed in the finest arts.   50
We have reared him in the lands watered by Parnassus,
    whence flow the waters of Bellerophon's wild mount,
and have allowed him to produce in the grandest prose
    works marked by weighty sayings and by gentle wit.
Hence, who doesn't know the noble books of learned Poggio,   55
    and all the knowledge that is crowded onto his pages?
Ah, how he blasts the greedy with his thunderbolt,
    the fools, how he brands them with deserved disgrace!
How fiercely he exposes those who, comely in outward show,
    in private rush headlong into every sort of crime.   60
Presently he teaches that nothing brings more evil
    to wretched mortals than the human state itself.
He teaches too the various ebbs and flows of Fortuna
    and how all things must move at her command,
and how unhappy is the palace of any given prince,   65
    although the ignorant mob would not have it so.
And rightly he casts doubt on whether old men should marry,
    since both states contain many seeds of evil.
But nobility itself, now far above the common herd,

70   laudibus a vulgo iam procul ipsa canit.
     Nec te praeteriit, rerum fortissime Caesar,
        nec te cui nomen Africa victa dedit.
     Sed longum est monumenta viri si cuncta revolvam,
        nec praesentis opus temporis esse reor.
75   Multa puer, iuvenis descripsit plura senexque
        plurima nec salibus nec gravitate carens.
     Quam variis redimita novi sub sidere Tauri
        floribus in verno tempore ridet humus,
     tam varia in doctis resplendent lumina chartis,
80   tam varius signat splendida verba color,
     ut qui purpurea distinguit veste lapillos,
        quo referat multum discolor aura decus.
     Quin etiam ut veterum erueret monimenta virorum
        nec sineret turpem tot bona ferre situm,
85   ausus barbaricos populos penitusque reposta
        poscere Lingonicis oppida celsa iugis.
     Illius ergo manu nobis, doctissime rhetor,
        integer in Latium, Quintiliane, redis;
     illius atque manu divina poemata Sili
90   Italicis redeunt usque legenda suis.
     Et ne nos lateat variorum cultus agrorum,
        ipse Columellae grande reportat opus,
     et te Lucreti longo post tempore tandem
        civibus et patriae reddit habere tuae.
95   Tartareis potuit fratrem revocare tenebris
        alterna Pollux dum statione movet,
     coniugis at rursus nigras subitura lacunas
        Euridice sequitur fila canora sui,
     Poggius at sospes nigra e caligine tantos
100   ducit ubi aeternum lux sit aperta viros.
     Rhetora, philosophum, vatem, doctumque colonum

sings of you in true praises from a generous heart.   70
Nor did Poggio omit you, Caesar, bravest in all things,
    nor you to whom defeated Africa gave up her name.
Still, it would take too long to run through all his works,
    nor do I think it is the task of the present moment.
As a boy he wrote much, as a youth still more,   75
    the old man most of all, with both wit and gravity.
As the earth, covering itself again with countless flowers,
    smiles in the springtime under Taurus' sign once more,
so countless varied insights gleam from his learned pages,
    and varied rhetorical figures stamp his brilliant words,   80
as one who makes his purple garment distinctive with gems
    so that its particolored hue might bring it high esteem.
Indeed, that he might resurrect the records of the ancients
    and not allow so many good things to suffer vile neglect,
he dared to make inquiries among the barbarian towns   85
    hidden high in the mountains of the Lingones.
Hence by his hand you, Quintilian, most learned of rhetors
    returned whole to us once more in Latium.
By his hand too that Silius' divine poems returned
    so that they might now be read by his fellow Italians.   90
And, lest the proper care of various crops be hid from us,
    he brings back with him the great opus of Columella,
and after ages long our Poggio restores you, Lucretius,
    to your land and fellow citizens to possess at last.
Pollux could call his brother up from the Tartarean shades   95
    while he moves successively down to take his place;
though she would return once more to the dark pit of Hell,
    Eurydice follows still her husbands' sonorous string:
but Poggio, unscathed, leads these great men from the mists,
    up to where the light is clear forevermore.   100
A barbarous hand had drowned in the thickest shades of night

merserat in nigra barbara nocte manus:
Poggius hos vita potuit donare secunda,
    dum mira turpi liberat arte situ.
105   Nec satis est ex se quod scripsit quodque vetusta
    eruit e tenebris multa labore suo;
verum etiam Graios nostro sermone libellos
    vertit in antiqua nobilis historia.
Et nunc, o mores, o tempora, debitus illi —
110   ferre quis hoc poterit? — eripietur honos.
Ah tantum vobis licuit, civilia iura,
    Pieridum casta pellere sede chorum:
formula quae vobis, quae competit actio summum
    per scelus audaces inseruisse manus?
115   Non ego Tyrrhena posco vos pellier urbe,
    nec sua causidicis praemia digna nego.
Auro cingantur nitido semperque superbos
    ingenti titulos ambitione gerant,
et pretio ingenti sanctarum aenigmata legum
120   arbitrio veniant discutienda suo;
denique si fas est inter mortalia regnent,
    illorumque brevis cuncta libellus agat.
A nobis tantum, si qua est reverentia divos
    quae colat, a nobis iam cohibete manus.
125   Nam quae vobiscum nobis commertia, quave
    consimilis vitae mos ratione fuit?
Nos neque clamores sequimur nec praemia voci
    poscimus et casta nil nisi serta iuvant;
vos inter strepitus fas est turbamque sonantem
130   spargere clamoso iurgia multa foro,
insanasque sequi lites rabidoque tumultu
    venali tristes voce citare reos.
Sed quid ego haec frustra, cum iam civilia iura

the rhetor, the philosopher, the poet and the farmer;
yet Poggio could give a second life to these men when
    with wondrous skill he freed them from shameful neglect.
Yet it was not enough that he had written his own works   105
    nor that his toil had brought from darkness many ancient
        things;
that noble man also translated in our Latin tongue
    books of the Greeks about ancient history.
And now — O *mores*, O *tempora* — the honor he deserved
    (who can bear it?) will be ripped away from him.   110
It was, alas, so far permitted you, O civil laws,
    to drive the Pierian chorus from their sacred seat:
what legal rule or action was applicable to you,
    letting you lay bold hands on him, the highest of crimes?
I do not ask that you be driven from the Tuscan city,   115
    nor do I deny to lawyers their merited rewards.
Let them be girded with shining gold; let them parade
    their arrogant titles, won through colossal ambition,
and let the mysteries of sacred law be cut into little pieces
    through their arbitration, at a colossal price.   120
In short, if it be right that they rule in human affairs,
    let a short brief accomplish everything for them.
But if there is any reverence for the gods above,
    keep now your hands from doing violence to us.
For what commerce can there be between yourselves and us,   125
    in what way do we share a similar way of life?
We don't go chasing uproars or seek rewards for talk;
    nothing but spotless garlands gives delight to us;
it's fitting that amid the din and the noisy crowd
    you spread many a quarrel in the noisy market-place,   130
pursue mindless lawsuits and with savage uproar
    summon sad defendants with a venal voice.
But why this vain speech, since by now the civil laws

per fraudem posito ius sibi iure parent?
135   Et poterit Medices veteres oblitus amores
    oblitusque mei talia facta pati?
Non poterit, neque enim Latiis est alter in oris,
    reddere pro meritis qui magis aequa velit.
Quin et Musarum sacro perculsus amore
140   et noctes studiis invigilatque dies.
Rhetores hinc omnes novit sanctosque poetas
    et veterum callet dogmata prisca patrum;
hinc etiam doctus doctis indulget amice
    atque inopes opibus consilioque fovet.
145   Nec Maecenatis fuerat clementia maior,
    communis vatum cui dedit astra favor.
Ergo huius gremio nostrum nomenque decusque
    ponimus: hic nobis rite patronus erit.
Hic etenim fessas e tempestate Camenas
150   in tutos referet restituetque sinus;
hoc duce nostra pio sedes reddetur alumno,
    et stabunt doctis praemia digna viris.
Nec tamen immemores dicet nos muneris ille,
    nec veniet merito gratia parva suo.
155   Nam surget quandoque meo de fonte poeta,
    qui magnum Petri nomen in astra ferat.
Qui referat magnumque Petrum Cosmumque parentem,
    egregium patriae lumen utrumque suae.
Ille modo niveo reddat sua flumina cygno,
160   impleat ut liquida voce canorus aquas.
Flumina reddantur cygnis, quae limpida quondam
    Bellorophonteos sint aditura lacus.
Qui nisi praeduros adamantas pectore gestet,
    solerti favos reddere nolit api?

make law of their own, though setting law aside by fraud?
And can Medici possibly forget his ancient love for him,   135
    and permit such actions, forgetting me as well?
No, he won't, for there is no man in Italy,
    who more wants to pay to merit its fair reward.
Indeed, he's overcome by sacred passion for the Muses;
    day and night he gives his studies care and watchfulness.   140
Hence he knows every rhetor and the holy poets
    and grasps the ancient teachings of our forefathers;
learned himself, he gives himself a friend to the learned
    and cares for the needy with resources and advice.
The kindness of Maecenas was not greater than his   145
    to whom the poets' common favor gave the stars.
Thus we cast our name and our glory on this man's breast:
    he will duly be a patron for us.
For he will bring back the Camenae, exhausted by the storm;
    he will restore them to the shelter of their harbor;   150
with him as guide, our homes will be restored to our devotee,
    and due rewards shall stand for all learned men.
Nor will he say that we forget his generosity,
    nor will small thanks only come to greet his deserts.
For one day a poet shall arise from my fountain,   155
    who shall bear the great name of Piero to the stars,
who will tell of great Piero and Cosimo his father,
    each a famous luminary of his fatherland.
Only let him give his waters back to the snowy swan,
    that its song may fill those waters with its liquid voice.   160
Restore to the swans the streams that as of old shall flow
    limpid back into the lake made by Pegasus's hoof.
Who, unless he carries the hardest iron in his heart,
    does not want to give the honeycomb back to the clever
      bee?

165 Reddite iam dulces apibus, iam reddite favos:
  hinc vobis posthac plurima mella fluent."
Haec et plura mihi: sed quis meminisse deorum
  cuncta queat? maesto Musa locuta sono est.
Mox sua dum celeri vertit vestigia passu:
170   "Cuncta—ait—haec Medici dixeris atque vale.
Cuncta!" Ait atque abiens, nequid sibi triste videret,
  conspectum fugit, Curia Tusca, tuum.

: 18 :

Eulogium in Cosmum puerum
Magni Cosmi nepotem

Me precor, ingenti subeunt dum funera luctu,
  aspice, seu civis seu peregrinus eris:
sic hominum vanas poteris cognoscere curas
  et solidum humanis rebus adesse nihil.
5 Nosces fallacis quot luserit aura sereni,
  quam fugiat celeri spes moritura pede;
haec te fortunae contemnere laeta monebunt,
  cum refluat lubricis mobilis illa rotis.
Nam mihi quid nomen generis, quid profuit aetas,
10   quid Medicum cunctis inclita fama locis,
quid mihi divitiae ingentes virtusve parentum,
  quid teneris annis pectus habere senis?
Vera loquar: pueri tu ne contempseris umbram,
  libera quae coelo iam leviore volat;
15 carcere nam caeco Manes vinclisque soluti
  mortalis terrae cernere vera queunt.

O give back now to the bees, give back their sweet   165
    honeycomb;
  henceforth a river of honey will flow for you here."
She said even more to me: but who can remember all
    the gods say? And the Muse spoke with a mournful voice.
Presently, with swift steps she turned around again:
    "All this," she said, "say to the Medici, and farewell!   170
All this!" She spoke and, leaving, lest she see something sad,
    she fled from your sight, O Senate of Tuscany.

: 18 :

Eulogy for the Boy Cosimo,
Grandson of the Great Cosimo

Look upon me, I pray, whether citizen or stranger
    while in great grief my funeral cortège passes you by,
for thus may you recognize how vain are the cares of men
    and how nothing lasting stands in human affairs.
You will see how many an air of false serenity fools,   5
    with how swift a step a dying hope runs away;
these things will warn you to contemn Fortune's joyful times,
    as she rolls away inconstant on her slippery wheel.
For what did it profit me to have my family name, my age,
    the glittering fame of the Medici known in every land?   10
What use to me was endless wealth and my parents' power,
    what use to have an old man's heart in my tender years?
I shall speak the truth: lest you scorn a child's shade
    which is flying free up to a lighter heaven now;
for, freed from bondage and blind prison, the souls of the dead   15
    are able to discern the truth about the mortal lands.

217

Cum me praecipiti periturum funere Clotho
    in lucem tristi conditione daret:
"I breve per spatium—dixit—puer! At breve vitae
20   hoc spatium longi temporis instar erit.
Namque capax rerum mens et prudentia velox,
    qualia iam magni dant mihi signa viri;
tu curas tenero gestabis corde viriles,
    oreque lactenti grandia verba fluent.
25   Adde bonae stimulos artis, primordia magni
    ingenii, et gravibus linguaque culta sonis.
Nec quisquam Lydos Fesula de gente Quirites
    impellet de se credere tanta puer,
ullo nec tantum Florentia mater alumno
30   confidet nomen tollere in astra suum.
Sed spes decipiet miseram surdisque deorum
    auribus in cassum tot pia vota cadent.
Nam tibi iam Lachesis, paene ipso in limine vitae,
    truncabit celeri fila refracta manu.
35   Sed vos o miseri tantum sperare parentes
    quid iuvat? An gravior luctus ut inde premat?
Discite iam pridem quid vobis fata minentur,
    nam praevisa minus fata nocere solent.
Fata domum Medicam cunctis celebrarier oris
40   et caput esse suis civibus usque dabunt;
sed nimium nimiumque potens foret illa, senectae
    si suus aspiceret tempora longa nepos.
Non tamen hinc ibit Stygias inglorius umbras;
    nam desiderii stant monumenta sui.
45   Ah quantos gemitus imo de pectore tollent
    Syllanidae, tota quantus in urbe dolor!
Te matres, te, parve, viri iuvenesque senesque

When Clotho with a stern condition brought me to the light,
    me who would be going soon to die too suddenly,
she said: "Go, boy, for a brief span! But this brief span for you
    will be equivalent in worth to a life that is long.   20
For your mind is capacious and your understanding swift,
    the sort that shows already the signs of a great man;
you will discharge a man's concerns with your tender heart,
    and great words will flow from your still-milky lips.
Add the stimulus of good teaching and the first fruits of   25
    a fine mind and a tongue schooled to weighty words.
No other boy of Fiesolan race will cause the Tuscan people
    to believe such great things of himself as Cosimino;
nor will mother Florence trust to any of her nurslings
    to raise her reputation to the stars so much as he.   30
But hope will deceive our wretched mother and many pious
        prayers
    will fall in vain on the deaf ears of the gods above.
For now Lachesis, almost at the threshold of your life,
    will cut short its broken thread with her rapid hand.
And O wretched parents, what help is it to hope so much?   35
    So that a heavier sorrow might oppress you thereafter?
Learn what Fates were threatening you a long time before,
    for a fate foreseen will usually harm you the less.
Fate will grant the Medici house to be praised in every land
    and ever to be chief among its fellow-citizens;   40
but it would be too, too potent if its young grandson
    were to live so long into the period of old age.
Still, he'll not go hence inglorious to the Stygian shades;
    for there are memorials of how much he is missed.
Ah, what groans from deep within their hearts the sons of   45
        Sulla
    will send up! what sorrow will besiege the entire city!
Mothers will weep for you, small one, and men young and old;

flebunt, te maesti, Curia sancta, patres.
Nec tantum Archemori fatum morsusque draconis
50   Argivum Nemeae flevit ab amne cohors,
Romula nec tantum puerili in corpore letum
    Marcelli tellus luctibus ingemuit.
Iam videor strepitus audire et rauca querentum
    murmura confusis evolitare sonis,
55 stiparique vias video et Laurentia templa
    turgidaque e lacrimis lumina cuncta piis.
Ergo ibis quo fata trahunt; sed qui tua condet
    parvus membra ferat disticha nostra lapis:
Hic Cosmus puer est, cui si via longa fuisset,
60   Cosmi virtutes aequiparasset avi."
Dixerat haec Clotho mihi iam sub liminis oras
    venturo: pariunt nunc sua verba fidem.
Namque duos primo lustro vix addidit annos,
    bisque etiam nonos invida parca dies,
65 et procul ah, dulcis distractus pectore matris
    pocula Letheo gurgite nigra bibam.
Iamque per Elysios veniens novus incola lucos
    mirabor Manes per sua prata pios.
Tu tamen o nobis genitor iustissima cura
70   aspera fortunae vulnera disce pati.
Et tua si flatu nunquam intumuere secundo
    pectora tam multis sollicitata bonis,
disce animum duris fortem quoque sumere rebus,
    nunc ne succumbat mens generosa malo.
75 Nam vir tunc fueris, sortem si invictus utramque
    sic tuleris, medio ne moveare gradu,
cum praeter culpam — stulti licet usque repugnent —
    nil sit quod sapiens non tollerare velit.
Quin etiam multi tranquillo pectore caros

and even our grieving elders, the holy Senate, will weep.
The Argive band did not so weep the death of Archemorus,
    dead of a dragon's bite by the river of Nemea,   50
nor did the land of Romulus groan so in lamentation
    over the young body of Marcellus when he was killed.
Now I seem to hear an uproar and the raucous murmur
    of mourners flying up with incessant cacaphony,
and I see the streets and the church of San Lorenzo   55
    thronged, and the eyes of all swollen with loyal tears.
Thus will you go, where lead the Fates; but let the little stone
    which covers your dear limbs bear my couplet upon it:
Here is Cosimo the boy, who if his life had been long
    would have matched the virtues of his grandfather Cosimo." 60
Clotho spoke these words to me as I was about to pass
    under the shores of light: now her words have proven true.
For in envy the Parca added scarce two years to five,
    and but twice nine days in addition to that.
And far, far away, torn from the breast of my dear mother,   65
    I shall drink black draughts from the Lethean flood.
And now, a new dweller coming to the Elysian groves,
    I shall marvel at the holy souls throughout its meadows.
Nonetheless, you, my father and my most rightful care,
    learn to bear up under the harsh injuries of Fortune.   70
And if your breast, solicitous of so many good things,
    has never swollen out with a favorable wind,
learn also to assume a manly spirit in harsh times,
    lest your noble mind now succumb to evil things.
For then you will be a man, if unconquered you so bear   75
    either fate, and are not shaken from the middle step,
since, except for sin — though fools may rebel against this —
    there is no evil that a wise man will not tolerate.
For many, indeed, with a tranquil heart, have even placed

80   arsuris natos imposuere rogis.
        Aemilii nota est fors invidiosa triumphi,
           perdita per septem pignora bina dies;
        et nati funus memorant spectasse Catonem,
           prospera qua sapiens cernere fronte solet.
85   At qualem natum, sella cui Roma curuli
           diceret ut praetor civica iura dedit.
        Et Fabius nati primos quem sumere fasces
           viderat arenti lumine fata tulit,
        nec te Tarpeios postes Pulville tenentem
90   tristibus infregit invida fama sonis.
        Sed nec Anaxagoras duxit nimis esse dolendum
           mortali genitum conditione mori.
        Facta virum memoro: fortis sed femina magnos
           aequarat nati morte Lacaena viros.
95   Audiit ob patriam certantem vulnere crudo
           in pugna natum procubuisse parens;
        tunc nec maternos conata est edere planctus
           nec per colla vagis exululare comis,
        sed: Genui, dixit, Spartam qui fortiter armis
100   dum tegit in vulnus fataque certa ruat.
        O vox in cunctis celebranda annalibus et quae
           legibus exurgat digna, Lycurge, tuis!
        Non ego Socraticis volvam licet omnia chartis
           his verbis quicquam grandius inveniam.
105   At tu qui magnas populi florentis habenas
           cum fratre egregio cumque parente tenes,
        unius in pueri succumbes morte, nec illis
           te similem quos nunc diximus esse voles?
        Immo voles nec te, quem facta domestica possunt
110   erigere, a patribus degenerare decet.
        Quin coeli numen tibi quo tua damna leventur

their dear children to burn up on a funeral pyre.   80
The envious ill luck is well known of Aemilius in triumph:
    two dear offspring lost in the same seven days;
it's recorded that wise Cato watched his son's funeral rites
    with the same expression that he used in happier times.
But such a son! A son whom Rome called to a curule seat   85
    that as praetor he might prosecute the civil laws.
And Fabius bore with unmoistened eye the fate of his son
    whom he had seen take up the chief magistracy,
nor did envious rumor with its dismal noise break
    your will, Pulvillus, as you clung to the Tarpeian gates.   90
And Anaxagoras, too, did not consider that a child
    should be mourned too much, for it is human to die.
I recount the deeds of men: but a Spartan women
    equaled these great men in courage at a child's death.
The mother heard that her child, fighting for his country,   95
    had fallen dead in battle from his bloody wounds;
then she did not venture to send up a mother's wails
    or howl with hair disheveled all about her neck,
but said: I bore a man who charged towards wounds and
        certain death
    while with his arms he protected Sparta courageously.   100
O words which should be honored in every chronicle
    and which rise to the standard of your laws, Lycurgus!
And though I should read everything written of Socrates,
    I would find nothing more sublime than these words.
But you who hold the mighty reins of a flowering people   105
    along with your outstanding brother and your father dear,
will you sink to the ground at the death of a single boy,
    don't you wish to be similar to those I've just described?
Indeed you will, and it's not fitting to disgrace your fathers,
    you whom domestic actions can raise up again.   110
Nay, the God of heaven (and may He lighten your losses),

progeniem fato iam meliore dabit.
Vive igitur nostrique memor, sed luctus abesto
    et te mortalem progenuisse puta!
115 Hoc age, sic nostrae demptum quod stamine vitae est
    adiungat pensis Parca secunda tuis,
sic superes felix grandaevi Nestoris annos
    et videas hominum saecula terna senex.

:   19   :

Ad Guidonem Guiduccium

Lusimus ardentes teneris haec Guido sub annis,
    ut canerem nostrae lumina sancta deae,
ut canerem Xandram cuius tantum uror ab igne,
    quantum Sicaniis non furit Aetna iugis.
5 Interdum nostri sic Maecenatis honores
    strinximus ut gracili qui canit alta pede.
At mea si Petro commendent carmina divae,
    quae iuga Permessi fluminis alta tenent,
prima haec Pierides Medici si grata reponant
10   ut sibi non penitus displicuisse putem,
auspicio tanto laetus maiore per altum
    aethera conabor carmine ferre virum.
Namque dabit magnas tanta haec fiducia vires,
    ut referam grandi grandia verba lyra,
15 inter et heroas Saturni tempore natos
    tentabo nomen inseruisse suum.
Nam Syllae aspicient hoc consultore Quirites
    aurea Dictaei saecla redire senis,
Icario aspicient geminas sub sidere lances
20   Erigonem iusto pondere ferre pares.

will now give you progeny with a better fate.
Live, therefore, remembering me, but let this grief be gone
    and realize that you had given birth to a mortal boy!
Do this, and may a favorable fate so add to your span of life   115
    the wool which was taken away from our life's thread;
thus may you happily overtake the years of aged Nestor
    and as an old man come to see three ages of men.

: 19 :

To Guido Guiduccio

We amused ourselves, Guido, in our tender years, aflame
    to sing of our goddess' heavenly eyes,
to sing of Xandra, in whose flame I burn as much
    as does raging Aetna in the heights of Sicily.
In the meantime I've secured honors from our Maecenas   5
    fit for one who writes in a high and slender meter.
But if the goddesses make my verses pleasing to Piero,
    they who dwell on the high banks of Permessus' stream,
if the Medici, Muses, store these first-fruits away,
    so I may believe I have not wholly displeased them,   10
under such auspices I'll try happily to raise
    that man to the heavens in a higher strain.
For this great trust will give to me an ampler vigor,
    that I may tell of noble deeds on a noble lyre,
and I shall endeavor to include his name   15
    even among the heroes born in Saturn's reign,
For with him as their advisor the Sullan People will see
    the golden ages of old Dictaean Jupiter return,
and under the star of Icarus they'll see Erigone
    bearing the twin scales of Libra balanced equally.   20

LIBRI PRIMI
FORMA ANTIQUIOR

:   1   :

Ad Leonem Baptistam Albertum

:   2   :

Ad Leonem Baptistam

Ne titulum nostri, dulcis Baptista, libelli
ignores, legito: disticha prima ferent.

:   3   :

De inscriptione libri

Xandra dedit quondam nobis in carmine vires;
nunc titulum libro candida Xandra dabit.

:   4   :

Ad Xandram

BOOK I
(EARLIER REDACTION)

: I :

To Leon Battista Alberti = 1.13

: 2 :

To Leon Battista

Lest you pay no heed, sweet Battista, to my booklet's title,
  Read it; for the first two lines will say it all.

: 3 :

On the Title of This Book

Once Xandra gave me energy and force to sing my song;
  Now fair Xandra will give a title to my book.

: 4 :

To Xandra = 1.3, lines 21–52

(longer version retitled: When He Was Crushed by Love)

: 5 :

Ad Bernardum

: 6 :

Ad Xandram

: 7 :

Ad Xandram

Quem tu, Xandra, cupis, multas amat ille puellas,
in quibus, ah demens, ultima semper eris!

: 8 :

Ad Xandram

∶ 5 ∶

To Bernardo = 1.4

(retitled: To Bartolomeo Scala)

∶ 6 ∶

To Xandra = 1.6

∶ 7 ∶

To Xandra

The man whom you desire, Xandra, makes love to many girls,
among whom, crazy girl, you will always be the last!

∶ 8 ∶

To Xandra = 1.19

: 9 :

Ad Thomam Cephium

Legimus in Xandram nuper tua carmina nostram,
    carmina quae Xandrae sint magis apta tuae.
Non etenim cunni — sapit etsi balsama cunnus —
    spurcide quod dicis, me trahit ipsus odor;
5 sed faciles oculi vultuque innata venustas,
    ingenui mores ingenuusque pudor,
atque color verus nullique obnoxius arti.
    Sponte sua nimium pulchra puella mea est,
nec me felicem neque haec fecere beatum.
10   O liceat tali semper amore frui!
Ergo si sapies, posthac dixisse cavebis,
    Cephi, quae dominae sint minus apta meae.
Aut narrabo, tuae Xandrae quam marcida vulva,
    marcenti vulvae quam variusque color,
15 et quam difficiles mores, et onusta quot annis
    sit vetula, ut multos luserit arte viros.

: 10 :

Ad Bernardum

O mihi praecipuos inter numerande sodales,
    Landinique decus delitiaeque tui!
En ad te mitto nostras, Bernarde, Camenas,
    quis mandata dedi grata futura tibi.
5 At si non statim veniant paulumque morentur,

: 9 :

To Tommaso Ceffi

Recently I read your verses on my Xandra,
    verses which better fit *your* Xandra than mine.
Indeed — though her cunt smells of balsam — it's not the odor
    of her cunt (as you obscenely call it) that attracts me.
but rather her quick eyes, the natural charm of her face,   5
    her noble manners and her noble sense of shame,
and her true complexion indebted to no craft.
    All on her own my girl is all too beautiful;
yet all this has made me neither happy nor blest.
    O that I might always delight in such a love!   10
So if you are wise, you will beware hereafter, Ceffi,
    of saying things inappropriate about my lady-love.
Or I shall describe how *your* Xandra's cunt is withered,
    how parti-colored is her flabby cunt,
how foul her disposition, the many years the old crone carries,   15
    so that she has to fool her many men by her skills.

: 10 :

To Bernardo

O man to be numbered among my special comrades,
    honor and delight of your very own Landino!
Look, I am sending you my Muses, Bernardo,
    to whom I gave orders to be pleasing to you.
But if they do not come at once and delay a little while,   5

imbribus attribues difficilique viae;
neve tamen nostras ex hoc culpare puellas,
    neve velis Musis iurgia ferre meis.
Nam pedibus teneris durum est transcendere montes,
10   qui valeant rigidos laedere saepe viros.
Nec tibi tam multam referent, Bernarde, salutem
    nomine cum dicent: Vive poeta! meo.
Exhinc scire volent, valeat nunc candida Xandra,
    extiterit semper num memor illa mei,
15 et numquid nostras acceperit ipsa tabellas,
    stet rescribendi reddere velle vices.
Formosae posthaec cupient dinoscere mores
    Franciscae et faciem saepe videre deae;
et mirabuntur crines et eburnea colla
20   artificesque manus et sine fraude decus.
Has tu deduces iter et monstrabis aperte,
    ut possint dominas visere saepe meas.
Inde domum revoca, tantisque Penatibus infer,
    ne noceat Musis turba molesta piis.
25 Post ubi tempus erit, subito dimittere cura,
    et mandata dabis, si qua ferenda voles;
Arretina mihi namque inter moenia prisca
    nil habeo nymphis dulcius ipse meis.

: 11 :

Ad Iohannem Antonium

Florentina cito pete moenia, parve libelle,
    Antonique mei quaere subinde domum,

ascribe it to the rainstorms and to a difficult road;
still, don't find fault with my girls on this account,
    and please don't hurl reproaches at my Muses.
For on tender feet it's hard to climb up across the mountains
    which often are able to harm even rugged men.   10
Nor will they pay you an elaborate greeting, Bernardo,
    when they say "Hail, poet!" in my name.
Then they will want to know how fair Xandra does now,
    whether she's on record ever as remembering me,
and whether she has accepted my letters herself,   15
    and stands willing to write an answer in return.
After that the goddesses fair will want to learn about
    the conduct of Francesca and gaze often on her face;
and marvel at her hair and at her ivory neck,
    her skillful hands and her undeceptive beauty   20
You shall lead them down and set them clearly on their way
    so that they can often pay my lady-loves visits.
Then call them home, bring them to your great household
        gods,
    so that no irksome crowd may harm my faithful Muses.
After that, when the time comes, send them quickly away   25
    and tell them if there's anything that you would like
        brought there;
for within Arezzo's ancient walls I have nothing
    that is sweeter to me than my fair young nymphs.

: II :

To Giovanni Antonio

Seek out quickly the walls of Florence, dear little book,
    and inquire right away for my Antonio's house,

233

nomine cui multam nostro dabis ipse salutem,
    utque valet post haec nostra puella, roga.
5   Dic me mirari quod tam iocundus amicus
    nil mihi rescribit, cura nec ulla mei est.

: 12 :

Ad Xandram

Ante fores pateris nostras astare tabellas
    nec tua licterulis limina, Xandra, patent.
Obsecro qui facias: non hic fera cena Thyestae
    narratur, non hic carmina Colchis agit;
5   nec tibi mordaci referuntur iurgia lingua,
    fallere nec temptat lictera nostra dolis.
Sed domini gestit modicas narrare querelas
    et veniam culpae poscere, Xandra, meae.
Durior ergo petra nisi sis, durissima, dura,
10   licterulas cupies, candida Xandra, meas.

: 13 :

De Gnognia

Arretina suis mihi dum blanditur ocellis
    cepit, nec mirum: pulchra puella fuit.
Candida nam roseo suffuderat ora colore
    atque auro similis ipse capillus erat,

whom you yourself will greet most warmly in my name,
    and after that please ask if my girl is doing well.
Say that I'm amazed that so delightful a friend   5
    doesn't write me back and doesn't care for me at all.

: 12 :

To Xandra

You let my little books stand outside your portal
    and you close your doors against my little notes.
Please, why do you do this? Thyestes' savage banquet
    is not recounted here; here Colchis performs no poems;
brawls with biting tongue are not laid out for you,   5
    and my writing doesn't try to trick you with its wiles.
But it's eager to narrate its master's modest laments
    and to ask your pardon, Xandra, for my faults.
Therefore, hardest of girls, if you're not harder than hard
      stone,
    you will want to see my little notes, fair Xandra.   10

: 13 :

About Gnognia

As long as that girl from Arezzo allured me with her eyes,
    she enthralled me and no wonder: she was a beautiful girl.
For her lovely face was suffused with a rosy glow
    and the hair of her head was similar to gold;

235

5   et faciles oculi, vultus moresque venusti
       nec vidi alterius mollius ire pedes.
    Sed postquam nomen demens inquirere cepi,
       illico displicuit: Gnognia nomen erat!

: 14 :

Ad Bernardum

: 15 :

De Gnognia

Gnognia non fuerat, fuit immo Antonia nomen
    isti, quae nuper ceperat esse mea.
Ergo infelicem vitam, Di, reddite matri,
    quae natae nomen vertit iniqua male!

: 16 :

Ad Iohannem Antonium

Sum Landinus ego, non sum Baptista, puellis
    qui dare formosis nomina pulchra queam.

her eyes were quick, her face and her manner were charming,   5
    nor have I seen another's feet move more pliantly.
But after I madly undertook to ask her her name,
    she displeased me right away: her name was Gnognia!

: 14 :

To Bernardo = 1.11

: 15 :

About Gnognia

She wasn't really Gnognia; in fact Antonia was her name:
    the girl who but lately had begun to be mine.
Well then, O gods, allot a joyless life to the mother
    who mispronounced her daughter's name so badly.

: 16 :

To Giovanni Antonio

I'm Landino, not Battista, and I know how to give
    names that are beautiful to shapely girls.

: 17 :

Ad [...]

: 18 :

De Gnognia

: 19 :

Ad Xandram

Nunc iuvat usque tuos fastus tolerasse superbos,
    cum meus accipiat praemia digna labor.
Nostrae felices sunt terque quaterque tabellae,
    quae dominae tepidos iam tetigere sinus.
5   Forsitan atque illis mille oscula, Xandra, dedisti,
    oscula vel Phoebo vel Iove digna deo,
inque tuo niveo fovisti pectore, Xandra:
    felix pro domino lictera nostra suo est.

: 17 :

To Alda = 1.12

(untitled in the earlier redaction)

: 18 :

About Gnognia = 1.20

(retitled To Filippo about his Sweetheart)

: 19 :

To Xandra

At this moment I happily bear your arrogance and pride,
　　as long as my sufferings get a worthy reward.
My notebooks are become thrice and four times blest
　　which now have touched the warm bosom of my lady-love.
Perhaps you have given them a thousand kisses, Xandra,　　　5
　　kisses worthy of Apollo or of the god Jove,
and you have warmed them, Xandra, against your snowy
　　　　breast:
　　my poems, at least, are happy in their master's stead.

: 20 :

Ad Xandram

Iam quater in girum fulgentia cornua torquens
    orbem complevit candida luna suum,
ex quo non licuit tua lumina cernere, Xandra,
    lumina purpureo splendidiora die.
5 Sed peream lustris ni longior usque duobus
    quaelibet ex istis nox fuit una mihi.

: 21 :

Ad Bernardum

Ardua virtutis res est superare cacumen,
    cui tenuis fuerit census, amice, domi.
En mala paupertas sacras me linquere Musas
    cogit et invitum discere iura fori.
5 Me miserum! Nostras hem sic, Bernarde, Camenas
    mittere compellar delitiasque meas!
Sunt coeli testes tamen et bona lumina coeli
    tangere me nullum crimen avaritiae,
sed iubet hoc pietas inopum miseranda parentum
10 et iubet hoc etiam nubilis ipsa soror.

: 20 :

To Xandra

The radiant moon has now filled out her orbit four times,
    turning in a gyre with her gleaming horns,
in which time they've not let me see your eyes, Xandra,
    eyes more brilliant than the radiance of day.
But may I die if every single night of them   5
    was not longer to me than twice five years.

: 21 :

To Bernardo

It's a hard thing, my friend, to climb up to virtue's peak,
    for one who has but little worldly wealth at home.
See how poverty's evils make me give up the Muses
    and master unwillingly the laws of the forum.
Poor me! Thus, Bernardo, I'm compelled to send away   5
    my Camenae, alas, who are my delight!
Still, I call to witness heaven and heaven's honest eyes
    that no charge of greed can be laid against me;
compassionate love of my impoverished parents bids me do
        this,
    and my yet-unmarried sister bids me do it as well.   10

: 22 :

Ad Bicem

Transibam, memini, tua prope limina, Bice,
    nescio quid meditans, immemor atque tui;
at tu subridens, vicinam forte locuta,
    speras me vocis flectere posse sono.
5   Nil, mihi crede, facis: quod si me flectere quaeris,
    cum dixti: Venias! ne mihi claude fores.

: 23 :

Ad Musas

: 24 :

Ad matrem puellae

Iam pudeat nitidae mater deforme puellae
    nomen, iniqua parens, imposuisse meae,
et te si qua suae tangit reverentia formae,
    nomine pro turpi da: Philomena! sibi.

: 22 :

To Bice

I was passing, I remember, just by your door, Bice,
    thinking over something and oblivious of you;
but you smiled and spoke to a neighbor, by chance,
    in hopes you'd make me heed you by the sound of your
        voice.
That's no good, believe me; if you want me to heed you,   5
    when you've said: come! don't close the doors to me.

: 23 :

To the Muses = 1.14

(retitled He Wonders Why He Feels Such Disquiet).

: 24 :

To My Mistress's Mother

As mother of my elegant lady-love, perverse parent,
    you should blush to have called her by so ugly a name,
and if any consideration for her beauty touches you,
    call her Philomena, and not that disgraceful name.

: 25 :

Ad Tubiam

Cum tibi sint crines, mea lux, vel Apolline digni
    et nitidos oculos cesserit alma Venus,
cumque genae flavam possint superare Dianam
    florentes et cum dentibus assit ebur,
5   cum facies roseo tibi sit perfusa colore,
    cygnea cum cervix, lactea cumque manus,
denique cum nulli cedas Tubia puellae,
    formosum nomen do, Philomena, tibi.

: 26 :

Ad Franciscum Castilionensem

Qui referam, quanta dulcedine nostra libellus
    pectora complerit, dulcis amice, tuus?
Phoebus enim et Phoebi, Parnasia turba, sorores
    carmina dictarunt, docte poeta, tibi.
5   Tu modo fata velint longinquam ducere vitam
    Callimaco aequabis nomen ubique tuum.
Lesbia nec tantum debebit amica Catullo,
    nec Nemesi tantum, docte Tibulle, dabis
Cynthia nec fiet tam carmine nota Properti,
10   Castilionensis quam Theoplasma sui.
Et nos o utinam cernat Florentia vatem!
    sic possem laudes dicere, Xandra, tuas.

: 25 :

To Tubia

Since, light of my life, you have hair worthy of Apollo
    and kindly Venus has ceded you her gleaming eyes,
and since your blooming cheeks can surpass golden Diana's
    and ivory just approximates your teeth,
since your countenance is overspread with a roseate color,   5
    since your neck is a swan's and your hand milky-white,
and since, in fine, Tubia, you give place to no other girl,
    I shall give you a lovely name — the name "Philomena."

: 26 :

To Francesco da Castiglione

How shall I relate, sweet friend, with what great sweetness
    your little book has so completely filled my heart?
For Phoebus and the Parnassan throng, Phoebus' sisters,
    have dictated poems for you, learned poet.
So long as the Fates want you to have a lengthy life,   5
    you'll match your name everywhere to that of Callimachus.
Not even his girlfriend Lesbia will owe Catullus so much,
    nor will you, learned Tibullus, give so much to Nemesis,
nor will even Cynthia become so known through Propertius'
      poems,
    as will Theoplasma be through those of her Francesco.   10
And O, would that Florence might take note of me, her poet!
    thus could I articulate your praises, Xandra.

: 27 :

Ad Leonem Baptistam Albertum

Baptista, Albertos inter celeberrime cunctos,
    et patriae nomen delitiaeque tuae,
tu seu bella cupis tumido depingere versu,
    digna Maronea carmina voce sonas,
5   grandia seu mavis pedibus dictare solutis,
    aequas divinum tunc Ciceronis opus;
seu iuvat historias et facta reponere prisca
    alter eris Crispus, Livius alter eris.
Tu faciles elegos cithara cantare latina,
10 atque potes Tusca ludere docte lyra.
Denique quicquid habet nostri nova temporis aetas,
    quis neget hoc nobis omne Leonis erit?

: 28 :

Ad Xandram

Qui dicam fieri? Quid nostras, Xandra, tabellas
    cum capias, nolis mittere, Xandra, tuas?

: 29 :

De aula

Qua ceno, semper residet rex Aeolus aula;
    sed non est Veneris coniugis illa capax.

: 27 :

To Leon Battista Alberti

Battista, most renowned of all the Alberti clan,
    glory and delight of your native soil,
if you want to represent wars in swelling verse,
    you sound out poems worthy of Maro's voice,
or if you prefer to speak of great events in prose,   5
    then you match the godlike work of Cicero;
if you'd like to preserve the ancient deeds of history,
    you will be another Crispus or another Livy.
You can intone facile elegies on the Latin zither
    and sport learnedly upon the Tuscan lyre.   10
In short, whatever this new epoch of our time holds,
    who among us will deny it all will belong to Leon?

: 28 :

To Xandra

How to describe what's happened? When you take my
    notebooks,
    why is it, Xandra, you don't want to send me yours?

: 29 :

Concerning a Hall

King Aeolus always sits in the hall where I dine;
    but that room isn't big enough for Venus' husband, too.

: 30 :

Ad Franciscum Tonsorem

Me petis ut nostram tibi dem, Francisce, puellam.
   Efficiam, nobis si dabis ipse tuam.

: 31 :

Ad Theoplasmam

: 32 :

Ad Gigiam

Dum nimios tremulo saltus pede, Gigia, tollis
   detexit casus candida crura tibi.

: 33 :

Ad Lucretiam

Nil respondebas quondam mihi multa roganti,
   nil respondebas, dura puella nimis.
Sed postquam nivibus tecum, Lucretia, cepi
   ludere, tum primos ora dedere sonos;
5   tum primum nobis posita feritate locuta es,

: 30 :

To Francesco the Barber

You solicit me, Francesco, to give my girl to you.
  I'll see to it, if you'll also give me yours.

: 31 :

To Theoplasma = 1.15

: 32 :

To Gigia

While you're taking those excessive leaps on fluttering feet,
    Gigia,
  chance has laid bare your lovely legs for you.

: 33 :

To Lucretia

Once you answered nothing though I asked many times;
  you answered nothing, you hard, too hard girl.
But afterwards, in the snow, when I began to tease you,
  then your mouth contributed its very first sounds;
then, all ferocity laid aside, you first spoke to me,   5

tum primum nobis vox tua blanda fuit.
Quidnam aliud credam nisi quod, Lucretia, victa est
nunc tua frigiditas frigiditate nivis?
Ergo utinam nivibus rigeant tua tempora semper,
10   quando aliter nobis reddere verba negas.

: 34 :

Ad Musas

: 35 :

Ad se ipsum

: 36 :

Pro Leonardo Arretino

: 37 :

Ad Iohannem Antonium

then, for the first time, your words were kind to me.
What should I believe, Lucretia, but that your frigidity,
   was overcome by the frigidity of the snow?
Would then that your temples be always numb with snow,
   since otherwise you may refuse to answer me.   10

: 34 :

To the Muses = 1.16

(retitled To Himself)

: 35 :

To Himself = 1.17

: 36 :

For Leonardo of Arezzo = 1.18

: 37 :

To Giovanni Antonio = 1.23

(retitled To Bartolomeo Opisco Scalam)

: 38 :

Ad Anastasium

: 39 :

Ad pedicatorem

Das vitio nobis teneras ardere puellas.
   At tu pedicas: rectius ergo sapis.

: 40 :

Ad Iohannem Antonium

Qui primus famae pernices addidit alas,
   ah, nimis egregio polluit ingenio!
Sensit enim primus nil hac velocius esse
   nec quicquam tanta mobilitate geri.
5   Quisnam Arretinae dulcissima furta puellae
   rettulit, heu, Xandrae nuntia dira meae?
Non possum assiduas voces tolerare, Iohannes,
   nec possum dominae iurgia ferre meae.
Nam clamat: "Nostros sic, perfide, ludis amores,
10   siccine servatur, perfide, pacta fides?
Quo valuit pellex mihi te mutare veneno,
   qua potuit sensus arte fugare tuos?

: 38 :

To Anastasio = 1.32

: 39 :

To a Sodomite

You tell me it's a vice to get hot over yielding girls,
    but you're a sodomizer: so your taste is more upright.

: 40 :

To Giovanni Antonio

He who was the first to add speedy wings to Rumor,
    polluted unbelievably his splendid talent.
For he was first to realize that there's nothing faster,
    and nothing gets about with such mobility.
Who, pray, reported on my delicious secret love   5
    for the Aretine girl, news dreadful to my Xandra?
I can't bear this constant shouting, Giovanni, my friend,
    and I can't endure more quarrels with my mistress.
She's shouting, "Traitor, do you mock our love this way?
    Is this the way you keep the love we've pledged?   10
What poison did your doxy use to change your mind about
    me?
    what trick did she use to deprive you of good sense?

Hic ego dum pro te cunctis celeberrima templis
    vota fero, nostras altera carpit opes.
15   Namque Reparatae nunc candida limina divae,
    nunc peto Baptistae splendida templa dei.
Quaeque auro fulgent aras et imagine cerae,
    accessi curis sollicitata tuis.
Nec Marci piguit miseram delubra beati
20   et petere et donis multa rogare datis.
Denique iam cunctis in templis omnibus aris
    effudi iustas et pia vota preces.
Interea niveo pellex te amplexa lacerto
    detinet et nostris utitur usque bonis.
25   Nimirum sapio, magna et prudentia nostra est,
    quam bene flexerunt ah mea vota deos!
Scilicet ut nostris frueretur adultera sacris,
    omnibus in templis anxia dona tuli.
Cecropidem iuvenem servavit Gnosia virgo,
30   passibus et dubiis fila sequenda dedit:
et quem iam monstro subduxerat ita biformi,
    germanae vidit se refovere sinu.
Atque auri custos serpens et dentibus atris
    Iasona fregisset terrigenaeque viri,
35   ni maga Thessalico consurgat Pontia suco,
    artibus et doceat vincere posse suis.
Quid tamen, ah, pretium tanto pro munere, Colchis,
    quod meritum rebus, praemia quanta capis?
Ah demens, demens, auro quid nobile vellus
40   surripis antiquo munera cara patri?
Matrem crudelis patriam dulcemque sororem
    deseris unius ducta furore viri.
Sed nescis quantos mox sis subitura dolores,
    quamque brevem teneat vir tuus iste fidem.

While I'm here making endless vows for you in every church,
    some other girl is snatching the treasure that is mine.
Now I entreat St. Reparata's fair doors,   15
    now the splendid church of the Baptist divine.
Worn out by concern for you I've been visiting altars
    that gleam with gold and images of wax.
Wretched, it didn't bother me to seek out St. Mark's shrine
    and make many appeals, and with votive offerings.   20
In short, in every temple, before every altar,
    I've poured out righteous prayers and pious vows.
Meanwhile, your doxy, locking you in her snowy arms,
    is taking up your time, and my property!
Of course I know—because I'm by no means a fool—   25
    how well, alas, my prayers have swayed the gods!
Evidently, I've been bringing gifts to every church
    to let that adulteress enjoy my sacred rites.
The Cretan maiden saved the life of the Athenian youth
    and gave a thread to follow for his hesitating steps;   30
then, having disenthralled him from the biform monster,
    she saw him reheat himself in her sister's bosom.
The serpent guardian of the gold with its blackened teeth
    and the earth-born men would have ground Jason to bits,
if the Pontic witch had not arisen with her Thessalian juice   35
    and taught him by her arts how he could win the Fleece.
Ah, but what reward do you have, Colchis, for such a gift,
    what requital, what great compensation for such things?
Mad, oh, mad, what noble fleece of gold do you steal,
    as a costly reward indeed for your old father?   40
Cruelly you abandon mother, country, and sweet sister,
    drawn by your passion for one man alone.
But you know not how many sorrows you will soon endure,
    and how briefly that man of yours will hold to his pledge.

45   En meritum victi tauri victique draconis,
      en veteris furti gratia quanta manet!
   Nempe Creontea ducta te pellice pellit:
      quid iuvat, heu, natos nunc peperisse duos?
   Parcite, formosae, nimium vos credere verbis:
50   nam solet haec levitas omnibus esse viris."
   Has ego non possum tantas perferre querelas,
      namque nimis doleo cum mea Xandra dolet.

: 41 :

Ad Bernardum

Humanae sortis vitio sic cuncta feruntur,
   ut post candidulam stet nigra saepe dies.
Nil here me fuerat, Bernarde, beatius usquam,
   nil hodie infelix me magis esse puto.
5   Quaeris tam subiti causas fortasse doloris?
     Quae promisit heri, nunc mihi Xandra negat.

: 42 :

Epitaphium Lisae Tedaldae

Lisa pudicitiam formae quae iunxerat olim,
   hoc sua nunc tumulo frigida membra tegit.
Et Venus hanc pulchram ploret castamque Minerva;
   namque ambas coluit sancta puella deas.

See the reward for a conquered bull and a conquered dragon,   45
    see how much good will remains for that theft long ago!
After he's married his doxy, Creon's daughter, he drives you
       out:
    what good did it do then, alas, to have borne two sons?
Refrain, lovely ladies, from trusting overmuch in talk:
    for fickleness like this is habitual in all men."   50
For my part, I can't bear up under all this great lamenting:
    When my Xandra is sorry, I am *really* sorry.

: 41 :

To Bernardo

All things are borne along by the defect of the human lot,
    as after a fine, clear day a black one often comes.
Nothing was ever happier than I, Bernardo, yesterday;
    nothing, I think, is more unhappy than I am today.
You want to know, perhaps, the reason for my sudden sorrow?   5
    What Xandra promised yesterday, today she denies me.

: 42 :

Epitaph for Lisa Tedaldi

Lisa, who had once united modesty to beauty,
    now hides her cold limbs in this burial-mound.
Venus and Minerva mourn her, beautiful and chaste;
    for that saintly girl worshipped both goddesses.

5   Heu, Tedalda domus, quanta privaris alumna,
coniuge vel quali, moeste marite, cares.
Quatuor addiderat ter quinis messibus annos,
quinta nec, ah, licuit cernere lustra sibi.

: 43 :

Ad Lucinam

: 44 :

Laudes Dianae

: 45 :

De abitu Xandrae

: 46 :

Ad Leandram

Alas, house of Tedaldi, what a daughter you have lost;   5
  grieving husband, of what a wife you are bereft.
She had just added four years to her thrice five,
  and was not allowed, alas, to see another five.

: 43 :

To Lucina = 1.21

: 44 :

In Praise of Diana = 1.22

: 45 :

About Xandra's Departure = 1.25

(*retitled On Xandra*)

: 46 :

To Leandra = 1.26

(*retitled To Ginevra*)

: 47 :

De reditu Xandrae

: 48 :

Ad Franciscum Albertum Altobianci filium

Magnanime Alberta clara de stirpe create,
per quem pauperiem quondam vitare molestam
curarumque acres licuit depellere morsus,
quando ego condignas potero tibi reddere laudes
5   pro meritis tantis? Quae praemia iusta rependam?
Namque domo primus, cum nos nec debilis aetas
nec tenues nostri possent nutrire parentes,
accipis et multo laetus me munere donas.
Tu primus nostrum generoso pectus honesto
10 imbuis et teneros sensus primamque iuventam
moribus ingenuis fingis, Francisce, tuoque
exemplo nostram tentas componere vitam.
Quaeque sequenda forent, quae sint vitanda vicissim
ostendis, nigros doctus defingere mores.
15 Nec Maecenati tantum debere fatetur
Flaccus et egregii facundia tota Maronis,
quantum ego Francisco. Sed me contingere laurum
pulcher Apollo vetat, Parnasia turba sororum
ora Meduseo prohibet me tangere fonte,
20 unde fit ut dignas nequeam tibi reddere laudes.
At mihi si faciles Musas mea fata dedissent

: 47 :

About Xandra's Return = 1.27

: 48 :

To Francesco d'Altobianco Alberti

Great-hearted man, sprung from the famous Alberti stock,
who once allowed me to steer clear of nagging poverty
and to drive away the bitter gnawings of my cares,
when shall I be able to return you proper praise
for such favors? With what fair rewards shall I repay you?   5
For first, when neither my humble parents nor my tender
    years
could care for me, you accepted me into your house
and cheerfully bestowed many presents upon me.
You first steeped my heart in a sense of noble honor
and formed the tender feelings of my early youth   10
in noble ways, Francesco, and by your example
you tried to give my life some order and shape.
Wise at reforming uncouth habits, you showed me
what mores should be followed and likewise what avoided.
Horace did not admit to owing so much to Maecenas,   15
nor did all the eloquence of extraordinary Virgil,
as I to Francesco. But fair Phoebus forbids me
to reach his laurel, and the group of sisters on Parnassus
keep me from touching my lips to the Medusean spring,
whence it is that I cannot offer worthy praise to you.   20
But if my torpid fate had made my Muses indulgent

pigra nec a gelido torperent sanguine corda,
non ego magnanimi cantarem Caesaris arma,
proelia nec Magni laudatave facta Catonis,
25   nec canerem praedas referentem ex hoste Camillum,
nec victum Hasdrubalem properataque castra Neronis.
Est quod pace queam de te memorare, tibique
quam sit firma fides, quam sit pia vita referrem,
et quibus egregiam mentem virtutibus ornes,
30   utque bonis faveas, ut sis adversus iniquis.
Nec te sollicitat magnorum tristis honorum
ambitio, nummi non inflammaris amore,
sed miseros opibusque tuis et mente benigna
protegis, et patriae caris et natus amicis.
35   Det modo Parca tuae longissima fila senectae,
et vivas casta semper cum coniuge felix,
illaque natorum faciat te prole beatum.

: 49 :

Ad Leandram

: 50 :

Ad Iohannem Antonium

: 51 :

Ad Xandram

and my heart not been numbed with icy blood,
I should not be singing of the wars of great-souled Caesar,
nor Pompey's battles and the lauded deeds of Cato,
nor should I be singing of Camillus with his plunder   25
or Hasdrubal conquered by Nero's forced marches.
What I would do is celebrate your acts in time of peace
and tell how firm your loyalty is, how godly your life,
with what virtues you embellish your outstanding mind,
how you help the good and how you thwart the wicked.   30
Grim ambition for great honors does not trouble you,
nor are you consumed with a passion for coin,
but you protect the wretched with kindly thought and deed,
a man born for your country, your friends and your kin.
May the Fates give to your old age the longest thread   35
and may you live always happy with your chaste wife,
and may she make you blessed with a long line of sons.

: 49 :
To Leandra = 1.31

: 50 :
To Giovanni Antonio = 1.30

: 51 :
To Xandra = 1.28

: 52 :

Ad Bernardum

: 53 :

Ad libellum

: 52 :

To Bernardo = 1.29

: 53 :

To His Book = 1.33

CARMINA VARIA

<In obitu Lisae>

Ergo sic nostro, saevissima pestis, amico
    non puduit dominam surripuisse suam:
tum Lisae nitidos ausa es extinguere ocellos,
    qui poterant Veneris exuperare iubar.
5   Et nunc umbra recens primo illa in limine Ditis
    iam sedet obscurum mox subitura nemus;
iamque iter ingreditur tenebrosum, unde impia nullum
    non prece non auro fata redire sinunt;
iam nigra cenosi vada gurgitis insilit et iam
10   aspicit inferni guttura terna canis:
Lisa meo quondam tantum dilecta sodali,
    quantum nunc oculos non amat ipse suos!
Quid tibi nunc prodest mores coluisse pudicos,
    quidve pia sanctos relligione deos,
15   dulcia quid nervis Phoebo instituente sonoris
    carmina tam doctis composuisse modis,
talibus indigna quando te exsolvere peste,
    nec potes extremum, Lisa, cavere malum?
Heu, heu quam surdas aures quamve impia tristi
20   inferni geritis pectora corde dei!
Nam quid vos flectet, quos nec pia verba puellae,
    nec flectunt miris carmina dicta modis?
Hoc meruit pietas, immo hoc pietate nefandum
    exitium exoritur? Sic nocet esse piam?
25   Nam dum vicinam miseranda in sorte salutas,
    non potes inde tuam, Lisa, redire domum.

MISCELLANEOUS POEMS

On the Death of Lisa

And so, most cruel disease, you were not ashamed
    to carry off his lady-love from my dear friend.
You have dared to blot out Lisa's shining eyes,
    eyes which could defeat the radiance of Venus.
And now, newly a shade, she rests at Dis' very doors   5
    ready soon to descend to the dark grove;
now she joins the shadowed path, whence the wicked fates
    allow no return, not for prayer, not for gold;
now she leaps the black shallows of the muddy river
    and now she gazes at the triple throats of the hell-hound: 10
Lisa, once as much beloved of my companion
    as he now himself despises his own eyes!
What does it profit you now to have practiced modest ways,
    or worshipped the holy gods with pious devotion,
what to have composed dulcet songs in learned modes   15
    on sonorous strings with Phoebus as your teacher,
when by such virtues, Lisa, you can't free yourself
    from undeserved sickness, nor avoid the final evil?
Alas, alas, infernal gods, how deaf are your ears,
    how wicked the hearts you bear in your grim breasts!   20
For what *will* sway you, gods, when a maiden's pious words
    and poems in wondrous meters fail to influence you?
Did piety merit this? Should so unspeakable a death
    be piety's reward? Does to be pious do one harm?
For while you visited, Lisa, a neighbor in distress,   25
    you could not return from her to your own home.

Heu, quam te saevi subito invasere dolores,
    quantus et in totis ossibus ardor erat!
Tum facies olim Punico perfusa rubore
30   et niveus toto languit ore nitor;
non aliter quam quae trunco decussa virenti
    liquit in aestivo lilia sole puer,
vel quae, iam sacris superant ubi forte peractis,
    paulatim siccis serta cadunt foliis.
35   Iam teneram sacer laeva de parte papillam
    ulceris impulerat morbus habere caput,
siccaque rigebant torrenti guttura febri,
    letalique arebat lingua perusta siti.
Illa tamen, nimio quamvis iam victa dolore
40   vix posset cubito nixa levare caput,
plorantes siccis comites suspexit ocellis,
    et dedit hinc placido talia verba sono:
"Di, quorum imperiis primo nunc flore iuventae
    ante diem Stygios cogor adire lacus,
45   vos mihi, vos testes nil me admisisse nefandum,
    quo tam crudeli morte premenda forem!
Namque ego maternum servavi casta pudorem,
    nullaque de nobis fabula turpis erit.
Ergo libens, quamquam nimis immatura, sub imos
50   descendam Manes et data fata sequar.
Alter erit tanti nostra quem sorte dolores
    vexent, ut sine me nil sibi dulce putet;
at vos, quae trahitis fatalia pensa sorores,
    hic facite ut videat saecula bina senex,
55   et quantum demptum est nostro de stamine vitae
    omne id vos annis accumulate suis."
Haec atque alia iis adnectere plura volentem

Alas, how suddenly the savage pains assailed you,
    and what burning you experienced in every bone!
Then the face that once blushed with Phoenician red
    over its snow-white glow grew dim and lost its sheen,   30
not unlike a lily, which, cut from its green stem,
    a child has abandoned in the summer sun,
or garlands which shed gradually their dried-out leaves,
    left over, perchance, after holy rites are done.
The cursed sickness now had forced your tender breast to   35
        show
    the beginnings of an ulcer on your left-hand side,
and your scratchy throat stiffened up with raging fevers,
    and your tongue grew dry, burned by a deadly thirst.
Still, though overcome now with excess of pain,
    scarcely able to lift her head supported by her elbow,   40
she surveyed her weeping companions with dry eyes,
    then uttered the words that follow in a tranquil voice:
"Gods, by whose command, though in the flower of my youth,
    I'm compelled to greet the Stygian waters before my time,
bear witness that I've not committed any wicked crime   45
    for which I should be crushed by so cruel a death!
For, a chaste girl, I preserved my mother's modesty,
    and no tale of shame will be told of me, ever.
Therefore, although much too early, I shall willingly go
    to the spirits of the dead and meet my destiny.   50
There will be another by great suffering beset
    through my fate, since he will find, without me, nothing
        sweet.
But you, O sisters, who spin out the wool of destiny,
    see to it that he may live long and see his grandchildren
and, however much is snipped from my thread of life,   55
    add that amount, O sisters, all to stretch out his years."
Then the sound of her voice deserted her parched throat,

269

deseruit sicco vocis in ore sonus,
et simul e gelido prolapsa est sanguine vita
60   et iacuit frigido corpus inane toro.
Exitus hic Lisae est, qua, si modo Xandra remota,
    Etrusca fuerat pulchrius urbe nihil.
Non tamen in prima sic, Lisa, extincta iuventa
    paeniteat mores excoluisse probos:
65   impia nam fugies sic Tartara nec tibi saevas
    incutiet poenas de tribus ulla soror;
non te Dictaei terrebunt iura tyranni,
    iura umbris nunquam diffugienda piis;
non rimosa nigris implenda paludibus urna,
70   non erit inter aquas dira timenda sitis.
Horrescant aliae falcatos vulturis ungues,
    et vetita extremum tangere saxa iugum;
horrescant volucresque rotas, scopulosque minaces,
    flammiferumque caput, saeva Chimaera, tuum.
75   At Lisa Elysios campos silvasque virentes,
    fortunatorum regna beata colet.
Tum positum quisquis subito mirare sepulchrum,
    quatuor haec cursim carmina nostra lege:
Cui Venus et Charites, cui Phoebus et ipsa Minerva
80   contulerant quicquid esset ubique boni,
hoc sua candenti tumulo nunc condidit ossa;
    ossa: beatorum spiritus arva colit.

: 2 :

Eulogium in Nerium Caponium
ad Iohannem Canisianum

Non ergo immerito tam clari in funere civis
    sollicitas pectus, Canisiane, tuum.

though she wished to add many other thoughts to these,
and at that moment life slipped away from her icy blood
   and her empty body lay on her cold couch.   60
Such was Lisa's end, than whom, excepting Xandra only,
   there had been no lovelier maiden in the Tuscan city.
Still, Lisa, though snuffed out in the first flush of youth,
   you should not be sorry to have cultivated virtue:
for thus you will escape unholy Tartarus and none   65
   of the sisters three will strike you with cruel penalties.
The judgments of the Cretan tyrant shall not frighten you,
   judgments which even pious shades never may escape.
You need never fill a cloven urn from the black swamps,
   dreadful thirst amid the waters won't be yours to fear.   70
Let others tremble at the crooked talons of a vulture,
   and at rocks forbidden to reach the mountain top.
Let others tremble at swift wheels and terrifying cliffs,
   and, savage Chimaera, at your flame-bearing head.
But Lisa shall dwell ever in the fields and flourishing groves 75
   of Elysium, the happy kingdom of the blessed.
Then you who marvel at her tomb so suddenly erected,
   in passing read this quatrain of my solemn elegy:
Venus and the Graces, Phoebus and Minerva too
   had bestowed on her every good thing the world holds.   80
She has now laid her bones in this shining tomb;
   but her spirit dwells in the fields of the blessed.

: 2 :

Eulogy on Neri Capponi
for Giovanni Canigiani

So you are right then to beat your breast, Canigiani,
   at the funeral rites of so illustrious a citizen.

Cernis enim magno testatus saepe dolore,
    suscepit quantum publica causa mali.
5   Nam quid tam miserum iam dudum tamque dolendum
    Lydius Etrusca vidit in urbe leo?
Nam qui pace bonus fuerat, qui magnus in armis,
    occidit omne togae militiaeque decus.
Ah, quanta in dubiis velox prudentia rebus
10   pectoris, impendens vaticinantis erat,
quamque graves casus, quam multa pericula quondam
    effugit monitis curia nostra suis!
Auctor enim pacis semper fuit: haec sua virtus,
    hoc fuit excelsae nobile mentis opus.
15   At si quem excierat nobis ut bella moveret
    improba regnandi saeva cupido ducem,
tum patre magnanimo Nerius, dum fortia contra
    arma movet, nusquam degener ipse fuit.
Gallia sit testis Gallique horrenda Philippi
20   agmina et undosi flumina magna Padi.
Testis et Anglari vallis, cum Braccia turpi
    Piccinine tibi signa relicta fuga.
Testis et Aragonum ductor Calabraeque cohortes
    et Lusitanis castra referta viris.
25   Hic Fesulos subito sperabat Marte Quirites
    turpiter insolito subdere colla iugo.
At vigilat Nerius, turmasque opponit amicas,
    ne manus excultos barbara vastet agros.
Ergo qui nuper nulli cessurus in armis
30   Iapygiis ruerat usque tremendus equis,
paulatim vires Fabia delusus ab arte,
    quae magnae fuerant, perdidit ille suas.
Hunc Roma inspexit contritis turpiter armis
    milite vix inopi signa referre domum.
35   Et dubitem Nerium patribus populoque salutem

For having witnessed it often with great pain,
    you see how much damage the public cause has suffered.
Has there ever been another event so painful and sad   5
    witnessed by the Lydian lion in the Tuscan city?
For he who was good in peacetime, great in war,
    the whole glory of arms and the toga, has fallen.
Ah, how great his swift prudence in uncertain matters,
    how well he expended his powers of forethought!   10
How grave the disasters, how numerous the dangers
    our senate once escaped through his warnings!
Always he was the author of peace: this was his virtue,
    this was the noble work of his lofty mind.
But whenever wicked greed for domination stirred   15
    some condottiere to make cruel wars against us,
then Neri proved worthy of his great-hearted father,
    and would give direction to courageous arms.
Let Gaul bear witness, and Filippo's frightful armies
    and the mighty stream of the wave-tossed Po.   20
Let the vale of Anghiari bear witness, Piccinino,
    when you left behind your Braccian flags in base flight.
Witness too the captain of Aragon and his Calabrian troops
    and the camps filled to bursting with men from Spain
He was hoping that of a sudden the citizens of Fiesole   25
    would basely put their necks under the unaccustomed yoke.
But Neri was vigilant, and sent out allied troops
    lest the barbarian force destroy our cultivated fields.
He, then, who but lately would yield to none in battle,
    rushed forward fearsomely with his Apulian horsemen,   30
till, deceived by an artfulness like that of Fabius,
    he gradually lost his forces, though they had been vast.
Rome then gazed upon him, his army shattered in shame,
    scarce able to bring home his flags, his soldiers destitute.
Is there any doubt that, by hesitation and long delay,   35

cunctando lenta restituisse mora?
Sed quis in Hesperia locus est, ubi magna Caponum
    hoc duce non fuerit cognita fama domus?
Sed quis in Hesperia dux est, qui plurima bello
40   consilium Nerii non valuisse neget?
Nec te, Sfortiada praesens mihi Caesar, in armis
    hunc comitem bellis saepe habuisse pudet.
Huius enim noras divini pectoris artes,
    et rerum certos in genus omne modos.
45 Ast heu nunc ipsum, quem fortis Etruria multis
    deploret lacrimis, abstulit atra dies.
Non ergo immerito tam clari in funere civis
    sollicitas pectus, Canisiane, tuum.
Nec te magnanimi casus nunc urget amici,
50   actum nec secum durius esse putas.
Nam civis quaecumque potest optare modestus,
    omnipotens illi fors cumulata dedit.
Florenti in patria natus, quae libera iusto
    Tyrrhenas urbes temperat imperio,
55 et patriae magnus dum tractat Cosmus habenas,
    proxima post Cosmum dignus habere loca.
Adde genus clarum simul et numerosa nepotum
    nomina et agnatis stemmata plena suis,
adde et Parrhasiae Pisano in litore gentis
60   victa genitoris moenia Marte sui,
adde animi vires, fortunae commoda, vitae
    quae validus duxit tempora longa senex.
Sed te communis populi iactura, tuaeque
    urbis amor magnus, Canisiane, movet.
65 Tempore nam duro tali privatur alumno
    publica res, qualem saecula rara ferunt.

Neri brought salvation to our fathers and the people?
Where in the Western world, thanks to his leadership,
   is the great Capponi house not known to fame?
Where in the Western world is there a man who'd deny
   that Neri's counsel was not worth the most in the war.   40
Nor are you, Sforza, a modern Caesar, ashamed
   to have often had this man as your comrade in wars.
For you knew the skills of his exalted mind
   and his sure moderation in all sorts of affairs.
But, alas, now a black day has carried off the very man   45
   whom brave Tuscany laments with many a tear.
So you are right then to beat your breast, Canigiani,
   at the funeral rites of so illustrious a citizen.
Yet the fall of a magnanimous friend does not weigh upon you
      now,
   nor do you think that it goes very hard with him.   50
For whatever an unassuming citizen can wish for
   all-powerful Fortuna gave him in abundance.
He was born with Florence as his native land, she who
   guides the Tuscan cities with just empire and free,
and while great Cosimo holds the reins of that land,   55
   he was worthy to hold the next place after Cosimo.
Add to that a famous family and a numerous list
   of grandchildren and a family tree full of male heirs.
Add, too, the walls on the Pisan coast of the Parrhasian race,
   a city vanquished by his father's power in war.   60
Add strength of mind, advantages of fortune and of life,
   which the healthy old man enjoyed for many years.
But the loss to the common people, and that great love
   you have for your city moves you, Canigiani.
For the republic is robbed in this hard time   65
   of such a son as only rare generations bring.

Ad Bernardum Bembum

Tale meo carmen resonet si pectore, quale
 Ismario vati Calliopea dedit,
non ego ad excelsos revocarem flumina fontes
 nec traherem fulvos per iuga summa lupos,
5 blanda nec auritae sequerentur carmina quercus,
 nec premeret gressus lynx stupefacta suos;
sed te, Tyrrheno sidus salutare leoni,
 qui nuper Veneta missus ab urbe venis,
sensibus amplectens imis et pectore firmo
10 cantarem laudes, maxime Bembe, tuas,
Bembe decus nostri, Musarum dulcis alumne,
 delitiae Charitum, Palladiumque caput.
Quod mihi principium, meritos dum reddere honores
 conor, Bembe, tibi, quis mihi finis erit?
15 Magna facit variis inopem me copia rebus,
 virtutes dubium me tenuere tuae,
ne, dum plura feram, plura et referenda relinquam
 immensumque novo carmine crescat opus.
Stultus sed tenui sublimia sidera penna
20 ire paro, Icarias mox subiturus aquas;
nam nec Calliope Rhodopei carmina vatis,
 nec Lini nobis praebet Apollo lyram,
sed curtis elegis Erato me iussit amantum
 usta cupidinea ludere corda face.
25 Quapropter Bembi castos ludemus amores,
 versibus ut surgat Bencia nota meis.
Bembus, pulchra, tuam miratur, Bencia, formam,
 caelestes valeas qua superare deas,

: 3 :

To Bernardo Bembo

If a poem should echo in my heart, one such as
    Calliope bestowed on the Ismarian seer,
I should not call rivers back to their lofty sources
    or draw the tawny wolves along the highest ridges,
nor would the listening oaks heed my enchanting songs   5
    nor the lynx in amazement follow in his tracks;
but embracing you with deepest feeling and steadfast heart,
    I would sing your praises, most illustrious Bembo,
who has lately come as a salutary star
    sent from the city of Venice to the Tuscan lion.   10
Bembo, you honor us, sweet offspring of the Muses,
    delight of the Graces, olive-crowned head.
What beginning shall I make, what will be my ending,
    as I try to pay you worthy honors, Bembo?
Your virtues give me pause: such extraordinary wealth   15
    in every point of praise leaves me destitute.
However much I say, I shall leave much unsaid,
    and a huge work may grow from the elegy I've begun.
But, fool that I am, I prepare to climb to the highest stars
    on my frail wing, soon to plunge into Icarian waters.   20
For Calliope does not give me songs like the Thracian bard's,
    nor does Phoebus offer me the poet Linus' lyre,
but Erato has bidden me to toy in crisp elegiacs,
    with lovers' hearts burned by the torch of Venus' son.
Hence I shall amuse myself with Bembo's chaste affairs,   25
    so that Bencia shall rise up made famous by my song.
Lovely Bencia, Bembo is in awe of your beauty,
    beauty which surpasses the goddesses in heaven,

quam magnus Veneris Mavors praeponere amori,
30   quam missa Europa Iuppiter ipse velit.
Sed magis antiquos mores pectusque pudicum
    miratur stupidus Palladiasque manus.
Semper amore pio calet hic, contagia tetrae
    nec possunt illum tangere luxuriae.
35 Nullam Helenem laudat Bembus, nullamve Corinnam,
    Cynthia nulla sibi, Lesbia nulla placet,
nec si qua est castum quae ausit violare cubile
    coniugis, et firmam voluit esse fidem.
Grata sed Alceste, grata et quae coniugis atros
40   Evadne voluit scandere viva rogos,
grata et Penelope, quam nec potuere parentes
    flectere, nec dites, turba proterva, proci,
et quaecumque olim duro succumbere leto
    maluit et Stygii nare per uda lacus,
45 debita legitimi quam rumpere foedera lecti,
    solvere vel sancti vincula coniugii.
Quapropter, tales artes imitata, puellis
    exemplar Tuscis, Bencia pulchra, venis.
Notus amor Paridis, fateor, <fur>orque Lacaenae,
50   sed turpi tamen est notus adulterio.
Pulchrior at Ledae partu iam, Bencia, cunctis
    gentibus es rara nota pudicitia.

: 4 :

Ad eundem

O te felicem! Lux o qu<am lactea> signet
    gemma et natali non su<peranda tu>o,

beauty which great Mars might prefer to Venus' love,
    which Jupiter himself might want, abandoning Europa.   30
But, stunned, he marvels more at your antique character,
    your bashful heart and Palladian hands.
He burns ever with a holy love, and the virus
    of foul dissipation can never lay its hand on him.
Bembo never praises Helen, praises no Corinna;   35
    no Cynthia or Lesbia does he find to please him,
And if any woman dared to stain her chaste marriage-bed,
    he always wished her loyalty to remain steadfast.
But Alcestis delights him, and Evadne, who desired
    to mount alive upon the funeral pyre of her husband;   40
Penelope delights him too, whom parents could not sway,
    nor her wealthy suitors in their impudent throng,
and whatever women long ago preferred to yield
    to hard death and cross the waters of the Stygian lake
rather than break the compact owed to a legitimate bed   45
    or loosen the fetters of holy marriage.
Wherefore, lovely Bencia, mirroring such conduct,
    you emerge as a model for the maids of Tuscany.
Paris's mad love for Helen is famous, I admit,
    but it's famous as foul adultery, nevertheless.   50
But you, Bencia, lovelier now than the offspring of Leda,
    are famous among all nations for your rare modesty.

: 4 :

To the Same Man

O you lucky man! O day not to be surpassed,
    that like a milk-white signet marks out your birth,

qua licuit dominam propter tibi, Bembe, sedere
    ludereque ac mutuo mille referre sales.
5   Fare, age, quis pallor, quis te rubor una timorque
    corripuit, tremulo qualis in ore sonus,
hospitis in mediis laribus nil tale putanti
    obvia cum facta est dia Ginevra tibi,
cumque salutanti respondit pauca modeste,
10   purpureus niveo crevit et ore calor.
Non ita concaluit, cum primum Sestia virgo
    vidit Abydenum nare per alta virum;
candida nec Dido, viridi residentis in antro
    cernens Dardanii membra decora ducis,
15   ut tu divinae subito fulgore puellae
    arsisti tacita gaudia mente ferens.
Es tibi tunc visus pinnatis, Bembe, quadrigis
    scandere lucentis regna superna poli,
colloquioque frui divum coetuque dearum
20   permixtus sanctos concelebrare choros.
Dic igitur: quae tunc renovatae in pectore flammae,
    et quibus, ah, durus ignibus ussit amor?
Sed dices nunquam; parvo namque igne calescit,
    qui quantum caleat dicere, Bembe, valet.
25   Dic Erato <quae sint flammae quae> pectus amantum
    incutiant; <nam tu> sola referre potes;
dic, quibus obstupuit verbis vel quae ora Medusae
    vertere eum in silicem sic potuere novam.
Surripuit Phrygium puerum Iovis ales in altum,
30   misceat ut regi pocula caelicolum;
Bencia sed Bembum divinae assistere mensae
    et dedit ambrosios sumere posse dapes.
Ludebat, lusum decuit; loquebatur, ab ore

when your mistress was allowed to sit beside you, Bembo,
    frolic and exchange a thousand witty sallies.
Come, tell us how you turned first white, then red with fear   5
    and what kind of sound came from your trembling lips,
when in the inner sanctum of your host you met
    Ginevra the goddess, when you least expected it.
As she answered modestly a few words to your greeting,
    a rosy blush spread also on her snow-white face.   10
The Sestian maiden did not glow so hot with love
    when first she saw Leander swimming through the deep;
nor was fair Dido, when she saw the fine limbs
    of the vigorous Trojan leader seated in the cave,
as you, when you burned with joy in your silent breast,   15
    at the sudden radiance of that godlike girl.
To yourself you seemed to fly up on a wingèd chariot
    to the celestial realms at the shining pole,
and to hold converse with the gods, and to mingle
    with a throng of goddesses in their holy dance.   20
So tell me: what flames have been rekindled in your heart,
    and what flames have burned you, sent by pitiless Love?
But you'll never say; for small is the flame that warms him,
    Bembo, who can say just how much he burns.
Erato, describe for us the flames that should strike   25
    the hearts of lovers; for you alone can tell.
Describe the words that struck him dumb, the Medusean
      looks
    that were able so to turn him newly into stone.
The bird of Jove stole the Phrygian boy away to heaven
    to prepare goblets for the king of the gods;   30
but Bencia has seated Bembo at the table of the gods,
    and given him a chance to sup ambrosial feasts.
She had fun and fun became her; she spoke, and you would
      swear

iurares Charites fundere verba suo.
35 Vidi ego post atros imbres, iam nube fugata,
   fulgentem subita luce redire diem;
at modico risu si forte Ginevra refulsit,
   tunc soles geminos emicuisse putes.
Candida lux igitur niveoque notanda lapillo
40 illa fuit, fateor; sed tamen una fuit.
Quod si felici redeat nunc altera fato,
   Bembe, immortalem te mea Musa canet.

: 5 :

Ad eundem

Hoc age nunc, Erato, Bembi referamus amores,
   sed quos caelestis comprobet ipsa Venus.
Hic nihil obscenum est turpive libidine tetrum;
   castus amor castam postulat usque fidem.
5 Talis amor Bembi, qualem divina Platonis
   pagina Socraticis exprimit eloquiis.
Namque amor a pulchro cum sit, perculsa cupido
   pulchrum amat et pulchris gaudet imaginibus;
at quodcumque bonum, pulchrum est, turpe omne nefandum:
10 sic bona deposcit, sic mala vitat amor.
His flammis Bembus talique accensus amore
   uritur, et medio corde Ginevra sedet.
Forma quidem pulchra est, animus quoque pulcher in illa:
   horum utrum superet, non bene, Bembe, vides.
15 Ergo nil mirum est, nam maxima semina flammis

that through her lips the Graces were pouring out their
    words.
I have seen that after storms, when the clouds have fled,   35
    the gleaming day returns with a sudden radiance;
but if perchance Ginevra glowed with but half a smile,
    you would think that doubled suns had then shone forth.
Thus the day was fair and to be marked with a snow-white
    stone;
    I admit that: still, it was only a single day.   40
But if by a happy fate another day should now return,
    my Muse will sing, Bembo, of your immortality.

: 5 :

To the Same Man

Come now, Erato, let us tell of Bembo's affairs,
    but only those that heavenly Venus might herself approve.
Here there is nothing filthy, or foul with shameful passion;
    for a chaste love always asks for chaste trust.
Bembo's love is of such a kind that Plato's divine page   5
    might express its quality with Socratic eloquence.
For when love from beauty comes, desire, being striken,
    loves the beautiful and joys in lovely likenesses;
But all things good are beautiful; all badness abhorrent,
    thus love demands the good, thus it shuns what is evil.   10
Bembo, afire with a love like this, burns with these flames,
    and Ginevra is seated at the center of his heart.
She is beautiful on the outside, and beautiful within;
    which of these is best, Bembo, you do not see well.
Thus it's no surprise, indeed, that your lady's virtue   15

virtus et dominae dant tibi forma tuis.
Teque etiam ingenio finxit natura benigno,
    solertemque animum stella secunda dedit;
hinc oculis priscas stupidis mirare figuras
20   sive hominum, seu sint haec simulacra deum,
si qua aut Parrhasio fulget splendore tabella,
    ductus Apellea si quis ab arte color.
Sed Cnidiae quondam Veneris simulacra retecta
    Praxitelis docta sunt tibi visa manu:
25   his tu non Italam, non Gallam, Bembe, puellam
    hactenus aut aliam conspicis assimilem.
Bencia sed nuper flavos redimita capillos,
    cum primum est oculis visa Ginevra tuis,
tunc ut plebeae reliquae de pectore formae
30   cesserunt! visa est sola Ginevra dea.
Tunc mens insolita stupuit, Bernarde, figura,
    cernere supra hominem nescio quid reputans.
Sed neget alatum quis te volucremque, Cupido,
    quo celere est toto iam nihil orbe magis?
35   Conspectu ut primo stupuit Bernardus, ut illi
    corripuit subito pectora tota furor!
Vidit, et internas irrupit flamma medullas,
    atque horrens subiit dura per ossa tremor.
Nam facies illi, qualem cum saepe videmus
40   candida purpureis lilia mixta rosis,
vel si Phoenicio veniat suffusa colore
    Indica Erythraeo gemma reperta mari.
Et Venus ipsa oculos divino spargit honore
    et Charitum tota gratia fronte nitet.
45   Ambulat: incessum iures Iunonis in illa.
    Est opus in manibus: Palladis extat opus.
Vidimus, horrisono Borea cessante, reducta
    candentem subito crescere valle nivem;

and her beauty give the greatest sparks to your passion.
For nature has formed in you a liberal temperament,
    and a lucky star has furnished an ingenious mind;
hence you marvel with astonished eyes at antique images,
    whether they be likenesses of men or of the gods,   20
if any picture glows with Parrhasian lustre
    or if any hue is painted with Apelles's skill.
A statue of Cnidian Venus, uncovered long ago,
    seemed to you fashioned by Praxiteles's learned hand:
hitherto, Bembo, you've seen no Italian girl,   25
    nor French, nor any other maiden like unto her.
But the first time Ginevra came before your eyes,
    Bencia, with her golden tresses freshly bound,
then the plebeian beauty of the others disappeared
    from your heart; Ginevra only seemed to be divine.   30
Then your mind was stunned by her extraordinary form,
    which reckoned it was seeing something more than human.
But who can say no to you, Cupid, winged and fleet,
    than whom is nothing faster in the entire world?
How stunned Bernardo was at his first sight of her,   35
    how passion quickly captured his whole heart!
He looked, and the flame shot through him to the marrow;
    a shuddering tremor passed through his strong bones.
For her countenance was like what we often see
    when white lilies mingle with red roses,   40
or if a pearl of India, found by the Arabian Sea
    should be suffused with Phoenician color.
Venus too sprinkled Bencia's eyes with godlike splendor
    and the Graces' charm shines full from her brow.
She walks: you would swear that Juno's gait was hers.   45
    Her hands are a work of art, Athena's living art.
After the North Wind has ceased his roar, we've seen
    a sudden snowfall shining in a valley far off;

at si cervicem spectes et colla Ginevrae,
50   candentem poteris temnere iure nivem.
Ardent purpurei vernali tempore flores;
        sed nihil ad dominae pulchra labella tuae.
Quid frontem nitidam et dentes referamus eburnos,
        et posita in roseis lumina nigra genis?
55   Nec mores qui sint, nec quales ore lepores
        humano sperem posse referre sono.
Ergo si casu in talem, Bernarde, furorem
        incidis aeternum, sors memoranda datur;
sin illam ex tota prudenter deligis urbe,
60   quis prorsus, quisnam te mage, Bembe, sapit?
Es felix igitur, sed non minus illa beata,
        quae quondam tanto vivat amata viro.
Nam quis nobilior Veneto cui prisca Senatu
        progenies multos enumeravit avos?
65   Est aetas viridis, pulchro est in corpore virtus,
        admixtusque decens cum gravitate iocus.
Smyrnaeo celebrem versu laudamus Ulixem,
        plurima qui magno viderat orbe loca.
Hic passus diros Ciconas belloque superbum
70   Ismaron, et forti proelia gesta manu.
Nam quid Cyclopas referam vel quas Polyphemus
        horrendo ferox edidit ore minas?
Hic vidit sociis falsa sub imagine captis
        dissutis ventos utribus ire leves,
75   Laestrygonum et diras epulas, fugiendaque Circes
        litora, et in varias corpora versa feras.
Sirenum fugit cantus, et nota Charybdis
        furta, et Scyllaeos, horrida monstra, canes.
Nec semel aequoreas enavit naufragus undas;
80   sic, Neptune, tibi, sic tibi, Phoebe, placet.
At si quas terras adiit, quos aequore tractus,

but if you will gaze upon Ginevra's neck and shoulders,
    you will be right to scorn that glistening snow.   50
Purple flowers glow in the season of spring;
    but they're nothing to your mistress's lovely lips.
What to say of Bencia's shining brow and ivory teeth,
    and her dark eyes set in rosy-colored cheeks?
I may not hope to tell in human speech   55
    the qualities of her witty words or her character.
Therefore, if by any chance, your passion proves eternal,
    Bernardo, you've been given a memorable lot;
but if you choose her wisely from the entire city,
    who, pray, Bembo, is wiser indeed than you?   60
You are fortunate, then, but she too is no less blessed,
    who may some day live to be loved of such a man.
For who is nobler than a man whose ancient lineage
    numbers many forebears in the Venetian Senate?
Vigorous in age, strength lies in his handsome body;   65
    he mixes tasteful humor with fine gravity.
In Homeric verse we praise the honored Ulysses,
    who saw many places throughout the great world.
He endured the dire Cicones, and Ismara, proud in war,
    and battles fought out with courageous hand.   70
What shall I say of the Cyclopes, what of Polyphemus,
    wildly spouting threats from his frightful mouth?
He saw the nimble winds come out of the torn bag,
    his comrades deceived by a fabricated image,
the Lastrygones' dire feasts, and the shores of Circe   75
    that he must flee, and bodies turned into varied beasts.
He fled the Sirens' songs and Charybdis' notorious tricks,
    and those bristling monsters, the Scyllaean dogs.
Shipwrecked more than once, he swam out of the sea waves:
    this you approved, Neptune, and you too, Apollo.   80
But if I should now describe the lands that Bembo has seen,

dum peragit patriae iussa verenda suae,
nunc referam, varias missus legatus in oras,
    Dulichium poterit vincere Bembus iter.
85   Nam qua Pyrene niveis ditata metallis
    splendida nubiferum tollit ad astra caput,
Herculis ad metas extremaque nomina Calpes
    et Gaditano litora tunsa freto,
innumeros populos variasque ex ordine gentes
90   circuit, et variis moribus ingenia.
Nec tantum geminos noster cognovit Iberos
    Bembus et occiduae litora longa plagae,
sed quae sunt gelido septem subiecta trioni,
    damnata aeterno frigida rura gelu.
95   Nam iuga Gallorum Rhodanumque et pervia ponte
    transivit Rheni flumina Caesareo,
atque omnes quos magna colit Germania montes
    et Morinum sedes Teutonicasque manus.
Atque aucta Venetum sic maiestate Senatum
100   colligat externis foedere principibus.
Magnarum hinc igitur sic experientia rerum
    egregium mira reddidit arte virum:
hinc callet quicquid civilia dogmata poscunt,
    quid dux, quid miles, quidve Senatus agat;
105   quae belli, quae summa bonae sint munera pacis,
    curia quod mandet, causidicumve forum.
Te decus egregium, Veneti te nominis omnes
    plebei lucem patriciique vocant.
Magna domi praestas magno de pectore promens
110   consilia in dubiis magnaque saepe foris.
His facilis rebus iam iam commota Ginevra
    (dura nec humano pectore saxa gerit),
perpetuo reddi cupiens insignis amore,

the seas he's crossed, to respect his country's commands,
sent as an ambassador to many different lands,
   Bembo could exceed even the journeys of Ulysses.
For from where the Pyrenees, enriched by silver mines,   85
   raise their cloudy heads up to the shining stars,
to the pillars of Hercules and Gibraltar, furthest name,
   and the shores beaten by the straits of Cadiz,
he's journeyed round various nations and unnumbered peoples
   with their varied mores and temperaments.   90
Our Bembo has come to know not just the twin Spanish races
   and the long littorals of the western shore,
but also those chilly lands condemned to everlasting frost
   which lie under Ursa Major's seven cold stars.
For he has crossed the Alpine heights that separate the Gauls   95
   and the rivers of the Rhine that Caesar's bridges spanned,
and all the mountains which great Germany inhabits
   and the seats of the Morini and Teutonic tribes.
And having thus augmented Venetian majesty,
   he links foreign princes to his Senate in a league.   100
Hence with wondrous skill this experience of great affairs
   has given the man an exceptional distinction:
hence he is an expert in that which politics demands,
   whatever a doge, a general, or the Senate might do,
what might be the greatest tasks of war or blessed peace,   105
   what the Curia or jurisprudence demands.
All the common people and patricians call you
   the special light and glory of the Venetian name.
Speaking from your mighty heart, you offer large counsel
   in doubtful matters both at home and, often, abroad.   110
Already Ginevra is all but won by these accomplishments,
   for her heart is not composed of unfeeling stone,
she wants to acquire distinction through enduring love,

optat adoptivae nomina clara domus,
115   mutatisque notis gentili e stirpe duabus,
Bencia quae fuerat, Bembia nomen erit.

: 6 :

Ad eundem

Quaeris, Bembe, diu sileat cur nostra Thalia,
nec Xandram nobis pagina muta sonet;
idque putas causae, curis quod forte solutum
insano sanum pectus amore vacet.
5   At, mihi crede, prius Pisanas Tuscus in undas
Arnus ab aereis desinet ire iugis,
quam nostro auratae vellantur corde sagittae,
meque suis faculis urere cesset amor.
Non Xandrae, ut quondam, flavent in vertice crines,
10   nec tantus, fateor, fulget in ore nitor.
Sic voluit stabili fatorum lege potestas,
ut quae sunt, ipso tempore nata cadant.
Sic formae decus omne perit fugiente iuventa,
paulatim et faciem ruga senilis arat.
15   Sed mihi nec flavi crines nec lumina nigra,
crede, olim tanti causa furoris erant;
sed mage me virtus muliebri in corde virilis
movit, et ingenii vis memoranda sui.
Inque dies crevit virtus, crescentibus annis,
20   inque dies nobis sic quoque crevit amor.
Nam quisquis sola forma vincitur amator,
lubricus instabili nititur ille gradu;

and desires the noble name of her adoptive house:
by changing only two signs of her family stock   115
   she who had been Bencia, will be Bembia by name.

: 6 :

To the Same Man

You ask why my Thalia has so long been silent, Bembo,
   and why my silent page no longer speaks of Xandra;
and this you think the reason: that perchance, released from
     care,
   my healthy heart is free of my unhealthy love.
But, trust me, the Tuscan Arno would cease to flow on down   5
   from its lofty mountains to the Pisan Sea,
before those golden arrows are plucked from my heart,
   and Love no longer burns me with his little torches.
Xandra's tresses are no longer golden on her head;
   I confess her face shines with a lesser radiance.   10
Thus the Fates' authority by stable law has willed,
   that things which are born shall die in due time.
Thus every ornament of beauty dies when youth takes flight,
   and by degrees age's wrinkles plow one's face.
But, believe me, it wasn't her dark eyes or golden hair   15
   that were long ago the reason for my great passion;
but more, the manly strength in her woman's heart moved me
   and the power, unforgettable, of her intellect.
Day by day her virtue grew, as her years increased,
   and thus, day by day, my devotion also grew.   20
For if any lover is won by loveliness alone,
   he's mounting insecurely on an unstable step;

si quis at egregiam mentem, si diligit acre
    ingenium et variis corda referta bonis,
25   hic pulchrum sequitur, quod nec vitiare vetustas,
    ulla nec a caelo magna ruina potest.
Discite mortales animo, non corpore formam
    optandam, et verum discite amare decus.
Hoc me iam sextum lustrum tenet, hocque tenebit
30   dumque animus stabit, dum memor ipse mei.
Nunc quia prima pios aetas cantavit amores,
    et lusit dominae cygnea colla meae,
quae posthac veniet maturis serior annis —
    nam sic, Bembe, decet — iam graviora canet.
35   Et tamen interdum dulcis tibi, Bembe, Ginevrae,
    sit modo Musa favens, nomen in astra feram.
Pierides, Bembo vos hoc praestabitis: orbe
    carminibus toto nota sit illa meis.
Hanc nostris soboles miretur Graia libellis,
40   hanc stupeant Latii me recinente viri.
Illi Smyrnaeo dicent te carmine dignam,
    hique Maroneo, Bencia diva, sono.
Quaeque Fluentina florebit in urbe iuventus,
    illa modo de te carmina nostra legat:
45   Heu, dicet, tersi cur non fecunda Petrarcae
    incidit in talem tempore lingua deam;
namque pudicitia, forma, comitate modoque
    haec Lauram et sanctis moribus antevenit.

but if anyone loves a noble mind or a keen wit
    and a heart filled with a variety of virtues,
he pursues a loveliness which age cannot taint,   25
    nor any great disaster that heaven might send.
Learn, mortals, to desire beauty of soul, not body;
    learn to love the kind of honor that is genuine.
This honor rules me now at thirty, and will rule me still
    while my spirit stands and my memory lasts.   30
Now since my first youth sang of that holy love,
    and amused itself with my mistress's swanlike neck,
the later age that came thereafter with my riper years—
    for this befits them, Bembo—will now sing of graver
        things.
And yet, meanwhile, if my Muse is well-disposed,   35
    I shall lift your dear Ginevra's name to the stars.
Muses, grant this to Bembo, that, through my poems,
    she may become well-known throughout the whole world.
Let the child of Greece marvel at her in my booklets,
    let the Latian men be amazed at my song's theme.   40
The one will say you're worthy of that old Homeric song,
    Bencia divine, the other of Vergilian tones.
Let whatever youth blooms in the City of the Lilies
    only read these elegies of mine about you.
Alas, they will say: why did not the fecund tongue   45
    of polished Petrarch fall in such a goddess's time?
For in chaste loveliness, restraint and courtesy
    she excels Laura, and in blameless conduct too.

∴ 7 ∴

Ad eundem

Non desiderio tali concussa Thoantis,
    cum subito Argoam vidit abire ratem,
nec tantum doluit Phrygio delusa marito,
    cum lucem dura fugit Elisa nece,
5   nec tulit Actaeam gravius discedere classem
    in frondes Phyllis mox abitura novas,
atque tuo deflet discessu, Bembe, Ginevra,
    et queritur surdos in sua vota deos.
Heu, surdos sua vota deos contemnere luget,
10   orbari et castis Bencia delitiis.
Delitias, ah, maesta pias sanctumque furorem
    nunc nimium celeri luget abire fuga.
Sed tamen excelsi testatur numen Olympi,
    si qua fides sanctae est, Bembe, pudicitiae,
15   se nunquam memori moturam pectore Bembum,
    Nestoreos annos vixerit ille licet.
Ergo ibis, caros felix visure propinquos
    et dulcis natos coniugiumque pium;
nam tandem exacto patria consistere lustro
20   sede tibi, magno munere functe, datur.
Tu tamen infixum generoso in pectore condes,
    qua tibi Landinus iunctus amicitia est.
Nec tantum Argivum Pylades dilexit Orestem,
    cui comes horrendo factus in exilio est,
25   Castora nec Pollux duris in caestibus audax,
    fortem nec fortis Thesea Pirithous,
quanto ego nunc Bembi teneor devictus amore,

: 7 :

To the Same Man

The daughter of Thoas was not stricken with such longing,
    when she saw the ship Argo suddenly departing,
nor did Dido, duped by her Trojan husband, mourn so,
    when by hard death she fled from the light,
nor did Phyllis, soon to vanish into new-grown leaves,   5
    bear more heavily the Attic fleet's departure,
than Ginevra weeps over your departure, Bembo,
    and in her prayers bewails the heedless gods.
Alas, Bencia moans that the deaf gods scorn her prayers
    and that she is orphaned of her virginal delights.   10
Grieving, now she moans that her faithful delights,
    and her holy passion go in a flight too swift.
But still she calls to witness the god of high Olympus,
    that if there is any trust in holy virtue, Bembo,
never, though he should live to the age of Nestor,   15
    will she cast Bembo from her heart or memory.
Thus will you go, glad to see your dear relations,
    your beloved sons and your dutiful wife;
for you've discharged your great task, your lustrum is
        complete,
    and now you're allowed to dwell at home in your country.   20
Still you will treasure, fixed in your noble heart,
    the friendship that unites your Landino to you.
Pylades did not so love the Argive Orestes,
    made his companion in frightening exile,
nor did daring Pollux with his boxing gloves Castor,   25
    nor brave Pirithous so love brave Theseus,
as much as I am won and held fast by love of Bembo,

295

quem iam nulla queat dissolvisse dies.
Magna Philoctetae potuit reverentia magnum
30   Alcidem obsequio conciliare pio;
tuque mihi Alcides, sed nec pietate fideque,
     Bembe, Philoctetes me superare potest.
Namque ego te tota complector mente animoque:
     virtutes mirae sic voluere tuae.
35   Prudentem admiror, facilem te diligo, Bembe,
     te doctum stupeo, te fruor usque comi.
Aetas germanum facit, at reverentia patrem
     te colit, ingenti natus amore venis.
Ergo perpetuum nostri sit pignus amoris,
40   quae colit Aonium turba canora nemus.
Vos, o Pieria doctae de rupe sorores,
     immo me Bembi condite corde mei;
atque viri ingentem laudem aspirate canenti,
     spiritus ut grandi surgat in ore novus.
45   Tunc noscet ventura aetas, Venetusque Senatus,
     quae fuerint civis munera magna sui,
quid patriae dederit varias legatus ad urbes,
     eloquio ante omnes consilioque potens.

: 8 :

Ad eundem

Nobilitas prisco si forte a sanguine surgit,
     quod gravis usque tamen Stoica secta negat,
quis te plura tulit ramoso in stemmate, Bembe,
     nomina vel plures enumeravit avos?
5   Sunt alii, patriae qui si moderentur habenas

a love which no future day shall ever undo.
Philoctetes's great devotion and his pious obsequies
    could endear the archer to great Hercules.   30
You, Bembo, are Hercules to me, but Philoctetes
    cannot surpass me in devotion or trust.
For I embrace you with my whole mind and spirit,
    for your admirable virtues have willed it so.
I admire your wisdom, Bembo, and love your easy ways;   35
    I marvel at your learning, I delight in your taste.
Age makes you a brother, but esteem reveres you as
    a father, you appear among us born of great love.
May then the tuneful throng who dwell in the Aonian grove
    be an everlasting pledge of our mutual love.   40
O learned sisters who dwell upon the rocky Pierian crag,
    rather, treasure me in the heart of my Bembo;
and inspire me to sing the man's abundant praise,
    that a new breath may produce a grander voice.
Then the age to come and the Venetian Senate will know   45
    how great are the gifts that their citizen possesses,
what his legations to various cities has given his country,
    his supereminent power in eloquence and counsel.

: 8 :

To the Same Man

If perchance nobility springs out of ancient blood,
    which the grave Stoic school always has denied,
who has borne more names in his branching family tree,
    and counted more ancestors than you, O Bembo?
There are others who, if they hold the reins of state   5

publica vel populi munera magna gerant,
sese Troiugenas et Cadmi semine natos
   Cecropiumque putant exuperare genus.
Sed si prima urbis Venetae repetatur origo,
10   quae latum imperium saecula longa tenet,
nunquam Bemba manum domus a temone remisit,
   sed semper dubiis addita consiliis.
At si sola potest virtus, nihil indiga rerum
   fortunae, quemvis nobilitasse virum,
15 Socrate iam gradibus convincam iudice Bembum
   omnibus exactum nobilitatis opus.
Namque illi est animus generoso incoctus honesto,
   quod sibi doctrina, quod sibi more parat.
Nam docilis subiens dudum penetralia sanctae
20   naturae, ad verum iam sibi fecit iter.
Hic salibus lepidus variis, huic ore rotundo
   grandibus in rebus grandia verba sonant.
Publica si dubio tractantur munera casu,
   atque opus est celeri mente praeire malum,
25 ingenii velox magni miramur acumen,
   rebus in ambiguis consiliumque grave.
Non aurum Xerxis, Siculi non monstra Perilli
   sperent robusto corde movere fidem;
Sirenas contra clausit nec firmius aures,
30   cuius ob ingenium Pergama celsa iacent,
atque voluptatum illecebras, Bernarde, dolosas
   et dirae Circes noxia philtra fugis.
Sed nullum est maius generoso in pectore signum
   Musarum sacros quam coluisse choros.
35 Nam, quem Pegaseo lavere in fonte sorores,
   ad gremium summi subvolat ille Iovis,
terrenasque odit labes, raptatur amore
   Caelestum, et patrias gaudet inire domos.

or carry out great public duties for the people,
think themselves to surpass the offspring of Troy
    and the seed of Cadmus and the Cecropian race.
But if one traces back the first origins of Venice,
    which for long ages has held far-ranging power,   10
never did the House of Bembo let go the tiller,
    but was always present in doubtful deliberations.
But if virtue by itself may ennoble any man,
    owing nothing to the goods of fortune,
with Socrates as my judge I'll now prove that Bembo is   15
    a product of nobility, complete in every degree.
For he has a soul steeped in generous rectitude,
    which he has built through learning and through habit,
for long ago he entered holy Nature's inner sanctum
    to study and to make his way towards the truth.   20
He is charming for his varied wit; and lofty words
    on lofty matters sound forth from his polished lips.
If public business must be handled on critical occasions
    and there's need to anticipate evil by rapid thought,
we marvel at the speed and keenness of his great mind   25
    and his grave counsel in uncertain affairs.
Neither Xerxes' gold nor the monsters of Perillus
    could hope to shake the loyalty of his sturdy heart.
He through whose intelligence high Troy lies in ruins
    did not more tightly stop his ears against the Sirens,   30
than you, Bernardo, flee the deceitful charms
    of pleasure and the harmful potions of dreadful Circe.
But there is no greater sign of his noble heart
    than his devotion to the Muses' sacred chorus.
For he whom the sisters have washed in Pegasus' font   35
    flies up to the bosom of highest Jupiter,
and despising earthly taints, is seized by godly love,
    and delights to enter their native dwelling-place.

Neve novum aut vilem iam, Bembe, putabis amorem:
40   nil magis antiquum, nobiliusve nihil.
Ante etenim caelos et clari sidera mundi
    stabat amor servans atria summa Dei.
Et si quos habeat genitores forte requiris,
    forma parens illi est, et pater ipse decor.
45 Te sine, dulcis amor, rerum natura creatrix
    nil agit, artifices nec movet illa manus.
Te duce, mortales imi licet infima mundi,
    heu, procul a patriis sedibus antra colant,
caelestis quoniam sunt haec simulacra decoris,
50   pulchrum adamant, siquid Daedala terra tulit.
Spiritus est homini superorum incensus amore,
    et cupit aeterno ponere fonte sitim.
At loca dum silvae peragrat tenebrosa profundae,
    nec caelum in tanta cernere nocte valet,
55 quae terrena sui genitoris imagine fulgent,
    haec amat, haec summi sunt simulacra boni.
Sic tu quam primum vidisti, Bembe, Ginevram,
    caelesti lapsam credis adesse choro.
Et certe aut diva est, aut munus tale deorum,
60   quale hominum generi saecula rara ferunt.
Namque caput Pallas dedit, et Venus aurea crines,
    a radiis oculi sunt sibi, Phoebe, tuis.
Iuppiter impressit clementi in pectore castum
    propositum et sanctae iura pudicitiae.
65 Cornibus at demptis faciem Semeleius affert,
    et Charites deceat, quod facit, omne iubent.
Dulce loqui dulci risu ingenuoque pudore
    Mercurius facili sidere, Bembe, dedit;
nam pudor et risus coëunt sic viribus aequis,
70   ut rubeat fulgor, fulgeat ore rubor.

You will not now think that love is new or vile:
    nothing is more ancient, Bembo, nothing more noble.   40
Even before the spheres and stars of the lucid cosmos,
    love stood, keeping safe the highest courts of God.
And if perchance you seek to learn what ancestors it has,
    beauty is its mother and its father is grace.
Sweet love, without you Nature, the creator of all,   45
    does nothing, nor does she move her skillful hands.
But with you as guide, men may plumb the lowest depths
    of the world below, alas, far from their native seats.
Since these are copies of grace sublime, it's Beauty that they love,
    if Daedalan earth brings forth somewhat of Beauty below.   50
Man has a spirit all afire with love of the gods above,
    and he longs to slake his thirst at an eternal spring.
But wandering through the shadowy places in the deep forests,
    he cannot make out the heavens in so dark a night.
The earthly things which gleam with the image of his Father,   55
    these he loves, these are semblances of the Highest Good.
Thus when first you saw Ginevra, Bembo, you believed
    that she had slipped down from the chorus of the gods.
And surely she is either a goddess or the gods' gift
    such as all the ages rarely bring to humankind.   60
For Athena gave her a mind, golden Venus her hair,
    and her eyes, Phoebus, are made from your rays.
Jupiter impressed upon her gentle heart
    a chaste purpose and the laws of holy modesty.
Semele offered her her face (but without the horns!)   65
    and the Graces bid that everything she does be seemly.
Mercury, under a favoring star, granted that she speak
    sweetly, with a sweet laugh and noble modesty;
for modesty and laughter join thus with equal strength,
    that in her face sparks blush, yet also blushes sparkle.   70

Hinc radii veniunt oculos qui luce retundant,
  quique urant flammis mollia corda suis.
Talis enim fulgor, qualis percussa nitenti
  gurgite de Tyrio purpura sole micat.
75 Uni igitur cedit generosum pectus amori,
  nobilibusque animis imperat unus amor.
Absit amor, nullae poterunt cohibere catenae
  nobile cor, nullis viribus impar erit.
Verum sponte sua sequitur meliora monentem,
80 pulchrum amat; in pulchrum nam rapit altus amor.
Quid, mala si mandent? Non, si ruat arduus aether,
  parebit; quoniam turpia vitat amor.

: 9 :

Eulogium in obitu Michaelis Verini

Estne levis rumor sic, oh, seu conscia veri
  fama? Sed heu nimis est conscia fama mali!
Occidit heu vestrum crimen, crudelia fata,
  occidit heu Michael, luctus amorque patris,
5 occidit Aonio quem vos nutristis in antro,
  Musae, Cyrrhaei quem lavit unda iugi,
occidit heu Michael, proprio nam nomine dixit
  princeps Aonii, Calliopea, chori.
"Quis Deus est" Michael resonat, modo nosse velimus
10 prisca Palaestino verba notata sono:
ipse Deus quid sit, vix puber nosse laborat,
  tempore quo reliquis ludus et umbra placet.
Verum id cum vera faceret ratione, putandum est
  Verini agnomen non sine sorte datum.

Hence come the rays that with their brilliance blind the eyes,
and that with their ardor consume tender hearts.
For their brilliance shines the way that purple taken from
the Tyrian sea shines when struck by the blazing sun.
Hence, a noble heart gives way to one love alone   75
and one love alone rules over noble minds.
Absent love, no chains can constrain the noble heart,
for it will be the equal of any violent force.
But willingly it follows one who urges higher things,
it loves beauty, for High Love ravishes it unto Beauty.   80
What if evils should command it? It will not obey,
even if the heavens fall, for love all baseness shuns.

: 9 :

Eulogy on the Death of Michele Verino

O is it just light rumor or does Fama know the truth?
But alas, it seems she knows it all too well.
Alas for your crime, cruel Fates, oh, he is fallen,
Michele, alas, is fallen, his father's grief and love.
He is fallen whom you nurtured, Muses, in the Aonian cave,   5
whom water from the Delphic heights has washed,
Michele, alas, is fallen, for by her own name,
he was called by Calliope, chief of the Aonian choir.
"Who is like to God" Michele echoes, should we wish
to grasp pristine words in the Palestinian tongue.   10
Scarcely a boy, he worked to grasp what God really is,
at an age when games and shadows please all the rest.
Since that Truth created by true reason, one must think
that his family name, Verino, was not bestowed by chance.

15   Quid pietas, quid casta fides, quid possit honestum
       a teneris annis hic monumenta dedit.
    Quique solet primam nimium vexare iuventam,
       expers obsceni semper amoris erat:
    vivebat caelebs, primis atque integer annis
20   contempsit Cypriae dulcia dona deae.
    Hoc tulit indigne, superat qui cuncta Cupido,
       cui parent superum numina magna deum,
    et parat ultrici puerum terebrare sagitta,
       altitonum valeat qua superare Iovem.
25   Sed frustra aurato tentat praefigere telo
       pectora, quae sanctae Palladis arma tegunt:
    hoc cernens aliosque dolos aliudque volutans
       consilium insolita callidus arte petit.
    Nam morbum immisit, quem nec queat ipse Machaon,
30   nec tua docta manus pellere, Phoebigena.
    Convocat hic medicos Paulus, quem cura nepotis
       anxia sollicitum nocte dieque premit.
    Conquirunt igitur veterum monumenta virorum,
       siqua datur morbo iam medicina gravi:
35   quae Galiene tuo divine volumine monstras,
       quaeque docet Coi pagina docta senis,
    quid velit Hippocratis magni doctrina, quid ille,
       cuius Arabs iusto paruit imperio,
    Mosaicosque manu versat, Latios Danaosque,
40   quique colunt ripas, advena, Nile, tuas.
    Denique perceptis cunctorum sensibus omnes
       huc veniunt atque haec mens fuit una viris:
    non posse extremae hunc tempus sperare iuventae,
       gaudia percipiat ni tua, pulchra Venus.
45   Res miranda quidem, rara et per saecula visa,
       exemplum in puero tale pudicitiae,

From his tenderest years he gave proof of what piety,   15
    what a sense of honor and pure faith could achieve.
He never took any part in the filthy love affairs
    that are wont to vex too much one's early youth:
he lived celibate and pure from his earliest years,
    and spurned the honied gifts of the Cyprian goddess.   20
Cupid, who rules all things, did not take this well,
    he whom the great spirits of the gods above obey,
and prepared to pierce the lad with a vengeful arrow,
    strong enough to overcome high-thundering Jove.
But vainly did he try to transfix with golden shaft   25
    a breast which wore the armor of sacrosanct Athena.
Seeing this, wily with unwonted skill he seeks
    to cogitate some other tricks and another plan.
He brought on a sickness which not Machaon himself
    nor even your learned hand, Asclepius, could expel.   30
Paolo, troubled day and night with worry for his nephew,
    summons doctors all together with anxiety.
They pore over texts, then, of the ancient authors, seeking
    if any cure might there be given for the grave disease:
what you, divine Galen, demonstrate in your book,   35
    and what say the learned pages of the old man of Cos,
what great Hippocrates' teaching orders, and what orders he
    to whose just imperium the Arabs submit.
He turns the pages of the Hebrews, Latins and the Greeks,
    and those who dwell along your banks, newcomer Nile.   40
Finally, the doctors, gathering views from every source,
    hither came and this one thought was shared by them all:
that he could not hope to outlast his youthful years
    unless he should taste your delights, lovely Venus.
Such an example, in a boy, of pure innocence
    was marvellous indeed, and rare in all the ages.   45
He was able to prefer a holy purity of life,

qui vitae sanctum potuit praeferre pudorem,
    viveret ut semper, tunc voluisse mori.
I nunc, Hippolytum verbis extolle superbis,
50   Bellerophonteum nomen in astra refer;
non hic Antiam, non pulchrae gaudia Phaedrae,
    omnia sed Veneris furta nefanda fugit.
At ne forte putes nullo hunc caluisse furore,
    nulla nec aligeri tela tulisse dei:
55 sunt geminae Veneres, gemini hinc oriuntur amores,
    terra haec demersa est, caelitus illa venit.
Altera vulgarem vero quam nomine dicunt,
    namque levis plebis vilia corda domat,
mortalesque artus homines, formaeque caducae
60   terrenum miseros corpus amare iubet.
Altera caelestis superis dominatur in oris,
    mater nulla illi est, Iuppiter ipse pater;
haec, quas nulla mali violant contagia sensus,
    divino mentes urit amore pias.
65 Hic Michael valido praefixus pectora telo,
    coelum amat, et coeli moenia mente capit;
nec quicquam puerile sapit puerilibus annis,
    tristis at in tenera fronte senecta sedet.
Sevocat a sensu mentem, tetramque perosus
70   luxuriem, aethereae scandit ad astra plagae,
cunctaque sub pedibus mittens quae mersa sub ipsa
    materia in tenebris corpora caeca tegunt,
et magni volitans mundi per curva supernos
    spirituum volucer tentat adire choros.
75 Interea pestis teneros depascitur artus,
    contrahit in rugas squallida membra lues,
et toto succum flaccescens corpore sugit
    pus solidum, innatus deserit ossa vigor,
donec ab assumptis animus discedere membris

and then to wish to die as he had always lived.
Go now, exalt Hippolytus with haughty self-esteem,
    lift the name of Bellerophon up to the stars;   50
this youth fled not Antea, not lovely Phaedra's joys,
    but all wicked stratagems that Venus could devise.
But lest perchance you think that he never burned with
       passion,
    nor endured any of the wingèd god's darts:
the Venuses are twins, and twin loves issue from them,   55
    the former sunk in earth, the latter heaven-born.
The first men call by its true name, the Venus of the vulgar,
    for it rules the vile hearts of the fickle plebs
and bids wretched men to love of fallen beauty
    only the earthly body and the mortal limbs.   60
The other, celestial, rules in the realms above;
    no mother has she, but her father's Jupiter himself.
She inflames the pious mind with celestial love
    a mind which no taint of evil sense violates.
Michele, heart transfixed by her mighty arrow, loves   65
    heaven, and storms its ramparts with his pensive mind.
Though of boyish years, he did not think as a boy,
    for age severe sits upon his tender brow.
He separates his mind from sense, and loathing foul excess,
    he climbs up to the stars of the aethereal zones;   70
and hurling beneath his feet all that's sunken into matter
    and wraps blind bodies in the shadowy dark,
he flies swiftly through the spheres of the greater cosmos,
    striving to approach the spirits' dance sublime.
Meanwhile, the plague feeds upon his tender limbs,   75
    his wasted members shrivel up beneath the scourge;
softening corruption sucks the liquid from his body,
    and his innate strength at length deserts his bones
until his soul is forced to leave his now-exhausted limbs

80   cogitur et putri carcere pulsus abit.
      Pulsus abit, sed laetus abit, vinclisque solutus
          cognoscit quantum mors habet ista boni,
      exilioque gravi liber caelestia summi,
          quae patria est, ardet visere templa Dei.
85   Sed quid te plorem puerum, Verine? Quid ultra
          fata tuae mortis stultus iniqua querar?
      Mortuus en vivis, sed nos dum nostra manebit
          vita, nimis blanda morte maligna premet.

: 10 :

In Dantis poetae sepulchrum

Fecerat egregia constructum ex arte sepulcrum
    Tyrrheno Danti prisca Ravenna novum;
invida sed sacris obsunt quoque fata sepulcris,
    et turpi obducunt omnia pulchra situ.
5   At tu, delitiae Veneti, Bernarde, senatus,
    tutela et sacri maxima, Bembe, chori,
livida mordaci quod triverat ante vetustas
    dente, novum niveo marmore restituis.

: 11 :

<Epitaphium Coluccii Salutati>

Multa licet stupidum rapiant spectacula templi,
    dum tamen ista legas, parva futura mora est.

and, expelled, departs from its decaying prison.   80
The soul, expelled, departs, but happy, free of bonds,
    and comes to know how much of good this death holds;
and free of exile's burdens, it is aflame to see
    the heavenly temple of God on high, its true fatherland.
But why should I weep for the boy, Verino? Why should I   85
    foolishly lament still more your death by an unjust fate?
Behold, though dead, you live, but while life remains to us,
    spiteful life afflicts us through your too tranquil death.

: 10 :

The Tomb of the Poet Dante

Ancient Ravenna had made a new tomb for Dante
    the Tuscan, built with extraordinary skill;
but envious fate is opposed to hallowed tombs,
    and envelops all things beautiful in ugly decay.
But you, Bernardo, darling of the Venetian Senate,   5
    you, Bembo, greatest bulwark of the blessed dance,
that which envious age with biting tooth had worn down
    you restore as new with marble white as snow.

: 11 :

Epitaph for Coluccio Salutati

Though many sights in this church enthrall dull-witted folk,
    still, your reading this will mean only a short delay.

Cantaram, nostri celebrati scriba leonis,
    Amphitryonidae maxima facta ducis,
5   unde Salutati viridantia serta Colucci
    cinxerunt vatis tempora cana. Vale!

: 12 :

< *Pro eodem in Palatio* >

Cuius Bebriacas perculsit epistola mentes,
    quantum equitum turmae non potuere decem,
hic caput exornas Phoebea fronde, Colucci,
    dum canis Herculeae maxima facta manus.

: 13 :

< *In laudem Iannotii Manetti* >

Haebreus, Graius quicquid Latiusve poeta,
    philosophus, rhetor scripsit et historicus,
Iannotius noram. Dubiis Florentia rebus,
    pontifices, reges me voluere sibi.

"I once sang as chancellor of our famous lion,
    and of the great deeds of Amphitryon's son."
Hence came the flourishing garlands binding the head   5
    of our seer Coluccio Salutati. Farewell!

: 12 :

For the Same Man in the Palace

You whose missive struck terror into the Milanese mind
    more than ten squadrons of cavalry could do,
adorn your head, Coluccio, with Apollo's leaves,
    while singing of the greatest deeds of Hercules' hand.

: 13 :

In Praise of Giannozzo Manetti

Whatever any Hebrew, Greek or Latin poet,
    philosopher, orator, or historian wrote,
I, Giannozzo, knew. In doubtful matters
    Florence, popes and kings required my services

CARMINA DUBIA

: I :

Ad Ugolinum Verinum

Felix quem suavi tangit Cypris aurea cura,
    mitior et solito cui venit ipse puer.
Iam, memini, teneros mandabas versibus ignes,
    e lacrimis inerat multa litura tuis.
5 Blanditiae molles et tunc tibi maxima cura,
    Flammea, materiam nequitiaeque dabant.
His dolor immixtus fuerat persaepe tabellis,
    spes brevis et semper longus ubique pavor.
In Venerem et puerum, lacrimis cogentibus ipsis,
10   impia non parvo verba furore dabas;
at rursus blandis ubi te aspiciebat ocellis,
    lenior et solito Flammea mitis erat,
vota precesque deis et tura Sabaea dabantur:
    augebant titulos carmina digna suos.
15 Abfuit alma procul tua Flammea: pectora cura
    tuta carent, et spes plena timoris abest.
Et siquid cantas, hoc totum Palladis, illud
    Delius a docto vindicat ore sibi,
aut nemora aut silvas laudas fontesque Dianae,
20   Nympharum turbas, Pieridumque choros,
cuncta refers elegis non discordantia nervis:
    solus cum blanda matre Cupido deest.
Quod non parva deis iniuria redditur: ambo
    sunt vati faciles et tua vota iuvant.
25 Ah, ne blanditias, praesentia numina divum,
    desere: sunt numeris apta, Verine, tuis.

DOUBTFULLY ASCRIBED POEMS

: 1 :

To Ugolino Verino

Happy is he whom golden Venus touches with sweet care,
    he to whom her boy comes more mildly than is his wont.
Once, I remember, you'd put your gentle flames in verse,
    and there was many a stain therein caused by your tears.
Flammea, then your greatest care, her alluring charms   5
    and her naughtiness gave you matter for your song.
Very often there was mingled in your writing-books,
    pain, brief hope and everywhere long, unending fear.
Tears themselves compelled you to say impious words
    to Venus and her boy, and with no little passion;   10
but when she looked at you again with her winsome eyes,
    Flammea was mild and more gentle than her wont.
Vows and prayers and Sabaean incense rose up to the gods,
    and worthy poems amplified their titles to distinction.
Your dear Flammea went away: your heart was safe from care;   15
    and hope, ever full of fear, went away as well.
And if you sing of anything, first it's all of Pallas,
    then Apollo defends himself through your learned mouth,
or you praise the groves or woods or fountains of Diana,
    the throngs of Nymphs, and the dances of the Pierides,   20
you tell of all that's not unsuited to elegiac verse;
    only Cupid and his mother are unaccounted for.
Because no small injury is paid to those gods,
    both are open to a poet and promote your prayers.
Ah, do not forsake the charms, the ever-present powers   25
    of the gods, Verino: they are suited to your verse.

313

Flammea iam rediit, redeant in pectore curae,
    et suavis redeat qui fuit ante calor.
Aspice quam miti tua dum vestigia lustrat
30   lumine te et grato suscipit ore dea;
nam dea vel prorsus comes est credenda Dianae:
    seu dea sive comes carmine digna tuo est.
Haec dedit ingenium; memini: laudare solebas,
    quod tibi discendi causa fuisset amor.
35 Si dedit ingenium, si Phoebi contulit artes,
    cur sibi, quae dederit sponte puella, negas?
Redde precor meritas laudes, amplectere digno
    carmine: felices Di tibi semper erunt;
sin minus, et Veneris saevique Cupidinis iram
40   iam tibi difficiles blanditiasque time.
Quique hilaris nuper potuisti et vivere felix,
    olim semper eris tristis et aeger amans.

: 2 :

Carmina super quaedam aenigmata

A

De me raduntur stipulae cultoris in agro:
"r" si tollatur, tunc sidus in aere fragro.

B

Quinque placent ori, quatuor in aere pendent,
sed tria pars hominis, duo sunt speciesque metalli.

Now Flammea has returned; let care return to your heart,
    and let the sweet warmth return that was there before.
See how that goddess, while she irradiates your steps
    with gentle light, takes you up with a pleasing voice.   30
You must believe that she's a god or one of Diana's girls;
    either way, she's a woman worthy of your song.
She gave you wit; I recall that you used to commend
    her love as the reason why you longed to learn.
If she gave you wit, if she brought you Phoebus' skills,   35
    why do you deny her what she willingly gave you?
Pay her back in well-earned praise, wrapped in fitting song,
    please, and the gods will ever favor your cause.
If you don't, beware the wrath of Venus and cruel Cupid,
    for now they will be charmingly impossible to you.   40
You who could just now have lived in joy and good cheer,
    will once again become the eternal sad and sickly lover.

: 2 :

Poems about Certain Riddles

1

By me the stubble in the farmer's field is razed:
if an 'r' is removed, then, a star, I stink in air.

2

Five are pleasing in appearance, four hang in the air,
but three are part of man, two a type of metal.

C

5   Sunt celsi montes quibus his si demitur "l" quae
crescunt nidificant: sed quis scit solvere solvat.

D

Est animal parvum quod nunquam pascit in arvum,
quod si vertatur, bos sonipes inde legatur.

E

Herba sum solis et sum de sole creata
10   et decies quinque quinqueque decemque vocata.

F

Iuncta fui Cereri, me divisere flagelli;
hunc quibus apponunt me pascunt bos et aselli.

3

There are lofty mountains from which, if an 'l' is taken, they   5
    build
nests which grow: but he who knows how to solve this, let
    him solve it.

4

There is a small animal that never feeds in the field,
which, if reversed, a loud-footed bullock may thence be read.

5

I am a plant of the sun and am created from the sun
and am called ten times five plus five plus ten.   10

6

I was joined to Ceres, but whips separated me;
the bullock and donkeys, for whom they set this out, feed on
    me.

APPENDIX

Bernardo Bembo Senatori Veneto, viro probitate ac litteris insigni, Christophorus Landinus s. d.

Quod ais te elegis nostris mirifice delectari, id me, ut verum fatear, immortaliter delectat. Tanti enim nostra semper facere consuevi, quanti illa ab iis viris fieri intelligo, quorum et ingenium perspicacissimum et doctrinam summam ac multiplicem et iudicium sapientissimum esse constat. Quid ergo, inquies? Tu carmen tuum verborum nostrorum lance ponderabis? Movent me profecto ea, quae dixi, quae quidem omnia in te maxima exactissimaque esse cognovi. Sed vereor interdum, ne mirificus tuus in me amor perstrigator assit. Novi enim quam indulgentes sint, qui amant, quamque lynceis, ut aiunt, oculis, siquid boni in amato est, admirari consueverint, quam contra ad omnes mendas Tiresiam agant. Verum ego quoque me ipsum amans mihi indulgebo atque in huiusmodi tuo de nobis iudicio, non quantum nos ames, sed quantum ingenio ac litteris possis, recordabor.

Librum autem ipsum cum iamdiu flagitanti tibi denegare non substineam, ad te mitto. Adiunxi etiam illi elegias nonnullas, quae mutui atque immortalis inter nos amoris testes futurae sint, quibus ego ingenuum omnino animi tui amorem exprimere conatus sum. Vidi enim te nihil terrenum quia terrenum sit, adamare, sed

APPENDIX

Letter of Presentation to Bernardo Bembo

The following letter, written in Landino's own hand, is preserved in a manuscript containing the *Xandra* and several of the *Carmina varia* (V, VI, VII and VIII), formerly owned by Bernardo Bembo (Vatican City, Biblioteca Apostolica Vaticana, Vat. lat. 3366). The text printed here is that of Perosa, 190–191; the manuscript is described ibid., xxv–xxvi.

Cristoforo Landino to Bernardo Bembo, Senator of Venice, a man renowned for probity and knowledge of literature, greetings.

Your saying that my elegies delight you wonderfully is something that, frankly, delights me immortally. I usually value my own works only as much as I understand them to be valued by men who evidently have the most penetrating minds, the greatest and most varied learning, and the wisest judgment. You'll say: what then? Will you weigh your poetry in the balance of my words? The qualities I've described, which I recognize to be all at their greatest and most exacting in you, certainly do influence me. But meanwhile, I'm afraid that your wondrous love for me makes you ready to scratch my back. For I know how indulgent lovers are, and how they usually admire anything good in the one they love with lyncean eyes, as they say, and how, on the other hand, they are as blind as Tiresias to faults. But I too, since I love myself, indulge myself, and in your judgment of this about me I shall remember, not how much you love me, but your intellectual power and literary ability.

I send the book to you as I cannot bear to deny your oft-repeated request. I've also added to it some elegies which shall bear witness in future to our mutual and immortal love. In them I have tried to express, for my part, my entirely frank and free love for your soul. For I see in you nothing earthly, since it is an earthly

ipsius divinitatis, a qua animi nostri sunt, similitudine, ubicumque illa reperiatur, vehementer delectari. Ea igitur in re si versiculos nostros generositati mentis tuae pares non reperies, erit eius humanitatis atque clementiae, quibus omnes facile superas, non quid potuerim, sed quid voluerim, considerare.

Vale!

thing to have a passion for someone, but it is a mark of divinity it-self to vehemently enjoy a similarity to divinity, from which our souls come, wherever it may be found. In that respect, if you do not find that our verses match your nobility of thought, it will be a mark of that humanity and clemency in which you have no equal to take into consideration, not what I was able to do, but what I wanted to do.

Farewell.

Note on the Text

ॐ৩৫

The text used as a basis for this translation is the one established by Alessandro Perosa, *Christophori Landini Carmina omnia* (Florence: Leo S. Olschki, 1939), in the series "Nuova collezione di testi umanistici inediti o rari" published by the Scuola Normale Superiore of Pisa. I am grateful to Prof. Michele Ciliberto and the Scuola Normale for permission to reproduce this text. Readers interested in the textual history of the *Xandra* and other poetry included in this volume, the dating of the individual poems and variant readings are encouraged to consult this superb edition.

The following changes have been introduced in Perosa's text:

1.5.11.	fabere *corrected to* fatere
1.8.6.	Sprituamque *corrected to* Spirituamque
2.3.14.	proveniet? Semper . . . velim *changed to* proveniet, semper . . . velim?
2.5.51.	immits *corrected to* immitis
2.7.38.	irrisae *emended to* irrisos
2.23.29.	reginas *emended to* Regias (*see Notes to the Translation*)
2.25.28.	penula *changed to* paenula
2.25.73.	tumidas *emended to* timidas
3.1.3.	tempus; graviori insurgite *emended to* tempus graviori insurgere *following some mss.*
3.4.59.	subido *corrected to* subibo
3.4.113.	nostrae frater persolvimus *changed to* nostrae, frater, persolvimus
3.5.42.	*semicolon added after* legibus
3.5.45.	reginas *emended to* Regias (*see Notes to the Translation*)
3.17.70	ipse *corrected to* ipsa, *following* V_1 *and* V_2
er1.41.6	munc *corrected to* nunc
Var8.49	decori *emended to* decoris
Var11.3	*Perosa's obelized* celeber † *has been emended to* celebrati

Notes

꽃Ꮆ?Ꮆ

XANDRA: BOOK I

1.1. To Piero de' Medici

Meter: elegiac distich

Piero de' Medici (1416–1469), son of Cosimo il Vecchio and father of Lorenzo il Magnifico, the unofficial ruler of Florence from 1464 to 1469. He took a deep interest in the humanist movement and was an avid book collector. It was through his influence and patronage that Landino received his position of professor of poetry and rhetoric at the University (Studium) of Florence.

5. Its twin brothers: Books II and III.

8. Maecenas (d. 8 BCE) was friend and unofficial minister of Augustus and the patron of Vergil, Horace and Propertius.

18. Medicean rock: A pun on Piero's name, which in Latin is *petrus* or rock.

1.2. To His Book

Meter: elegiac distich

15. Xandra: Landino's name for his beloved, a familiar form of Alessandra (and metrically more convenient).

25. Mountains of Haemus: A mountain range in Thrace.

26. Pontus was a kingdom in the northwest of Asia Minor from which Medea came.

29. Acheron: The river of the Underworld by which the spirits of the dead gathered.

33. Medea: Daughter of Aeëtes, King of Colchis, who by means of magic helped Jason to secure the Golden Fleece. See Ovid, *Metamorphoses* 7.9 ff.

1.3. WHEN HE WAS CRUSHED BY LOVE

Meter: elegiac distich

3. Erato: The muse of love poetry.

4. You have the name of love: Erato means "lovely" in Greek, but Landino may have connected the word with *erōs*, love or passion.

22. Aries: The constellation of the Ram (or the Golden Fleece) that rescued Phrixus and Helle from being sacrificed.

45. Sprung from the blood of Uranus, the Giants attacked Olympus but were destroyed by the gods and buried under Etna and other volcanos.

51. The giant Typhoeus was buried under Etna.

52. In their war against the gods the Giants piled Mt. Pelion on Mt. Ossa in an attempt to reach Olympus. See Ovid, *Metamorphoses* 1.151–155 and Propertius 2.1.19–20.

1.4. TO BARTOLOMEO SCALA

Meter: elegiac distich

Bartolomeo Opisco Scala (1430–1497), humanist, a member of the household of Piero de' Medici, treasurer to Lorenzo de' Medici, chancellor of the Florentine republic from 1465. See Alison Brown, *Bartolomeo Scala, 1430–1497, Chancellor of Florence: The Humanist as Bureaucrat* (Princeton, 1979).

9. Tityos: A giant thrown into Tartarus for attempting to rape Latona (Leto); he lay stretched out on the ground while two vultures pecked at his liver. See Ovid, *Metamorphoses* 4.457.

11. Tantalus: He was punished in Tartarus by being placed in a lake whose waters receded every time he tried to slake his thirst. See Ovid, *Metamorphoses* 4.458.

1.5. TO XANDRA

Meter: elegiac distich

2. Ascra: A town on Mt. Helicon where Hesiod ("the old man") lived.

23–24. Lucifer . . . Hesperus: Venus is called both the morning star and the evening star in a lost play of Euripides, the *Melanippe*, which Landino probably knows via a famous quotation in Aristotle's *Nicomachean Ethics*; see Bruno Snell, *Tragicorum graecorum fragmenta*, vol. 2, ed. Richard Kannicht and Bruno Snell (Göttingen, 1981), 140.

27. Sidon: Ancient city of Phoenicia, 20 miles from Tyre, both famed for the purple dye obtained from the murex.

47–50. I.e., even though his mind and heart are with Xandra, his body continues to live, in violation of the principles of Aristotelian biology.

1.6. To Xandra

Meter: elegiac distich

In part modelled on Catullus 8.

1.7. A Sestina in Imitation of Petrarca

Meter: dactylic hexameter

The sestina, a form used by Provencal troubadors and made famous by Petrarca, consists of six six-line stanzas and one three-line envoi. It requires that the end words of each six-line stanza be the same, but arranged in a differing order, such that the last word of the last line of each stanza must be the last word of the first line of the following stanza, and the six end words must appear at the middle and end of the three-line envoi. For examples see *Petrarch's Songbook* (*Rerum vulgarium fragmenta*), tr. James W. Cook (Binghamton, NY, 1995), nos. 22, 30, 66, etc.

23. Apollo is leader of the Muses and the patron of music and poetry; Landino will devote himself to the Muses rather than to love. *Furor* (madness) is the word most commonly used in the fifteenth century to translate the *mania* of Plato's *Phaedrus*.

24. Make poetry of: *Ludere*, a verb used especially with reference to the making of light literary entertainments and love poetry.

37. Under the Aeolian Fleece: The Golden Fleece. For the epithet, compare Valerius Flaccus 7.517, and the note to 1.3.22, above. The constellation Aries is most visible in winter.

1.8. Alfonso, the Lame Lover
Meter: elegiac distich

3. The church of Sant' Ambrogio, on the eastern edge of Florence in Landino's time, is thought to have been founded in the fifth century CE and is one of the three oldest churches in Florence.

5. Oltr'arno: Literally "beyond the Arno," the southern district across the river from the heart of the city.

7. Galphunda: The area behind S. Maria Novella in the western part of Florence between Via della Scala and Via Valfonda, now occupied by the railroad station.

8. Landino often uses the adjective "Braccian" to signify a connection with *condottieri*. The adjective comes from Braccio da Montone (1368–1424), a famous Umbrian *condottiere* who worked for Florence, the pope, and other Italian powers. According to Michael Mallett, "The names of Sforza and Braccio were battle cries for almost the whole [fifteenth] century, and even as late as the Pazzi War in 1478–9, many of the Florentine and Venetian troops still marched under the banner of the black ram (*montone*) on a yellow ground." See Mallett, *Mercenaries and Their Masters* (London, 1974), 74.

9. The sign of the Zodiac associated with the month of July. In the myth of the Labors of Hercules, the crab Cancer seizes the hero's toe with its claws while he is fighting the Hydra. See Coluccio Salutati, *De laboribus Herculis* 3.10 (ed. Ullman 1: 205–7).

1.9. A Dissolute Theological Demagogue
Meter: elegiac distich

5. Smooth of tongue: For *ore rotondo*, see Horace, *Ars Poetica* 323

6. Chrysippus (280–207 BCE): A philosopher, born in Cilicia, who became head of the Stoa in Athens.

1.10. To Lupo

Meter: elegiac distich

6. Fools . . . stupidity: Puns on the word *bardus* (foolish). A large section of the Oltr'arno along the river southeast of the Ponte Vecchio was occupied at one time by houses belonging to the Bardi family, one of the great banking families of fourteenth century Florence; it had fallen on hard times by Landino's time.

1.11. To Bernardo

Meter: elegiac distich

Bernardo Nuti was a secretary of the Florentine republic and one of the four candidates in the Studium Florentinum controversy (see Introduction). Ficino gave him a role in his commentary on Plato's *Symposium*. *Xandra* 1.29 and 2.12 are also dedicated to him.

1.12. To Alda

Meter: elegiac distich

1.13. To Leon Battista Alberti

Meter: hendcasyllabics

Leon Battista Alberti (1404–1472), famous Italian humanist, athelete, architect, artist, and principal founder of Renaissance art theory. Landino dedicated the first redaction of Book I of the *Three Books of Xandra* to him and later introduced him as a character in his *Camaldulensian Disputations*.

2. Trembling step: Pun on foot as extremity and metrical measure; the allusion is to Landino's use of the hendecasyllabic measure.

4. The Aonian sisters: The nine Muses, so-called because they dwelt on Mt. Helicon in Aonia.

5. Ancient city: Rome, where Alberti was at the time of composition.

33. The Sparrow: The poetry of Catullus, specifically 2 and 3.

34. The Spanish Dog: The epigrams of Martial, who was a native of Bilbilis in Spain.

35. The Fly (*musca*): Lucian 's *Praise of a Fly*, translated from the Greek by both Alberti and Guarino da Verona. Margarethe Billerbeck and Christian Zubler, *Das Lob der Fliege von Lukian bis L. B. Alberti* (Bern, 2000), includes Alberti's Latin translation.

1.14. HE WONDERS WHY HE FEELS SUCH DISQUIET
Meter: elegiac distich

2. Goddesses of the Pierian spring: The Greek Muses. Pieria, on the southeast coast of Macedonia, was one of the earliest seats of their worship.

3. Camenae: The Latin Muses. The Camenae were originally fountain nymphs who eventually became identified with the Greek Muses.

1.15. TO THEOPLASMA, MISTRESS OF FRANCESCO DA CASTIGLIONE
Meter: elegiac distich

Despite Perosa, p. 201, the Francesco da Castiglione (or Castiglionchio) referred to here is probably not the priest who was a student of the famous humanist schoolmaster Vittorino da Feltre and the secretary of Archbishop (later Saint) Antoninus of Florence and who taught Greek at the Florentine Studio, but rather another Franciscus Castilionensis, a love poet and a much more obscure figure. See Francesco Bausi, "Francesco da Castiglione fra umanesimo e teologia," *Interpres* 11 (1991): 112–181, especially 126–129. See also er1.26. Theoplasma means "shaped by God."

4. Survive the pyre: With reference to Dido, who achieved immortality thanks to Vergil.

1.16. TO HIMSELF
Meter: elegiac distich

4. Compare Catullus 7.2.

1.17. To Himself

Meter: elegiac distich

7. Compare Catullus 8.2.

1.18. Epitaph for Leonardo of Arezzo

Meter: elegiac distich

Leonardo Bruni (1370–1444) of Arezzo, humanist, historian and translator. The poem refers to his two greatest achievements, his *History of the Florentine People* (1416–1442) and his translations of the moral philosophy of Aristotle into Latin. The Lion or *Marzocco* was the symbol of Florence.

1.19. To Xandra

Meter: elegiac distich

The poem is modelled on Propertius 2.14 and 2.15, as is noted by La Penna.

1. The fleece of Phrixus: The Golden Fleece, stolen by the Argonauts under Jason from King Aeëtes of Colchis.

4. See Vergil, *Aeneid* 6.56 ff., for the prayer of Aeneas in the Sibyl's cave.

5. Andromeda was chained to a rock in order that a sea-monster, ravaging her father's kingdom, might devour her. She was saved by Perseus, who slew the monster and claimed her for his bride. See Ovid, *Metamorphoses* 4.470 ff.

17. Nauta: Sextus Propertius (c. 51–c. 19 BCE), one of the principal Roman elegiac poets. See Propertius 1.3. Propertius' name was long believed to be "Propertius Aurelius Nauta" owing to an error in the manuscripts; see D. F. S. Thompson, "Propertius." The error was corrected by Beroaldus later in the Quattrocento.

1.20. To Filippo about His Sweetheart

Meter: elegiac distich

2. St. Lucy's holy rites: The feast of St. Lucy, patron of virgins, is December 13. The incident described must have taken place at the Church of Santa Lucia in Prato, near Ognissanti in Florence, or at the Church of Santa Lucia de' Magnoli, in Via de' Bardi in Oltarno, near the Ponte Vecchio.

7. For *cervix reflexa* see Virgil, *Aeneid* 8.633.

1.21. To Lucina on Behalf of Xandra in Childbirth
Meter: elegiac distich

Juno Lucina, as the bringer of light, was the goddess of childbirth and newborn children.

1.22. In Praise of Diana
Meter: Sapphic

Diana was an ancient Italian fertility goddess early identified with the Greek goddess Artemis, much of whose story and attributes she assumed; the Grove of Nemi was sacred to her, and like Artemis she was identified with Hecate, goddess of the underworld, and Selene, the moon.

8. For Diana as Juno Lucina see 1.21, above.

9. Niobe's scorn for Leto and her pride in the number of her children brought down the vengeance of Apollo and Artemis. See Ovid, *Metamorphoses* 6.165 ff.

10. Latona (Leto): Mother of Apollo and Artemis.

13. Actaeon: A hunter who saw Artemis bathing with her nymphs, was turned into a stag in consequence, and devoured by his hounds. See Ovid, *Metamorphoses* 3.206 ff.

1.23. To Bartolomeo Scala
Meter: elegiac distich

2. Keep the mean: In Aristotelian ethics, virtue is held to reside in the mean between extremes of behavior.

3. Myrrha: Daughter of Cinyras and, by her father, mother of Adonis, for which crime she was changed into a myrrh-tree. See Ovid, *Metamorphoses* 10.312 ff.

4. Medea: See note to 1.2.33, above.

5. Scylla: Daughter of Nisus and Megara, who, because of her love for Minos, cut the purple hair on which her father's power depended, so that Minos might conquer the kingdom. See Ovid, *Metamorphoses* 8.81 ff.

7. Pasiphaë: Wife of Minos, king of Crete; in one version of her myth she has Daedalus build a wooden bull, inside of which she was able to enjoy a sacrificial bull, and thus gave birth to the Minotaur. See Ovid, *Metamorphoses* 8.131 ff., and *Ars Amatoria* 1.295 ff.

9. Phyllis: She committed suicide when her beloved, Demophon, journeyed to Attica for so long that she thought he had abandoned her.

13. The loves of Zeus and Leda, Apollo and Isse, Saturn and Philyra are all pictured in Arachne's fatal web. See Ovid, *Metamorphoses* 6.105 ff.; Vergil, *Georgics* 3.92 ff.

21. Paphos: The birthplace of Venus, a town in southwest Cyprus where Venus/Aphrodite was said to have come ashore after her birth amid the waves. Cythera (Kythira): an island off the Peloponnese sacred to Venus.

23. Panchaea: A mythical island in the Indian Ocean where Myrrha gave birth to Adonis, the beautiful youth beloved by Venus. See Ovid, *Metamorphoses* 10.478 ff.

1.24. TO BARTOLOMEO SCALA ON HIS OWN ANCESTORS
Meter: elegiac distich

4. Cecropian stock: Cecrops was the first king of Athens.

5. Julian house: Julius Caesar's clan, claiming descent from Venus and Iulus, Aeneas' son.

7. The *pietra serena* of the quarries of Monte Cocari, southeast of Fiesole near the present site of the Villa I Tatti, was widely used for buildings in Florence.

10. Santo Spirito, the largest of the Oltrarno churches.

18–19. I.e., he did not need to disguise the fact that his ancestors were Ghibellines, as many Florentines did. At the battle of Campaldino (near Landino's family estates) on 11 June 1289, the Guelf party defeated the Ghibellines and their Aretine allies.

22. Black whips, etc.: The coat of arms of the Landini family.

25. Francesco Landini (c.1325–1397), Cristoforo's great-uncle, was a leading composer of fourteenth century Italy, famed for his musical memory, his improvisational skill and his virtuosity on the organ. For an extended description of his life and music see *The New Grove's Dictionary of Music and Musicians*, ed. Stanley Sadie (New York, 2001), 14: 212–221.

27. Amphion: The son of Zeus and husband of Niobe, he was king of Thebes whose walls he built by the magical music of his lyre.

29. Tyrrhenians: Dwellers by the Tyrrhenian or Tuscan Sea, hence the Tuscans; for this association see Leonardo Bruni, *History of the Florentine People*, ed. and tr. James Hankins, 3 vols. (Cambridge, Mass., 2001–2007), Book I.

31. Arion: Lyric poet and inventor of the dithyrambic poetry who, when cast into the sea, was saved by music-loving dolphins who carried him safely to land.

33. Orpheus: Given his lyre by Apollo and taught by the Muses, he could cause trees and wild beasts to follow his music. See Ovid, *Metamorphoses* 10.86 ff.

37. A Muse as his ancestor: I.e., Calliope, the Muse of epic poetry; see line 85, below.

41. Sirens: Sea nymphs who had the power of attracting all who heard their song, most famously in Homer's *Odyssey* 11.

45. Phthone: For a vivid picture of her (known as Invidia in Latin) and her dwelling see Ovid, *Metamorphoses*, 2.761 ff.

54. Lachesis: That one of the three Fates who assigns to humans their lifespan.

56, 68. Linus: A son of Apollo who was killed by his father because he ventured to contend with the god in song. Alternatively, an ancient Thracian bard who challenged the Muses in song and was struck blind.

58. Clotho: The Fate who spins the thread of life.

61. Helicon: The mountain range in Boeotia sacred to Apollo and the Muses.

92. Lydian: I.e., Etruscan. The Etruscans were believed to have come originally from Lydia. See Virgil, *Aeneid* 9.10–11, and Bruni, *History*, 1.13.

97. The cathedral church of Florence: Lit., the church of the Fluentine bishop: i.e., S. Maria del Fiore, the Florentine Duomo. Fluentia was supposedly the original name of Florence according, again, to Bruni, ibid. 1.3.

101–104. Landini was supposed to have been interested in natural philosophy according to Filippo Villani's *Liber de origine civitatis Florentiae et eiusdem famosis civibus* and according to Landino's own commentary on Dante; he also wrote a poem in honor of William of Ockham; see *Grove Music Online*, Biographies, s.v. Landini, Francesco.

110–111. The old church of San Lorenzo where Landini was buried was being rebuilt by its most famous parishioner, Cosimo de' Medici, in the middle years of the fifteenth century, when this poem was written.

115–118. Yet Landino's tomb, placed in San Lorenzo in 1397, was found in Prato in the nineteenth century and was moved back to San Lorenzo (and placed the second side-chapel to the right) only in the twentieth. Cosimo de' Medici's own tomb was placed exactly in the center of San Lorenzo, under the crossing.

125. Gabriele Landino (d. 1430), uncle of Cristoforo, a poet and prominent member of the Camaldolese Order. The latter was an order founded in the early eleventh century that followed a rule similar to that of the later Carthusians.

127. Ambrosian milk: A reference to Ambrogio Traversari (1386–1439) Florentine humanist and monk, translator from the Greek, later (1431) minister-general of the Calmaldolese Order.

128. Gorgons' waters: Hippocrene, a fountain on Mt. Helicon sacred to the Muses.

134. Arcadian people: I.e. the Pisans, whose city according to legend was founded by Pelops, fleeing from the Trojan War. Pelops gave his

name to the Peloponnesus, hence Arcadian or (as the Latin says) Parrhasian. According to Servius's commentary on Vergil's *Aeneid* 10.179, the Greek town of Pisa, "a city of Arcadia," was "the place from which came the men who founded Pisa in Italy, so called from the original city." Florence conquered the Pisans in 1406; Gabriel was evidently in the midst of a work describing the victory when he died.

142. Cirrha: The port of Delphi.

144. Permessus: A river rising on Mt. Helicon, sacred to the Muses.

1.25. About Xandra

Meter: Sapphic

13. The nightingale is Philomela, raped by her brother-in-law Tereus, who subsequently cut out her tongue when she began to reveal his deed; her sister Procne in revenge killed her own son, Itys, Philomela's nephew, and served him to Tereus for his supper. The gods changed Philomena into a nightingale. See Ovid, *Metamorphoses* 6.440 ff.

1.26. To Ginevra

Meter: hendacsyllablic

1.27. On Xandra's Return

Meter: Sapphic

1. Raven: The raven in classical literature was thought to give omens by its behavior. See Cicero, *On Divination* 1.12.

1.28. To Xandra

Meter: elegiac distich

2. Croesus: Last king of Lydia, legendary for his power and wealth.

12. The conceit of the sleepless lover fills Latin elegiac poetry. See, for example, Tibullus 1.275–79 and Propertius 1.1.33–34.

39. The Pactolus: A river in the kingdom of Lydia, which derived much of its wealth from the river's golden sands.

40. The Tagus: A river of Iberia whose waters were said to run with gold.

1.29. To Bernardo

Meter: elegiac distich

For Bernardo Nuti see the headnote to 1.11.

3. Ambiguous cases and specious pleas: Subjects treated in Quintilian's *Institutes*. Bernardo is studying rhetoric while Landino is studying to be a notary (an official something like a British solicitor); see Introduction.

7. Lisa (or Elisabetta): Sister of Bernardo, whose death is the subject of 2.12.

14. For the phrase *insani fori* see Virgil, *Georgics* 2.502.

19. The celebrated pool: The Castalian Spring, a fountain on Mt. Parnassus, sacred to Apollo and the Muses; by metonymy a source of poetic inspiration. See line 38.

38. The Aonian grove: The grove of the Muses.

40. The learned Linus: See note at 1.24.68.

1.30. To Giovanni Antonio

Meter: Sapphic

Giovanni Antonio has not been identified, but he was evidently a close friend of Landino and is mentioned in 1.30, 2.29, er10, er16, er37, and er40.

3. Our precious native town: I.e., Pratovecchio, in the Casentino north of the castle of Poppi. See Introduction.

1.31. To Leandra

Meter: elegiac distich

4. The play on *menta* (mint) and *mentula* (the male sex organ) is found throughout classical literature. For a Renaissance example see Pietro Bembo's *Carminum Libellus* 8.77 ff., in Pietro Bembo, *Lyric Poetry*, ed. Mary P. Chatfield (Cambridge, Mass., 2005), 29. See J. N. Adams, *Latin Sexual Vocabulary* (London, 1982), 9 ff.

5. The *ruta* or rue-plant causes rigidity, according the to pseudo-Virgilian poem *Moretus*, line 88.

1.32. To Anastasio

Meter: elegiac distich

No contemporary named Anastasio has been identified. The name is perhaps a mask, meant as an allusion to Anastasius the Librarian, a learned Roman cleric of the ninth century who, unusually for the time, knew Greek.

1.33. To His Book

Meter: elegiac distich

9. Maecenas: I.e., Piero de' Medici. See Introduction.

11. Perform the rites: I.e., throw yourself into the fire.

XANDRA: BOOK II

2.1. To Piero de' Medici

Meter: elegiac

For the circumstances of the dedication to Piero de' Medici, see the Introduction.

11–14. P. Cornelius Scipio Africanus Maior (236–c.184 BCE), extraordinary battle commander from his youth onwards, decisively defeated Hannibal ("the African general") at Zama in 202 BCE, thus ending the Second Punic War. The story of his amusing himself by collecting shells and pebbles on the seashore was a famous example of the simple pleasures of the great; see Valerius Maximus 8.8.1, quoted in the famous educational tract of Pier Paolo Vergerio *De ingenuis moribus*; see *Humanist Educational Treatises*, ed. Craig W. Kallendorf (Cambridge, Mass., 2003), 85, §69.

16. M. Porcius Cato Uticensis (95–46 BCE), Roman statesman and Stoic philosopher known for his stern morality.

18. Unmixed wine: I.e. strong wine. The ancients usually diluted their wine with water and so regarded the drinking of unmixed wine as intemperate.

2.2. To Piero de' Medici

Meter: elegiac

5. Pelion: A mountain in Thessaly. The king of Pelion was Peleus, the father of Achilles; or possibly Chiron the centaur is meant.

2.3. Against the Covetous

Meter: elegiac

24, 26. Persia . . . India: Both Persia and India were fabled in ancient times for their wealth.

41. Trumpet of Smyrna: Homer, who according to one ancient legend was born in Smyrna.

2.4. To Xandra

Meter: elegiac

1. Callimachus: Hellenistic poet, native of Alexandria and cataloger of its famous library.

3. Assisi: The native town of the elegist Sextus Propertius (c. 50–c. 15 BCE), an important model for Landino.

5. Francesco Petrarca (1304–1374): The first humanist, the first modern Italian poet, and the inspiration of six succeeding centuries of writers.

16. Paestum: An ancient city of Magna Graecia south of modern Salerno, renowned in classical times for its roses; compare Propertius 4.5.61.

17. An ancient poet: Ennius (239–169 BCE), who wrote an epic poem entitled *Scipio* and translated or reworked many tragedies from the Greek, including some of Euripides' and probably some of Sophocles' as well. For the judgement about Ennius' "thin" style see Aulus Gellius 12.2.

18. Scipio and his sons: Several of the numerous descendants of Publius Cornelius Scipio (consular tribune 395 BCE) were famous figures in Roman public life.

22. Learned Mantua: Vergil, who was born near Mantua.

21–24. The diction is rather strained and imprecise, but the thought seems to be that both Vergil and Xandra were treated unjustly by Fate, as he was not able to devote himself to describing her virtue in verse, while her virtue went unsung by a poet of Vergil's caliber.

32. The Iulii: The descendants of Aeneas' son, Ascanius (Iulus).

33. The Aonian sisters: The Muses, so-called because their dwelling-place, Mt. Helicon, is in Aonia (Boeotia).

43–44. Move rocks, move iron hearts . . . and drive shaggy beasts: Powers attributed to the great poet-seers of antiquity, like Amphion and Orpheus.

46. Erato: The muse of love poetry.

2.5. TO XANDRA

Meter: elegiac

32. Niobe: See the note to 1.22.9.

35–38. For Mars' love-affair with Venus see Ovid, *Metamorphoses* 4.171 ff.

39. Neptune (Poseidon): The god changed himself into a horse to deceive Demeter: ibid. 6.117–118.

49. Daphne: She refused the love of Apollo and while running from him was changed into a laurel tree: ibid. 1.548 ff.

50. She who shut the path: Herse, one of the three daughters of Cecrops: ibid. 2.724 ff.

2.6. TO PIERO DE' MEDICI: ON HIS PRAISES AND THOSE OF MAECENAS

Meter: elegiac

8. Virgil's *Aeneid* opens with the words *Arma virumque cano* (I sing of arms and a man).

9. Pauper child: Horace (65–8 BCE), Roman poet, to whom Maecenas gave a small estate at Sabinum (in modern Lazio, not Campania).

10. Sing of Lalage: See Horace, *Odes* 1.22. Horace was one of the first authors on whom Landino lectured after being appointed a professor at the Florentine Studium.

13. Lesbos: Aegean island birthplace of Terpander, Alcaeus and Sappho. Horace made wide use of Alcaic and Sapphic meters in his poetry.

17. Tuscan shores: Etruria, Tuscia, Tyrrhenia and Lydia are used interchangeably by Landino to refer to Florence and its fifteenth-century territory.

22. The old Aonian: Hesiod, whose *Works and Days* deals with the pursuits of ordinary life.

35. Father: Cosimo il Vecchio (1389–1464), *pater patriae*, unofficial ruler of Florence between 1434 and 1464, spent vast sums on the arts and public works and sponsored the first public library in Florence.

43. The lion or *marzocco* was the symbol of Florence, Lydia the mythical country of origin of the Etruscans; see the headnote to 1.18 and the note to 1.24.92, above.

2.7. TO XANDRA

Meter: elegiac

3. The mother of love: Venus. For Venus and Adonis see Ovid, *Metamorphoses* 10.519 ff.

5–6. The girl from Pontus . . . the child of Aeson: Medea and Jason. To obtain the Golden Fleece Jason had first to yoke two brazen bulls and sow a field with dragon's teeth, but thanks to Medea was able to accomplish this and other tasks; see ibid. 7.100 ff.

12. The maid of Colchis: Medea.

26. Adder's ears: Adders were supposed in folklore to stop up their ears to prevent hearing a snake charmer; compare Psalm 58:4.

39. Oenone: Daughter of Cebren, a river-god, she was a mountain-nymph and the first wife of Paris, who left her for Helen of Troy;

Oenone committed suicide after his death. See Ovid, *Heroides* 5, Landino's main source here.

2.8. A Description of Monte Asinario
for Lorenzo Cresci

Meter: elegiac

Lorenzo Cresci was a Florentine statesman, brother of Migliore Cresci, who was a disciple of Ficino. Monte Senario, as it is known today, is the site of a convent built in 1231 by seven Florentine nobles who founded there the Servite Order, a community devoted to the Virgin Mary. It is located north of Florence in the Medici lands of the Mugello.

15. Leo: The fifth sign of the Zodiac, associated with the month of August.

18. The urban toga: The cares of urban government, of which Lorenzo often complains in his own poetry.

45. A full lustrum: A period of five years, a name derived from the ceremony of purification or lustration performed every five years by the censors in ancient Rome.

2.9. He Rails about Love

Meter: elegiac

2. Argos: The hundred-eyed son of Aegenor whom Juno employed to guard Io.

2.10. To His Muse

Meter: elegiac

The poet seems to be imagining himself somewhere on the wooded ridges to the east of Fiesole.

1. Thalia: The muse of comedy and idyllic poetry.

4. Bellerophon's waters: By transference, the waters of the fountain of Hippocrene, which sprung from the footprint of Pegasus, the winged horse captured by Bellerophon.

7. Dryads: Spirit-nymphs of the trees.

11–12. Mugello: An agricultural area north of Florence, where lay the traditional lands of the Medici.

14. Bright temples: If the plural is not merely poetic, Landino might be referring, in addition to the Duomo (Santa Maria del Fiore), to Santa Maria Novella and Santa Maria del Carmine, all clearly visible from Fiesole. The word "Christ-bearing" might be an allusion to his own first name, Cristoforo.

2.11. About a Nightmare
Meter: elegiac

5. Tablets: I.e., writing tablets, such as the wax-covered boards used in antiquity. Xandra is reading his rival's poetry and approving it.

17. Endymion: A youth, known for his perpetual sleep, whose beauty attracted the love of the moon (Cynthia).

27. Palinurus: The pilot of Aeneas' ship who was overcome by Sleep (Morphus) and fell into the sea as the Trojan fleet neared Italy.

2.12. The Dying Elisabetta to her Brother Bernardo
Meter: elegiac

The poem is spoken in the voice of Elisabetta Nuti, the younger sister of Bernardo Nuti, referred to in 1.29.7. Some of the themes reappear in Var1.

12. Dis: A name both for Pluto, as King of the Underworld, and his realm.

20. Manes: The spirits of the dead.

21. Tartarus: The deepest portion of the Underworld where the wicked are punished.

23. Dictaean king: From Mount Dicte on Crete. The Dictaean king is Minos in his role as judge of the shades passing to the Underworld. See *Aeneid* 6.568–572; Dante, *Inferno* 5.4 ff.

25. The punishments referred to in lines 25–29 are those imposed upon the Danaides (filling sieve-like vessels), Tantalus (unslakable thirst), Prometheus (hooked claws), Sisyphus (rock), Tityos (vulture), and Ixion (wheel). The Chimera is a fire-breathing monster associated with Lycia in southeastern Asia Minor.

2.13. About Bindo the One-eyed

Meter: elegiac

It is unclear why a poem to "one-eyed Bindo" should address a Marco in its first line. One pair of manuscripts has the title *De Marco lusco* (Perosa, 63) and entitles the next poem (XIV) as *De Bindo bibone*. Bindo, perhaps an imaginary comic character, is also mentioned in 2.19 and 2.24, below.

3. See the note at 2.9.2 above.

2.14. On the Same Man

Meter: elegiac

2.15. Epitaph for the Architect Filippo

Meter: elegiac

Filippo Brunelleschi (1377–1446), Florentine artist and the foremost architect of the early Renaissance, builder of the cupola of the Duomo in Florence, the largest groin-vault ever built.

2.16. Another Poem for the Same Man

Meter: elegiac

2. The cathedral church of Florence, Santa Maria del Fiore.

2.17. To Francia

Meter: elegiac

2.18. To Xandra

Meter: elegiac

9. Sicily in ancient times was proverbial for its cruel tyrants, men such as Dionysius of Syracuse and Phalaris of Akragas.

13. Having addressed first Xandra, Landino now addresses himself down to line 29, at which point he begins to address Jupiter.

29–32. To escape Jupiter's embraces Asteria took the form of a quail and, hurling herself from heaven into the sea, became the island of Delos. Zeus took the form of a white bull in order to carry Europa off to Crete.

33–37. How Neptune deceived Theophane (daughter of Bisaltes), Apollo deceived Issa (whom Landino seems to confuse with the river Issos), and Bacchus deceived Erigone, as well as the deceptions of Zeus to in the preceding lines, are some of the many stories of the gods' treachery described in Arachne's fateful tapestry, as recounted by Ovid in *Metamorphoses* 6.108 ff.

56. Stern sailor: Charon, the Stygian ferryman.

58. Lethe: The river of forgetfulness in the Underworld that causes souls to forget their previous lives.

2.19. To Bindo

Meter: elegiac

On Bindo see above, 2.13 and 2.14, and below, 2.24.

2.20. To Francia

Meter: elegiac

On this poem see the articles of Charlet and Murgatroyd cited in the Bibliography. The poem is technically a *paraclausithyron*, a poem "from behind a locked door," of which a number of examples survive from antiquity, including love elegies by Catullus (67), Ovid (*Amores* 1.6), Tibullus (1.2) and Propertius (1.16); the latter seems particularly in evidence here.

24. To enable Jason to yoke the brazen bulls and perform other heroic endeavors (see note to 2.7), Medea gave him powerful herbs and potions.

37–38. Referring to the custom for lovers to festoon their girlfriends' doors with garlands of flowers; see above, 2.7.21. The poet continues to apostrophize the doors through line 41.

2.21. To Leandra

Meter: elegiac

2. A pledge: She has pawned her ring with him which will be redeemed when she comes to see him on a future night.

2.22. Epitaph for Paolo
Who Died While Having Sex

Meter: elegiac

2.23. To the City of Florence

Meter: elegiac

6. The war of the Seven Against Thebes is described in Statius' heroic poem *Thebiad.*

11. Flourishing children (*florentes alumnos*): A common trope for Florence, which had considered herself the daughter and successor of Rome since the thirteenth century. For the story of the founding of Florence by Sulla's Roman veterans see Bruni, *History* 1: 1–11. The historical events alluded to in lines 11–30 are all treated in Bruni's official history of the city, written between 1416 and 1442.

13. Poggibonsi: See Bruni, *History* 2.118–21. After the siege, the Florentines destroyed the original town, built on an impregnable height, and transferred the town to the valley below.

15 24. The defeats of Pisa, Siena, and Volterra in 1254—the "Year of Victories"—are described by Bruni, *History* 2.5–15, 32. The story of Florence's victory over Volterra is also recounted in Bruni's well-known *Panegyric of the City of Florence* (1404).

18. The She-wolf: The symbol of Siena, the wolf that suckled Romulus and Remus.

26. For the etymology of the name Fluentia see Bruni, *History* 1.3.

27. For the story of the giant Casca, who was defeated according to one report in single-hand combat by Foresi de' Adimari, leader of the Florentine Guelf exiles, see Bruni, *History* 2.82.

34. Pleasure-craft (*phaselus*): Probably with reference to the yacht described in Catullus 4, just as the *libellus* of line 38 probably alludes to Catullus 1.1.

42. No girl of old: The *quondam* of 42 links back to the *quondam* of line 9. Just as ancient history is meaningless to him compared with the history of Florence, so the girls in old books are lifeless next to the his living experience of Xandra.

52. Your carriage: Probably an allusion to the famous line of Vergil, *vera incessu patuit dea*, "the true goddess was revealed by her carriage," *Aeneid* 1.405.

65–72. The story of Daphne and Apollo is found in Ovid, *Metamorphoses* 1.452 ff.

76. Arethusa's flight from the river-god Alpheus is found ibid. 5.576 ff.

80. How the poor youth Iphis was scorned by the proud Cretan princess Anaxarete and hanged himself in despair is found ibid. 15.699 ff.

2.24. To Bindo

Meter: elegiac

For Bindo see above, 2.13, 2.14 and 2.19.

2.25. To Xandra

Meter: elegiac

8. Moon: The moon (the goddess Luna or Selene) was famously obsessed by her love for Endymion.

12. The goddess Aurora was married to Tithonus, brother of Priam, hence the epithet "Phrygian spouse."

38. Bactria: A province of Persia, near the furthest bounds of Alexander the Great's eastern conquests.

45. A mountain: Probably Monte Falterona in the Casentino is meant, the source of the Arno; it lies just north of Pratovecchio, the *paese* of the Landino family.

67. Philomena: The nightingale. See the note to 1.25.13. Landino seems to be mistaken about the fate of Itys.

73. Shy she-goats: Reading *timidas* for *tumidas* (swollen—pregnant?—or angry).

2.26. To Xandra

Meter: elegiac

3–4. Metaphorically, the ends of the earth: Ultima Thule, an island in the northern part of the North Sea, sometimes identified with Norway, and the river Indus, flowing from the Himalayas through Pakistan into the Arabian Sea.

12. Darius I (521–485 BCE), king of Persia.

13. The Parcae: Another name for the Fates, Clotho, Lachesis and Atropos, the spirits that attend the birth of a child and determine his or her fate.

2.27. The Way Rome Marvels at Xandra

Meter: elegiac

3. Cynthia: The girlfriend of the Roman poet Propertius.

5. Lesbia: The girl to whom Catullus wrote some of his most ardent, as well as his most angry, poems.

7. Corinna: The beloved of Ovid in his *Amores*.

9. Nemesis: The fictitious name of a woman addressed in Book II of Tibullus.

2.28. To Giovanni Antonio on the Poems of Burchiello

Meter: elegiac

Domenico di Giovanni (1404–1449), called Il Burchiello, a barber-poet, who wrote burlesque and satiric poems in the vernacular. He left Florence because of his anti-Medicean sentiments. For Giovanni Antonio see 1.30.2. The wit turns on the double sense of *lego* to mean both "read" and "choose, select, pick." You can read but you won't find anything select or elegant. *Quid tum?* ("What then?" or "What next?") was the motto of Leon Battista Alberti.

2.29. To His Muse to Hurry to Giovanni Antonio in Florence

Meter: elegiac

On Giovanni Antonio see the headnote to 1.30.

3. Sienese Gate: The southern gate of the city, now called Porta Romana; the street straight ahead is the Via Romana.

8. The silk-makers shops were in Por S. Maria that leads to the Mercato Nuovo and the Mercato Vecchio ("The Merchant's Forum"), now the Piazza della Repubblica.

9. Evil Lane: The brothels in Renaissance Florence were located along the north side of the Mercato Vecchio.

13. Crossroads named for Pales: Or "from the straw." Possibly the present-day Via dei Pecori, Pales being the tutelary deity of flocks and herds.

14. San Lorenzo: In the years following 1442 the church of San Lorenzo, the parish church of the Medici, was rebuilt and enlarged through the generosity of Cosimo il Vecchio. See the note to 1.24.110–112.

17. Mighty palace: The present-day Palazzo Medici-Riccardi on the Via Cavour.

20. Via San Gallo: Proceeding northward from Piazza San Lorenzo, it keeps the same name today.

2.30. On the Near Ruin That Is Rome

Meter: elegiac

On this poem see the article by Charlet cited in the Bibliography.

6. The seven hills of Rome are the Capitoline, Palatine, Esquiline, Quirinal, Viminal, Coelian, and Aventine. The Circus Maximus, which

in its heyday could seat 200,000 people, is located between the Palatine and Aventine hills.

7. Tarpeian rock: Part of the Capitoline hill named after Tarpeia, who opened the gates of the fortress to the besieging Sabines; in later Roman history the Tarpeian Rock was a site of execution.

10. Will there come a time: Sarcastic. What is the point of rehabilitating Marius and damning the memory of his great rival, Sulla, when all such memorials are now lost to time?

11. Your lofty Colosseum: More properly known as the Flavian amphitheater, it was begun by Vespasian and finished by his son Titus in 80 CE.

12. In Landino's day the practice of burning the marbles of old Roman buildings for their lime had not yet died out.

13. Nauta: I.e., Propertius; see the note to 1.19.17, above. For the poem to the temple of Apollo Palatinus, see Propertius 4.6.

15. Scopas: A distinguished sculptor and architect, native of Paros, who flourished between 395 and 350 BCE.

17. Praxiteles: Athenian sculptor who flourished in the fourth century BCE.

20. Phidian art: Phidias was the greatest of Greek sculptors (c. 490–c. 417 BCE), whose chief works were the Parthenon and the Propylaea.

20. Mentor: Friend of Ulysses and proverbial as a wise and faithful counselor. "Wise Mentor has perished" means that the example of great art no longer remains to provide counsel to modern artists.

21. Augustus: The emperor Octavian (63 BCE–14 CE), great-nephew of Julius Caesar and first Roman emperor. He was credited by Suetonius with having made Rome a city of great monuments, "finding it brick and leaving it marble," in his famous phrase.

XANDRA: BOOK III

3.1. TO PIERO DE' MEDICI

Meter: elegiac

The poem contains numerous echoes of Propertius 2.1 and 2.10, the elegies of *recusatio*, where Propertius attempts to renounce lighter poetic meters and subjects.

18. Ten of War: The *Dieci di Balìa* (the "Ten of War"), a civic board with special powers in wartime. Piero served on this board in 1453 (Perosa, XLI).

25. The Peace of Lodi (1454).

33. Our Senate: The Signoria, the ruling body of Florence.

35. The Calabrian tyrant: Alfonso I of Naples and V of Aragon (1396–1458), who acquired the Kingdom of Italy, based in Naples, in 1443; he made war against the Florentines in 1452–54.

42. A captain: Francesco Sforza, the famous condottiere who became Duke of Milan in 1450, and was an ally of the Medici in Italian politics.

43. Francesco Sforza is referred to here as "Sforza's son" because he was himself the son of the a famous condottiere of the previous generation, Muzio Attendolo Sforza.

46. The Lombard tyrant: Filippo Maria Visconti (1392–1447), duke of Milan.

50–51. The man: Francesco Sforza, whose military power was sustained by Florentine financial resources, chiefly those of the Medici themselves. "The people of Sulla" are the Florentines, as Florence was supposedly founded by veterans of Sulla's armies; see the note to 3.3.3, below.

55. Fabius: Fabius Maximus Cunctator, five times consul, famous for his delaying tactics against Hannibal in the Second Punic War. The son and father: Publius Cornelius Scipio (father) and Publius Cornelius Scipio Africanus Major (son), both heroes of the Punic Wars.

3.2. TO PIERO DE' MEDICI, HIS MAECENAS
Meter: elegiac

7–8. Spring of Hippocrene . . . Clarian Apollo: Famous ancient sites for poetic and prophetic inspiration, respectively.

10. Rock (petra): A favorite pun on Piero's name; see 1.1.18. The image of water flowing from a rock is Biblical; see Exodus 17:6.

3.3. To Antonio Canigiani on the Beginnings of the City of Florence

Meter: elegiac

Landino mentions Antonio Canigiani twice in his *Commentary on Dante* and introduces him as a character in the *Camaldulensian Disputations*. The poem in general is reminiscent of Propertius 4.1.

3. Sulla's soldier: Florentines from the time of Salutati and Bruni believed that their city was founded under the Roman republic by veterans of Sulla's armies. Modern opinion inclines to the view that the land beneath Fiesole was first drained and centuriated when Octavian was triumvir in 41 BCE.

14. Aqueduct: See Bruni, *History* 1.4.

15. High tower: The Palazzo Vecchio or Palazzo della Signoria, the town hall of Florence.

17. Baptistery: An octagonal building opposite the Duomo, built during the thirteenth century and noted for its bronze and gilded doors.

19. The temple of the Cross: Santa Croce, the chief church of the Franciscan Order in Florence.

20. The monument to the Alberti clan: The Palazzo Alberti.

25. Mountain air: Sulla's soldiers were thought to have originally settled in Fiesole before moving down to the plain below.

31. Not unmindful of the Capitoline citadel: Landino echoes Bruni's view that ancient Florence was modelled on Rome; see Bruni, *History* 1.5.

34. A Curia: The Senate House of ancient Rome.

35. A temple: The Florentines believed falsely that their Bapistery had originally been a pagan temple to Mars.

48. A bronze moon upon snowy marble: the coat of arms of the Canigiani family. Later examples, such as that preserved in the Raccolta Ceramelli Papiani (see *www.archiviodistato.firenze.it/ceramellipapiani*) con-

sists of a blue crescent moon facing upwards on marble; the bronze moon described by Landino may be a variant.

55. I.e., the Medici cannot trace their ancestry back to immemorial antiquity; their eminence only emerges by comparison with the worth of other citizens.

59. That temple: Santa Maria del Fiore.

62. Vieri di Cambio de' Medici (1323–95) who, during a popular uprising in 1393, declined to seize power and acted instead as a mediator. He was among the few fourteenth-century Medici who were reliable supporters of the oligarchic regime.

71–84. For the famous metaphor of a raging crowd as a stormy sea, see Vergil, *Aeneid* 1.148 ff.

71. Pelorus: The promontory forming the northeast corner of Sicily.

73. Scylla . . . Charybdis: Two great rocks between Italy and Sicily: Scylla containing a cave with a monster having the heads of six dogs with enormous teeth, and Charybdis, which thrice a day swallowed and regurgitated the waters of the sea. See Homer's *Odyssey* 12.73 ff.

97. Aristides . . . Cato: Famous ancient examples of incorrupt government.

99. Crassus: M. Licinius Crassus, member with Pompey and Caesar of the First Triumvirate, proverbial for his love of money.

101–102. Cosimo divided his inheritance from his father Giovanni di Bicci with his brother Lorenzo, and was famous for the churches he built or restored, including San Lorenzo and San Marco, among others; he also built or restored a number of churches outside the city that were less visible, hence Landino's remarks here.

107. Lofty home: The Palazzo Medici on Via Larga, which was being built for Cosimo by the architect Michelozzo during the years when Landino was writing the *Xandra*.

111. The king: King Alfonso I of Naples; see the note to 3.1.35, above.

113–114. The lion or *marzocco* is the symbol of Florence; Tyrrhenia is a classical name for Etruria or Tuscany.

134. For Cosimo as patron of the arts and embellisher of Florence one need look no further than the architects and artists he employed: Brunelleschi, Michelozzo, Donatello, and Masaccio, to name but a few.

135. Holy ones (*divi*): The Christian saints.

137–138. Probably a reference to the elegant tempietto designed by Michelozzo and built at Piero's expense to house the image of the Blessed Virgin in the Church of Santissima Annunciata (1448).

3.4. Eulogy for His Brother

Meter: elegiac

1. No shame to the Fates: An anti-Stoic sentiment. The fact that he suffers the passion of grief is no challenge to the inevitability of fate.

7. Astrologically a malign combination.

20. See Catullus 101.

21. Pollux . . . Castor: Twin brothers of whom one, Castor, was mortal and the other, Pollux, was immortal. When Castor was slain, Zeus, at the request of Pollux, allowed him to share Castor's fate and each lived alternately one day under the earth and one in heaven.

27. Spanish tyrant and his Calabrian wedge: King Alfonso I of Aragon and his Neapolitan cavalry; see the note to 3.1.35 above.

75–90. These lines owe much to Evander's farewell to his son, Pallas; see Vergil, *Aeneid* 8.560 ff.

99. A lake near Cumae said to lead to the lower world. Near it was the cave of the Cumaean Sibyl through which Aeneas descended to the Underworld; see ibid. 6.236 ff.

102. Avernus: The three-headed dog that guarded the entrance to Hades.

111. Gate of horn: According to Virgil, there are two gates of sleep, the gate of ivory, through which false dreams are sent, and the gate of horn *qua veris facilis datur exitis umbris* (by which an easy departure is given to true dreams); see ibid. 6.893 ff.

119. Compare Propertius 2.15.1–2.

3.5. ELEGY ON THE ARAGONESE WAR
Meter: elegiacs

28. Decemvirs: The Ten of War; see the note to 3.1.18.

29. Lower Gaul (*Gallicanis*): I.e., Lombardy.

36. Braccian cavalry: the condottiere Braccio da Montone died in 1424; Landino is referring elliptically to his followers, the Braccheschi, a famous mercenary company. See the note to 1.8.8, above.

39–41. Landino is calling for a return to the days of the thirteenth century when Florence's wars were fought in large part by her own citizens. The "old laws" referred to in line 41 are the laws that obtained before the changes of 1351, which allowed military service to be commuted by cash payments; see Bruni, *History* 7.101.

44. The Wolf: Siena; see the note to 2.23.18.

45. Rhegian squadrons: See the note to 2.23.27.

47. The Battle of Campaldino in 1289, one of Florence's greatest victories; see Bruni, *History* 4.5; see also the note to 1.24.18–19, above.

49. Volterra: See the note to 2.23.24.

51. Nola: A Campanian city east of Naples, not known for its military valor.

59. The contempt for Campania is perhaps to be explained by its ancient reputation as a region owing its wealth to agricultural slavery.

3.6. TO PAOLO, NOT TO FEAR THE ARAGONESE WAR
Meter: elegiac

Paolo dal Pozzo Toscanelli (1397–1482), a highly esteemed mathematician and geographer whom Landino included as a character in his dialogue *De anima*. He was the chief Italian advocate of the theory that one might reach the east by sailing west, later adopted by Columbus. This poem was probably written in the summer of 1452, when Florence was being menaced by the army of Ferrante, son of Alfonso of Aragon; Landino attempts to encourage Paolo, and presumably other Florentines, by reminding him of other occasions when Florence has been in a tight spot militarily.

15. Emperor Henry: Henry VII of Luxemburg (1274–1313), elected Holy Roman Emperor in 1310; for his threat to Florence and its territory, see Bruni, *History* 5.1–21.

18. Fiesolan: Not Fiesole itself, but the town of Florence, founded by settlers from Fiesole.

19. San Salvi: The ex-convent of San Salvi, which lies just outside the walls to the east, was Henry's headquarters during the siege of Florence in 1312.

23. Montopoli: A battle in 1252 when the Lucchesi, allied to the Florentines, were defeated disastrously by the Pisans, leading the Florentines to counterattack immediately and defeat the Pisans; see Bruni, *History* 2.7.

27. Piccinino: Landino refers to an incident in the summer of 1440 when the Milanese commander, Niccolò Piccinino, marched through the Mugello, causing great fear of an invasion in the unprotected city of Florence. See Bruni's *Memoirs* 109 (included in Bruni's *History of Florence*, vol. 3, as cited above). Piccinino was defeated soon after at Anghiari (see below).

29. Bebriacus: More commonly Bedriacus, a village in the Po valley, here stands for the might of the Milanese massed against Florentine-led Tuscany; the latter is here called "the empire of the Lydians," from Etruria's supposed foundation by settlers from Lydia in Asia Minor; see 3.1.45, above.

31. Exiled Florentine: Probably Rinaldo degli Albizzi, the former Florentine oligarch and Cosimo's chief rival, who after his exile from Florence joined forces with the Duke of Milan.

39. Divine beings: The Christian saints, as is shown by the phrase "sprung from mortal seed."

42. Filippo: Filippo Maria Visconti, Duke of Milan from 1412 to 1447, and his Lombard ("Insubrian") forces.

45. Anghiari: In the battle of Anghiari (3 July 1440) the Florentines defeated the Milanese and Venetians under the leadership of Piccinino.

The victory was quickly followed by the conquest of all the Casentino, mentioned in lines 51–54. The war with Piccinino and its aftermath are all described at the end of Bruni's *Memoirs*, cited above, although Landino would have had a living memory of the events.

51. A kinglet: Francesco of the Guidi of Battifolle, count of Poppi.

55. Pistoia: Pistoia became a Florentine protectorate in 1253 in order to avoid the civil strife that would follow from its adherance to the Ghibelline cause with Florence as its Guelf neighbor (see Bruni, *History* 2.10); this situation seems to have reminded Landino of the effects of the Catilinarian conspiracy in 63 BCE, which led to insurrections in various cities of Etruria.

57. Prato: Prato and its territory, watered by the streams of the Bisenzio and Ombrone, were threatened by Castruccio Castracane, despot of Lucca, in 1323 but recovered by the Florentines; see Bruni, *History* 5.66.

59. The great contest: The struggle for preeminence between Florence and Pisa lasted down to 1406, when the Florentines finally conquered the port town.

60. Parrhasian city: Parrhasia is a poetic name for Arcadia, the epithet being transferred to the Pisans; see the note at 1.24.134.

62. People: The Florentine *popolo* or People, formally the sovereign body of Florence, which in Bruni's account often shirked the expenses associated with building its empire in central Italy.

71–72. Empoli: See Bruni, *History* 2.67. After the great Florentine defeat at the battle of Montaperti in 1260, a meeting of Florence's enemies was held at Empoli which called for the complete destruction of Florence; this fate was only averted by the intervention of the Ghibelline leader Farinata degli Uberti. See also 3.13, below.

84–86. As in a Roman triumph.

91–92. I.e., he would rather see Florence triumph than live to see his next birthday.

93. Saturn: Mythical king of Italy identified with Cronos, whose reign was thought of as a Golden Age.

97–98. Lines reminiscent of Vergil's famous lines in *Aeneid* 6.851–853: "You, Roman, remember to rule peoples with your power—these shall be your arts: to impose the custom of peace, to spare those who submit and to subdue the proud."

3.7. EULOGY FOR CARLO ARETINO

Meter: elegiac

Carlo Marsuppini (1398–1453) of Arezzo, humanist scholar and chancellor of Florence, professor at the University of Florence, where he was Landino's teacher. He died in the midst of translating the *Iliad*. His tomb, by Desiderio da Settignano, is in Santa Croce. This poem seems to have been composed in part to record his elaborate public funeral on 27 April 1453 in the Church of Santa Croce (see line 24, below). For biographical details, see Giuseppe Zippel, "Carlo Marsuppini da Arezzo, notizie bibliografiche," in his *Storia e cultura del Rinascimento italiano* (Padua, 1979), 198–214; a description of the funeral is on 211. On this poem, see also the letter of Landino to Piero de' Medici published in Perosa, 180–187 (Document I).

9. The Aeonian mount: Olympus.

12. Propertius: Nauta in the Latin; see the note to 1.19.17, above.

13. For the phrase *masculo Sappho* ("manly Sappho"), see Horace, *Epistles* 1.19.28.

20. An ancient stag: See Cicero, *Tusculan Disputations* 3.69.

22. Saturn's circuits: Saturn takes twenty-nine and one-half years to orbit the earth.

24. A state concern: After his death Marsuppini was given an elaborate public funeral, laid out on a bier with a poet's wreath; a funeral oration was pronounced by Matteo Palmieri. Landino here seems to recall the scene, or perhaps the poem may have been written originally to be read at the funeral obsequies.

29. The Latin bishop: Pope Nicholas V (1447–1455), at whose request Marsuppini began his Latin translation of the *Iliad* and who confirmed

him in the title of honorary Apostolic Secretary, first given him by Eugene IV.

31. French King: Charles VII (1403–1461), allied by treaty with Florence against the Venetians.

32. Duke of Milan: Francesco Sforza, a close ally of Cosimo de'Medici; see 3.1.42, 51.

40. The Ten of War: See the note to 3.1.18, above.

41. The eight guardians: The *Otto di Guardia*, an important civic board with police duties.

43. The Guelf Party: A Florentine patriotic society; the Green Dragon was a *gonfalone* or electoral ward in southwest Florence near the church of the Carmine.

54. Cosimo de' Medici: Marsuppini was an *habitué* of the Medici palace, a close friend of Cosimo and one of the few who followed him into exile in 1433, as well as the teacher of Cosimo's brother Lorenzo and his son, Giovanni; Zippel writes that he was "among the most intimate friends of the Medici family."

60. Calliope: The muse of epic poetry, from whom Homer drew inspiration for the *Iliad* and *Odyssey*.

67–68. See Propertius 3.3.1–2.

73–78. Only a few verses in lyric meters survive written by Marsuppini. The *Carmina illustrium poetarum italorum* (Florence, 1719–26), 6: 267–87, contains a poem in honor of Leonardo Bruni as well as poems to Tommaso Pontano, Cyriac of Ancona, Poggio Bracciolini, Maffeo Vegio, and the condottiere Braccio da Montone, but no love poetry. The poem alluded to in praise of virtue may be his poem on the death of Bruni, while the poem on true nobility can be identified with the poem written to Poggio.

81. Apollo: Lit. "the Cyrrhan one" (*Cirrhaeus*), from Apollo's love of this peak of Parnassus.

84, 89. Old man of Maeonia . . . the Smyrnaean: Epithets of Homer.

90: In Italic verse: I.e., Latin. As Zippel notes, what impressed contemporaries most about Marsuppini was his verse translation of Homer, of which only Book I and parts of book IX were finished at his death.

95. Cecropian page: Greek manuscripts.

95–106. Subjects that can be studied in Greek: Natural philosophy and ethics are emphasized.

108. Memory divine: Contemporary sources stress Marsuppini's phenomenal powers of memory.

115. Chryse: A city near Troy with a temple to Apollo. The daughter of its priest was captured and given as booty to Agamemnon, but Apollo sent a plague into the Greek camp in reprisal so Agamemnon was forced to return her to her father (*Iliad* 1.11 ff.).

147–148. See the note to line 108.

150. The master of life (*vitae magistrum*): Virtue, according to Socrates (Valerius Maximus 3.3.4.ext.1); time according to the proverb *Tempus vitae magister*; history according to Cicero (*On the Orator* 2.9.36); love according to the younger Seneca (*Hippolytus* 183). Landino seems to be thinking of the second alternative.

153–154. Roman law: For Marsuppini's knowledge of law, see Zippel, "Marsuppini," 205.

155–158. Landino here credits Marsuppini with a knowledge of cosmography and chorography, otherwise unattested.

163. Senate house: the Palazzo Vecchio, home of the Florentine Signoria, for which Marsuppini worked as chancellor.

168. No envious tongue: Probably alluding to the many attacks on Marsuppini by his former rival, Francesco Filelfo, which included hiring an assassin to kill him.

191. The Dog Star: The brightest star in the heavens, Sirius in the constellation Canis Major was proverbial for signaling hot weather (dog days). Arcturus, the fourth brightest, is on the northern constellation Boötes.

197. He who sang: Claudian (b. ca. 370 CE), a court poet of the Roman emperors, born in Alexandria, was falsely held by Florentine tradition to be a native of Florence; his most famous work is *The Abduction of Proserpina*, an unfinished epic in three books.

199. Earth, stars and spirits (*Manes*): I.e., the *Inferno, Paradiso* and *Purgatorio* of Dante Alighieri (1265–1321). But compare 3.7b.1 and 3.17.23–24 below.

201–202. The man: Francesco Petrarca (1304–1374); Landino refers to his *Canzoniere*, written in Italian in various meters, and his *Africa*, an epic in Latin hexameters.

203–204. Giovanni Boccaccio (1313–1375); Landino is not necessarily alluding only to his most famous work, the *Decameron*, especially as the latter is in prose, but may also mean by *opus* his entire *oeuvre* as a love poet.

205–206. Leonardo Bruni (1370–1444), whose *History of the Florentine People* Landino equates with its model, Livy's history of Rome.

3.7A. Another Epitaph for Carlo Aretino

Meter: elegiac

Epitaphs 7a and 7b are included after 7 in only one of the 36 manuscripts used as a basis for Perosa's edition.

2. Walls of the shining cosmos: *Moenia mundi* is a favorite Lucretian phrase, e.g. *De rerum natura* 1.73 and 3.16.

3.7B. Another

Meter: elegiac

1–2. The earth, the stars and spirits: See the note to 3.7.199–200, above.

2. Dust and shade: For the phrase *pulvis et umbra* see Horace, *Odes* 4.7.16.

3.8. Epitaph for the Poet Dante

Meter: elegiac

3.9. Another

Meter: elegiac

4. The Tuscan lyre: I.e. poetry in the Tuscan dialect of Italian.

3.10. Epitaph for Francesco Petrarca, the Poet

Meter: elegiac

Francesco Petrarca (1304–1374), humanist scholar, a famous poet in Italian as well as a major writer in Neo-Latin prose and verse. Landino here celebrates his contribution to Italian poetry, particularly his *Canzoniere*, in which he sang of his love for Laura. He is here seen as holding a position in Italian poetry superior to that held by Pindar (b. 518 BCE?) and Horace (Quintus Horatius Flaccus, 65 BCE–8 BCE) in Greek and Latin poetry, respectively.

3.11. Another

Meter: elegiac

3.12. The Cumaean Sibyl

Meter: elegiac

One manuscript adds the adjective *Cumana* after *sibylla* in the title.

4. See Vergil, *Eclogues* 4.4–5. These famous lines led Christians in later centuries to believe that the Cumaean Sibyl had prophesied the birth of Christ.

3.13. About Farinata degli Uberti

Meter: elegiac

Farinata degli Uberti (d. 1264), the great Ghibelline leader who after the battle of Montaperti (1260) by the river Arbia, when the Sienese and Pisans wished to destroy Florence in order to destroy the Guelf party, dissuaded them by the force of his personality. According to Bruni, *hoc uno tum patria stetit* ("our country survived because of this one citizen"), *History* 2.68. Even though Dante places him in the Sixth Circle of hell for his heretical beliefs, he calls Farinata *magnanimo*, great-souled (*Inferno* 10.73), an adjective echoed in Landino's *mens magna*.

2. An allusion to *Inferno* 10.86: *Che fece l'Arbia colorata in rosso*.

3.14. TAMYRIS, QUEEN OF THE SCYTHIANS

Meter: elegiac

Tamyris, queen of the Massagetae tribe of Scythians, lured Cyrus' army into the mountains and massacred thousands. In revenge for the death of her son in battle, she had the head of the dead Cyrus plunged into a leather bag of blood. See Boccaccio, *Famous Women*, tr. Virginia Brown (Cambridge, Mass.: Harvard University Press, 2001), 198–203, no. 49. Boccaccio's story is based on Justinus' *Epitome* 1.8 and Orosius 2.7, but Landino's identification of the mountains as those of the Massagetae (a detail not found in Justinus or Orosius) may show that he knew the relevant passage of Herodotus 1.201–214 (Books 1–7 had already been translated by Lorenzo Valla in 1453/54).

3.15. TO GIOVANNI SALVETTI ON THE PRAISES OF COSIMO THE GREAT

Meter: elegiac

Giovanni Salvetti was a humanist friend of Poggio Bracciolini, otherwise obscure. The poem contains echoes of Propertius 2.1 and 2.10; see also Landino's 3.1, above.

6. For the phrase *surda bucina* see Juvenal 7.71.

15–16. Julius Caesar, P. Cornelius Scipio Africanus Major and L. Cornelius Scipio Asiaticus; the latter two drove the Carthaginians out of Spain during the Second Punic War. For *fulmina bina* as an epithet of the Scipios, compare *duo fulmina belli* in Vergil, *Aeneid* 6.842–3.

17–18. Nero . . . Hasdrubal: Son of Hamilcar Barca, Carthaginian general and brother of Hannibal. He was killed by the consuls Nero and Salinator, who cut off his head and threw it into Hannibal's camp.

19. Latian axes: The axes carried in the fasces of a Roman magistrate as a mark of authority.

41. Cosimo was in fact accorded the title of *pater patriae* by the Signoria after his death, and it is inscribed on his tomb in San Lorenzo.

44. Your greatness lies in the urban toga: I.e., as a statesman. Contrasts between arms and the toga were a staple theme of ancient as well as Renaissance rhetoric.

59–60, 64. Publius: Vergil's *praenomen*. The "Trojan father" is Aeneas; Aeneas' mother is the goddess Venus.

71–76. Three building projects supported by Cosimo: The church of San Lorenzo, the Medici parish church; the restoration of the church of San Marco and its cloister (the latter is presumably the "portico" with its "sacred wood"), and the cloister added to south of the church of Santa Croce, near to the Arno. See Dale Kent, *Cosimo de' Medici and the Florentine Renaissance: The Patron's Oeuvre* (New Haven: Yale University Press, 2000), chapter X.

82. Julian house: Iulus was an alternative name for Ascanius; Julius Caesar's clan, the *gens Iulia*, claimed to be descended from Ascanius/Iulus.

86–87. Probably referring to the occasion in 1451 when Cosimo's elder son, Giovanni, returned from his embassy to Venice, leading to a rupture in Florentine-Venetian relations and to an open alliance with Francesco Sforza, the Duke of Milan, formalized by a treaty in 1451. The latter is called "the Lombard serpent" (*Gallicus anguis*) because Sforza, after marrying the daughter of the Filippo Maria Visconti and inheriting the dukedom from him, quartered with his own the Visconti arms, which depict a basilisk or serpent devouring a child.

89. The treaty: Probably the Peace of Lodi (1454).

92. Of an epic: Literally, "of a large buskin," the buskin being a shoe worn by tragic actors in ancient Greece; but here Landino simply means, generically, an elevated style.

3.16. To Jacopo Acciaiuoli in Praise of Cosimo the
Great and of the House of Acciaiuoli

Meter: dactylic hexameter

The Acciaiuoli were one of the great merchant banking families of Florence and close allies of the Medici from the 1430s through the 1460s. Jacopo Acciaiuoli was the son of the important statesman Angelo Acciaiuoli, Cosimo's right-hand man in diplomatic affairs; Jacopo was a student of the Greek émigré John Argyropolos and a friend of Landino.

3. Scorning elegaics: Landino has in fact departed from writing elegiac couplets in this poem, composed entirely in hexameters, the meter of epic poetry.

8. Buskin: See the note to 15.92, above.

18. That great name: Humanist poets often played on the double meaning of "Cosimo" (*Cosmus*) as "universe".

25. Campanian armies: The army of Alfonso I, King of Naples.

25. Siena: Lit. "the Wolf," a symbol of Siena.

32. Citadel of Athena: The Acropolis in Athens. The Acciaiuoli ruled the Latin crusader kingdom of Athens as dukes from about 1390 to 1460; Neri I Acciaiuoli (d. 1394) conquered the Acropolis in Athens from the Ottomans in 1388.

33. Thebes, born of dragons: The mythical ancestors of the Thebans were five soldiers remaining from those who had sprung up when Cadmus sowed the ground with the teeth of the dragon-son of Mars. Mercenary forces hired by Neri I Acciaiuoli took control of Thebes in 1379.

35. Apulia: The heel of the Italian boot, here standing for the Kingdom of southern Italy generally. The Acciaiuoli were bankers to the kings of Naples and Sicily; Nicola Acciaiuoli (1310–1365) was grand seneschal of the Angevin kingdom and held numerous fiefs in the Latin kingdom of Greece.

38. Most famously the Certosa di Galluzzo in Florence, a monastery founded by Nicola Acciaiuoli in 1342.

40. Angelo Acciaiuoli, father of Jacopo (see above). He was sent as ambassador to France in 1449–50 and again in 1452 to negotiate a treaty with Charles VII, and was responsible for bringing René of Anjou to It-

aly in 1453 to help Florence and Milan in their war against Venice and Alfonso of Aragon.

46. Francesco Sforza, a famous condottiere, later Duke of Milan. At the moment of which Landino speaks (1452), Sforza was fighting both the King of Aragon and the Venetians.

48. Braccian: See the note to 3.5.36, above. Many of the Bracceschi at the time were under the control of Sforza.

51. Brescia: In 1453, after the arrival of 1700 French cavalry under the command of René of Anjou, troops under the command of Sforza repeatedly raided and sacked the territory around Brescia, a border city then under Venetian rule. Sforza's control of Brescian territory was surrendered at the Peace of Lodi in 1454. Many towns in Brescian territory surrendered without a fight after the French troops committed a series of atrocities.

53. Venetians: Landino uses the word *Marcicolae*, those who dwell in the lands of St. Mark, the patron saint of Venice.

3.17. To Piero de' Medici in Praise of Poggio
Meter: elegiac

Poggio Bracciolini (1380–1459), humanist, papal secretary, and chancellor of Florence from 1453 to 1456. He wrote a continuation of Bruni's *History of the Florentine People* that was left unfinished at his death; other, earlier works are mentioned below. The context of the poem is the scandal that arose in August 1456, when a popular, anti-Medicean Signoria failed to reappoint the famous Poggio to his office as chancellor. See Field, *Origins*, 39–44. The call to keep the chancellorship out of the hands of lawyers in lines 113 ff. may reflect hostility to the rise of Benedetto Accolti, a professor of jurisprudence, of dubious loyalty to the Medici, who unofficially began to take over Poggio's duties in February of 1457 before being officially appointed to the post in 1458. See Robert Black, *Benedetto Accolti and the Florentine Renaissance* (Cambridge, 1985), 90–98. On this poem see also the letter dated 7 May 1458 from Landino to Piero de' Medici published by Perosa, 187–190 (Document II).

3. The planet Venus is Lucifer, the Day Star.

16. Apollo: "The Clarian god" (*Clarius deus*) in the Latin. The epithet comes from the celebrated temple and oracle of Apollo in the town of Claros on the Ionian coast.

18. Mugello . . . Casentino: An agricultural basin to the north of Florence and a mountainous region to the east of Florence, respectively.

22. Flowers (*floret*): A conventional pun on the name of Florence.

23–24. Compare 3.8 and 3.9, above

25–28. Compare 3.10 and 3.11 above.

29. Compare 3.7.203–204.

30. Coluccio Salutati (1331–1406), humanist, chancellor of Florence from 1375 until his death; he was the author of a number of learned works in Latin.

33. One described: Leonardo Bruni. See 1.17.

35. The other: Carlo Marsuppini. See 3.7.

41–42. A near-quotation of the last two lines of 3.7.

57. The following lines refer to various of Poggio's works; in order, the *De avaritia* (1428), *Contra hypocritas* (1449), *De miseria humanae conditionis* (1455), *De varietate fortunae* (1448), *De infelicitate principum* (1440), *An seni sit uxor ducenda* (1435), *De vera nobilitate* (1439/40), *De praestantia Scipionis et Caesaris* (1435) and the *Defensio de praestantia Scipionis et Caesaris* (1435).

72. You whom defeated Africa: Scipio Africanus. See the notes to 3.1.56 and 3.15.15, above.

78. Taurus: The second sign of the zodiac associated with the month of May.

83–94. Poggio was revered by later humanists for the rediscovery of ancient Latin works that were lost or little known in the Middle Ages, principally on journeys he took to the monasteries of Northern Europe during the Council of Constance. Included were the works alluded to in these lines: a complete copy of Quintilian's *Institutio oratoria*, Silius Italicus' epic poem *Punica*, Columella's *De re rustica*, and Lucretius' *De rerum natura*.

86. Lingones: A Celtic people of the Vosges mountains, in what is today Burgundy.

107–108. Poggio, though not among the more accomplished Greek scholars of the Renaissance, translated into Latin the history of Diodorus Siculus, Xenophon's *Cyropaedia* and some dialogues of Lucian.

109. A much-quoted phrase from Cicero's *Catilinarian Orations*, 1.2.

111. O civil laws: Possibly a reference to Accolti (see headnote). Accolti's two humanistic writings were both written after his appointment as chancellor; before that time he had written only brief legal opinions (*consilia*); see Black, *Accolti*, 86n., 190, 225–6.

126. The incompatibility of law and literary studies was a staple humanist theme, going back to Petrarch, Boccaccio and Leonardo Bruni.

133–134. These lines encapsulate the argument of Poggio's own invective, *Contra fidei violatores*, written around this time; see Field, *Origins*, 40–42.

159, 161. Swan, swans: Let Poggio, and by implication men of letters in general, be given back their traditional office of Florentine chancellor.

3.18. Eulogy for the Boy Cosimo, Grandson of the Great Cosimo

Meter: elegiac

Cosimino de' Medici (1452–1459) was the only son of Giovanni de' Medici, Piero's younger brother. His death in November 1459 provides us with the latest securely datable event in the *Xandra*. He is imagined as the speaker in this elegy.

15–16. A broadly Platonic sentiment. For *carcere caeco* see Vergil, *Aeneid* 6.734.

49. Archemorus: Son of the Nemean king who was killed by a dragon and in whose honor the Seven Against Thebes instituted the Nemean games.

53. Marcellus: Nephew and heir-designate of Augustus whose early promise and much-lamented death are described in Virgil, *Aeneid* 6.860–885.

62. Compare *lumen oris* in Lucretius 5.1455.

76. The middle step: An allusion to the Aristotelian doctrine of the mean.

77–78. That wrongdoing is the only evil that can befall a wise man is a Socratic doctrine, later adopted by the Stoics.

82. Aemilius: Aemilius Paulus Macedonicus. According to Plutarch (*Life of Aemilius Paulus* 35), his two sons by his second marriage died, one five days before, one three days after the triumphal celebrations for his conquest of Macedonia.

83. For Cato see the note at 2.1.16. A curule seat was the chair of state, inlaid with ivory, that high Roman magistrates used. For the story here, see Plutarch's *Life of Cato the Elder* 24.6.

88. Fabius Maximus Cunctator: See the note to 3.1.56; for the story about the death of his son, see Plutarch, *Life of Fabius Maximus* 24.4.

90. M. Horatius Pulvillus who dedicated the temple of Jupiter on the Capitoline. For the story see Valerius Maximus 5.10.1.

91. Greek philosopher (500–428 BCE) of the Ionian school; for the quotation see Diogenes Laertius 2.13.

102. Semi-mythical lawgiver of Sparta, whose life was written by Plutarch.

117. King of Pylos for three generations who, though advanced in age, sailed with the other heroes to Troy.

3.19. To Guido Guiducci

Meter: elegiac

Nothing is known of Guido Guiducci except that he was a correspondent of Cosimo de'Medici and may have been an officeholder in the Florentine territory.

8. Permessus: A river of Boeotia whose source is Mount Helicon and is sacred to the Muses; see Propertius 2.10.26.

9. store . . . away (*reponant*): Or "repay"; the ambiguity is perhaps intentional.

19–20. I.e., they will enter an age of justice. Erigone, daughter of Icarus, is a star in the constellation of Libra, seventh sign of the zodiac.

XANDRA, BOOK I (EARLIER REDACTION)

2. To Leon Battista
Meter: elegiac couplet

3. On the Title of This Book
Meter: elegiac couplet

7. To Xandra
Meter: elegiac couplet

9. To Tommaso Ceffi
Meter: elegiac couplets

Tommaso di Lorenzo Ceffi was a member of the *contubernium* of Niccolò della Luna, a friend of Leon Battista Alberti and Leonardo Dati, and the author of priapic verses; later a prominent Florentine officeholder. See Arnaldo della Torre, *Storia dell'Accademia Platonica di Firenze* (Florence, 1902), 294–319.

10. To Bernardo
Meter: elegiac couplets

Bernardo Nuti, on whom see 1.11. He is here imagined in Arezzo with Xandra and another female friend, Francesca.

11. To Giovanni Antonio
Meter: elegiac couples

For Giovanni Antonio see 1.30.

5. Friend: I.e., Giovanni Antonio, not Landino's girlfriend.

12. To Xandra
Meter: elegiac

3. Thyestes: Brother of Atreus; his brother famously fed him the flesh of his sons at a banquet.

4. Colchis: Native land of Medea, famous for poisonings and murders.

13. ABOUT GNOGNIA

Meter: elegiac

The name "Gnognia" sounds something like the word *vergogna*, which would mean something like "ribald" or "disgrace," but in er15 it turns out to be a dialectal form of Antonia.

15. ABOUT GNOGNIA

Meter: elegiac

16. TO GIOVANNI ANTONIO

Meter: elegiac

On Giovanni Antonio see 1.30, above.

2. For the point of this distich, compare it with the characterization of Alberti in 1.13, above, and er1.27, below.

19. TO XANDRA

Meter: elegiac

5. See Catullus 5.7 ff.

20. TO XANDRA

Meter: elegiac

21. TO BERNARDO

Meter: elegaic

1–2. A paraphrase of the famous line of Juvenal 3.164–65.

4. On Landino's early studies of civil law, see the Introduction.

22. TO BICE

Meter: elegiac

24. To My Mistress's Mother

Meter: elegiac

See er1.13 and er1.15, above.

25. To Tubia

Meter: elegiac

8. On the poet's role as a namer of women, see er1.16, above.

26. To Francesco da Castiglione

Meter: elegiac couplets

For Francesco da Castiglione or Castiglionchio see the headnote to 1.15.

6. Callimachus: The great Hellenistic scholar-poet, cataloguer of the library at Alexandria.

27. To Leon Battista Alberti

Meter: elegiac

28. To Xandra

Meter: elegiac

29. Concerning a Hall

Meter: elegiac

2. Aeolus, king of the winds, and Vulcan, god of fire. In other words, the hall is drafty and unheated.

30. To Francesco the Barber

Meter: elegiac

32. To Gigia

Meter: elegiac

33. To Lucretia

Meter: elegiac

39. To a Sodomite

Meter: elegiac

40. To Giovanni Antonio

Meter: elegiac

For Giovanni Antonio see 1.30, above.

16. Reparata . . . the Baptist: Santa Reparata, the traditional name of the Florentine Duomo. The Baptist: The baptistery of the Florentine cathedral, dedicated to St. John the Baptist, patron saint of Florence.

19. St. Mark's shrine: The Dominican priory and convent of San Marco.

29–32. For the story of Ariadne and Theseus, see Ovid, *Metamorphoses* 8.172 ff. Theseus abandoned Ariadne on Naxos and married her sister, Phaedra.

36. See the note to 2.7.6. For the full story of Medea as limned in the following lines, see Ovid, *Metamorphoses* 7.297 ff. Jason abandoned Medea to marry Creusa, daughter of King Creon of Corinth.

41. To Bernardo

Meter: elegiac

42. Epitaph for Lisa Tedaldi

Meter: elegiac

For information on the Tedaldi, an old and rich Florentine family with deep interests in literature and the fine arts, see P. O. Kristeller, "Una novella latina e il suo autore, Francesco Tedaldi, mercante fiorention del Quattrocento," *Studies in Renaissance Thought and Letters II* (Rome, 1985), 386–410.

48. To Francesco d'Altobianco Alberti

Meter: dactylic hexameter

Francesco d'Altobianco Alberti (1401–1479) was Landino's first patron (see Introduction).

NOTES · NOTES ·

POEMS POEMS

1. On the Death of Lisa

Meter: elegiac

Possibly this is the same Lisa (Tedaldi) whose death Landino mourns in er1.42. Elisabetta Nuti was also known as Lisa, however. The title was added by Perosa. For its themes, compare 2.12, above.

14. Compare Tibullus 1.3.25.

35–38. The symptoms described seem to be those of bubonic plague, endemic in Europe through much of the Renaissance.

74. For these tortures of the damned see the notes to 2.12, above.

2. Eulogy on Neri Capponi for Giovanni Canigiani

Meter: elegiac

Neri di Ginò Capponi (1388–1457) was a leading Florentine stateman. He served frequently as the Florentine republic's military commissioner, for example in the failed war against Lucca (which Landino does not mention) and at the great Florentine victory of Anghiari in 1440 (which he does). He also served as Florentine ambassador a number of times, especially in Venice during the Aragonese War, and was the republic's mediator between Francesco Sforza and Pope Eugene IV. He was the author of several historical works and was allied politically with Cosimo de' Medici. His life was written by the Roman humanist Bartolomeo Platina. See the article on him by Michael Mallett in the *Dizionario biografico degli italiani* (Rome, 1977), 70–75. Giovanni Canigiani was the son of Antonio Canigiani (see headnote to 3.3) and is also mentioned in the preface to Landino's Dante commentary.

17. His great-hearted father: Gino Capponi (1350–1421), Neri's father, served on the special war commission (the "Ten of War") in the siege of Pisa in 1406; this was Florence's greatest conquest in Tuscany. See the note to 3.1.18, above.

19. Filippo: Filippo Maria Visconti, Duke of Milan, controlled most of Lombardy ("Gaul," i.e. Cisalpine Gaul); his forces were defeated in the battle of Anghiari.

21. Piccinino: Niccolò Piccinino was the condottiere in charge of the Milanese forces, some of whom belonged to companies once commanded by Braccio da Montone. See notes to 1.8.8 and 3.5.36, above.

29. He then: Ferrante of Aragon, commanding the troops of his father Alfonso of Aragon.

31. Fabius: Fabius Maximus Cunctator; see the note to 3.1.55.

33. Rome: Pope Eugenius IV was allied with Alfonso V and Filippo Maria Visconti against the armies of Florence and Francesco Sforza.

36. Our fathers: I.e., to the achievements of the Florentine's forebears. Political speeches urging Florentines to defend their territory often speak of the necessity of not wasting the patrimony left them by their fathers.

41. Landino glosses over Capponi's opposition to Cosimo's policy of supporting Sforza in his bid to become Duke of Milan and of shifting Florentine alliances from Venice to Milan.

59. Parrhasian race: For Landino's use of the adjective "Parrhasian" to mean Pisan see 1.24.134 an 3.6.60 and the note to 1.24.134.

3. To Bernardo Bembo

Meter: elegiac

Bernardo Bembo (1433–1519), Venetian diplomat and bibliophile, father of Pietro Bembo, whose relationship with his son is painted in the latter's *Etna*: see the translation of Betty Radice in Pietro Bembo, *Lyric Poetry — Etna*, tr. Mary P. Chatfield (Cambridge, Mass., 2005). His first embassy to Florence in 1475–6 cemented the league between Florence, Venice and Milan. It was during this embassy that the platonic affair between the 42-year old Bembo and the sixteen-year old Ginevra de' Benci, both married, took place. Bembo's second embassy in 1478–80 sealed the friendship between the Bembo and Medici families. He was also close friend of Ficino's and Landino's circle and an *habitué* of Ficino's gymnasium. See Giannetto, *Bembo*, for a full account of his life. The poet Alessandro Braccesi also celebrated the platonic love between Bembo and "Bencia."

2. Ismarian seer: Orpheus, a mythical poet and seer from Thrace, where Mt. Ismarus is located.

3–6. For these ancient images of poetic power, see above, 2.4.43–44.

15–16. See 3.15.38.

21. Thracian bard: Orpheus.

22. Compare Vergil, *Eclogues* 4.57 ff.

26. Ginevra da Benci, Bembo's *inamorata*, was the subject of a famous portrait made in 1474 by Leonardo da Vinci, now in the National Gallery (Washington, D.C.). On Ginevra in Landino's poetry, see Walker, "Ginevra de' Benci," who gives the texts and a prose translation. For the theory that Leonardo's painting was in fact commissioned by Bembo (whose device with the motto *Virtutem forma decorat*, "Beauty is the ornament of virtue," is on the reverse of the panel), see Fletcher, "Bernardo Bembo."

32. Palladian hands: I.e., artistic hands; see 5.45 below and Seneca, *Medea* 366. Ginevra was among other things a poetess and an artist in needlepoint. Sadly, though they were originally a prominent feature of the painting, Ginevra's portrait by Leonardo now lacks her hands. There does, however, survive a silver-point study of them by Leonardo at Windsor Palace; see Fletcher, "Bernardo Bembo," figure 8.

35–36. Women sung in Roman love elegy; see the notes on 2.27, above.

39–42. The women referred to in these lines are all models of wifely devotion: Alcestis, wife of Admetus who saved him from death by dying in his stead; Evadne who when her husband was struck by a thunderbolt from Zeus leapt onto the flames in order to die with him; and Penelope whose 20 years' devotion to Odysseus underlies Homer's *Odyssey*.

51. Leda's offspring: I.e., Helen of Troy.

4. To the Same Man

Meter: elegiac

1–2. Milkwhite signet (*lactea gemma*): A variation on the classical expression for marking out happy days with white stones (*lapillus niveus, candidus*); see Catullus 68.148 for a famous poetic example.

11–12. Hero ("the Sestian maiden"), priestess of Aphrodite, beloved of Leander of Abydos (*Abydenum . . . virum*), who swam the Hellespont every night to visit her; the story is told in Ovid's *Heroides* 18 and 19.

14. Trojan leader seated in the cave: See Vergil, *Aeneid* 4.160–172.

17. Chariot: Lit. *quadriga* means a chariot drawn by four horses as used in race courses in the ancient world.

30. Zeus/Jupiter in the guise of an eagle stole the boy Ganymede to be cup-bearer to the gods. See Ovid, *Metamorphoses* 10.155–161.

5. To the Same Man

Meter: elegiac

2. The doctrine of the two Venuses, a heavenly and an earthly one, is central to Marsilio Ficino's famous commentary on Plato's *Symposium*, known as the *De amore* (1469).

11. These flames: I.e. the virtues. Celestial love brings forth virtue, a typically Ficinian doctrine.

14. You do not see well: Bembo was notoriously an Averroist, i.e., a follower of the school of Aristotelian interpretation that denied personal immortality; see Giannetto, *Bembo*, 136–37.

22, 24. Apelles (fourth century BCE) . . . Praxiteles (fourth century BCE): By repute the greatest Greek painter and sculptor, respectively. The Aphrodite of Cnidus was the most famous work of the latter. The Medici later owned a famous Roman copy, the Venus de' Medici, now in the Uffizi, but it is not known at what date they acquired the statue.

39–42. Common classical descriptions of female beauty.

69–80. A synopsis of Ulysses' (or Odysseus') various perils.

85–98. Bembo was Venetian ambassador to Castile in 1468–69, to the Burgundian court in 1471–74, to Austria in 1474.

91. Both Spanish races: the Portuguese and the Spaniards.

98. Morini, Teutonic tribes: Belgic and German tribes described in Caesar's *Gallic Wars* 2.4 and 4.

100. Referring to the league between Venice, Florence and Milan negotiated by Bembo in 1475–76.

6. To the Same Man

Meter: elegiac

29. At thirty: lit. "during my sixth lustrum," i.e from 30 to 35. Landino is being either vain, fictional or very approximate here, as it is implausible in the extreme that he could have written a poem to Bembo between 1454 and 1459.

7. To the Same Man

Meter: elegiac

1. Daughter of Thoas: Hypsipyle, who bore twin sons to Jason when the Argonauts landed at Lemnos and who was then deserted by him.

5–6. Phyllis: See the note to 1.23. After committing suicide she was changed into a tree. She is the subject of Ovid's *Heroides* 2.

23–26. Three classical examples of manly devotion. For Philotectes and Hercules, see the *Hercules Oetaeus* of Seneca, 1618 ff. Philoctetes' devotion was expressed by lighting the funeral pyre of Hercules, who was dying in agony, poisoned unintentionally by a love philtre applied by Hercules' wife, Deianira, in an attempt to regain his lost love. Hercules in gratitude to Philoctetes left him his bow and arrow. An allegorical meaning may be intended.

39–40. These lines may be intended as an explicit reference to a manuscript of his poems presented by Landino to Bembo (see Appendix), though the last lines seem to promise a new poetical work by Landino in honor of Bembo. Bembo was the recipient of dedications from many humanists.

8. To the Same Man

Meter: elegiac

The poem contributes to a long-standing humanist debate over true nobility, for which see *Knowledge, Goodness and Power: The Debate over Nobil-*

ity among Quattrocento Humanists, ed. and tr. Albert Rabil, Jr. (Binghamton, NY, 1991).

18. Habit: Aristotle taught that virtue was a stable habit learned by repeated acts in accordance with good.

19–20. Bembo received degrees in arts (1455) and law (1456) at the University of Padua, the most famous center in Europe for the study of natural philosophy.

28. Perillus was the sculptor who made a hollow bronze bull for Phalaris, the tyrant of Akragas in Sicily, who used to torture his enemies inside of it. The story was famous among philosophers in antiquity who asked, in order to test Stoic doctrine with an extreme case, whether anyone could be happy inside the bull of Phalaris.

29–30. He through whose intelligence: Ulysses.

39–40. I.e., he will not confuse the earthly with the heavenly Venus.

42–56. For Landino's theory of love here, see Ficino's *De amore* (1469).

53. Forest (*silvae*): *Silva* is also a philosophical term for matter.

9. Eulogy on the Death of Michele Verino
Meter: elegiac

Michele Verino (1469–1487), a gifted student of Landino whose early death was mourned by many contemporary poets. See the undated letters of his father Ugolino Verino and Landino published by Perosa, 192–193 (Document Va and Vb).

8. Calliope in Greek means "beautiful voice."

9. "Who is like to God:" The Hebrew meaning of Michael. See Exodus 15:11.

20. Cyprian goddess: Venus

29. Machaon: Surgeon to the Greeks during the Trojan War, son of Asclepius, god of healing. Asclepius was himself the son of Apollo, hence the epithet *Phoebigena*.

36. The old man of Cos: Hippocrates.

37–38. He to whose just imperium: Avicenna (980–1037 CE), the chief medical authority of the Arab world.

40. For the phrase *advena Nile* see Ovid, *Fasti* 5.268.

43. The doctors recommend venereal pleasures as an antidote to plague (see line 75), a common remedy of the time, exemplified, for example, in Boccaccio's claims for the prophylactic effects of his *Decameron* upon people living through a plague.

49. Son of Theseus whom Asclepius restored to life at Aphrodite's request.

51. Hippolytus rejected the advances of Phaedra, as Bellerophon did those of Antea.

55–64. See Var5.2, above. The doctrine of the two Venuses as developed by Marsilio Ficino in his *De amore* (1469) is discussed by Landino in Book IV of the *Camaldulensian Disputations* (1472).

66. With his pensive mind: I.e., through contemplation.

70, 74. Loathing foul excess . . . aetherial zones . . . spirits' dance sublime: Like Dante in the *Paradiso* Michele after purgation ascends first through the region of the heavenly spheres, made of aether but still material, then rises to the immaterial realm of the angels and disembodied spirits. The ascent mirrors the mystical ascent through stages of *purgatio*, *illuminatio* and *unio* in the Christian tradition.

10. The Tomb of the Poet Dante
Meter: elegaic

After being exiled in 1302, Dante never returned to Florence, but traveled from court to court, dying in Ravenna in 1321, where he was buried in the church of San Francesco. Bernardo Bembo was the Venetian governor of Ravenna in 1481–83 and restored Dante's tomb in May 1483. On this poem, see the undated letter of Landino to Bembo published by Perosa, 191–192 (Document IV).

6. Blessed dance: The chorus of the Muses.

· NOTES ·

11. Epitaph for Coluccio Salutati

Meter: elegaic

Coluccio Salutati (1331–1406), first in the great series of humanist chancellors of Florence. This epitaph seems to have been written for his tomb in the Duomo, Santa Maria del Fiore, in Florence. On Salutati, see Ronald G. Witt, *Hercules at the Crossroads: The Life, Work and Thought of Coluccio Salutati* (Durham NC, 1983).

4. Amphitryon's son: Hercules. Salutati composed a long moral-encyclopedic work on ancient mythology entitled *On the Labors of Hercules.*

12. For the Same Man in the Palace

Meter: elegiac

In Palatio here means "in the Palazzo Vecchio." Landino's poem was composed for the now-lost paintings belonging to the cycle of Famous Men, which included the famous Florentine chancellors such as Salutati and Bruni. These were accompanied by verse inscriptions, painted on the walls of the *Saletta* on the second floor; see Nicolai Rubinstein, *The Palazzo Vecchio, 1298–1532: Government, Architecture and Imagery in the Civic Palace of the Florentine Republic* (Oxford, 1995), 52. Rubinstein does not identify these as verses by Landino (but see ibid., 61, for Landino's role in elaborating the decorative program of the Palazzo Vecchio in the 1480s).

2. For the source of the tradition that Giangaleazzo Visconti remarked that a letter of Salutati was worth a thousand horses see Witt, *Hercules*, 159, note 40.

13. In Praise of Giannozzo Manetti

Meter: elegiac

Giannozzo Manetti (1396–1459) a distinguished Florentine humanist and diplomat, learned in three languages. The epigram refers to his service as ambassador for the Republic of Florence to Pope Nicholas V and King Alfonso I of Aragon.

DOUBTFULLY ASCRIBED POEMS

1. To Ugolino Verino

Meter: elegaic

Ugolino Verino (1438–1516), Neo-Latin poet and close friend of Landino. He was the father of Michele Verino whose death Landino mourns in Var9. In his book *De illustratione urbis Florentiae* Ugolino wrote an elegy on Landino's death entitled *Ad Christophorum Landinum rhetorem ac poetam Florentinae insignem.* The present poem is preserved, as far as is known, in a single manuscript and was assigned to Landino by Alfonso Lazzeri, *Ugolino e Michele Verino* (Turin, 1897), 61; the attribution was placed in doubt by Perosa, xvii–xviii. Verino's *domina* was called Flametta in Verino's poetic cycle of the same name (1458–63), hence the attribution.

2. Poems about Certain Riddles

Meter: dactylic hexameter

These riddles are preserved only in a single eighteenth-century codex, copied from an older codex, apparently Florence, Biblioteca Nazionale Centrale MS Magl. VII 1120, written in Florence in 1454. The older MS, once in the possession of the Strozzi family, no longer contains them. The later codex claims they were written in Landino's youth. See Perosa, xxi–xxii.

Bibliography

❧❧❧

TEXT

Christophori Landini Carmina omnia. Edited by Alessandro Perosa. Florence: Olschki, 1939.

STUDIES

Bandini, Angelo Maria. *Specimen literaturae Florentinae saeculi XV, in quo . . . Christophori Landini gesta enarrantur.* 2 vols. Florence: Rigaccius, 1747–1751.

Cardini, Roberto. "La critica del Landino dalla *Xandra* alle *Disputationes Camaldulenses*." *Rinascimento,* n.s. 7 (1967): 177–234.

———. *La critica del Landino.* Florence: Sansoni, 1973.

———. "Landino e Dante." *Rinascimento,* n.s. 30 (1990): 175–190.

———. "Landino e Lorenzo." *Lettere Italiane,* 3 (1993): 361–375.

Charlet, Jean-Louis. "Permanence et mutation d'un genre littéraire antique au Quattrocento: un paraclausithyron de C. Landino, *Xandra* 2.20." *Res publica litterarum,* 7 (1984): 39–51.

———. "Une meditation poétique sur les ruines de Rome: Landino, *Xandra* II, 30." In *Lettere e arti nel Rinascimento: Atti del X convegno internazionale: Chianciano-Pienza, 20–23 luglio 1998,* ed. Luisa Secchi Tarugi, 123–131. Florence: Franco Cesati, 2000.

Coppini, Donatella. "Properzio nella poesia d'amore degli umanisti." In *Colloquium Propertianum (Secundum), Assisi, 9–11 novembre 1979, Atti,* 169–201. Assisi: Accademia Properziana, 1981.

———, "Cosimo *togatus.* Cosimo de' Medici nella poesia latina del Quattrocento." *Incontri triestini di filologia classica,* 6 (2006–2007): 101–119.

Field, Arthur. "The *Studium Florentinum* Controversy, 1455." *History of Universities,* 3 (1983): 31–57.

———. *The Origins of the Platonic Academy of Florence.* Princeton: Princeton University Press, 1988.

Fletcher, Jennifer. "Bernardo Bembo and Leonardo's Portrait of Ginevra de' Benci." *Burlington Magazine*, 131, no. 1041 (December, 1989): 811–816.

Giannetto, Nella. *Bernardo Bembo: umanista e politico veneziano*. Florence: Olschki, 1985.

Kallendorf, Craig W. "Cristoforo Landino." In *Centuriae Latinae*, ed. Colette Nativel, 477–483. Geneva: Droz, 1997.

———. *In Praise of Aeneas, Virgil and Epideictic Rhetoric in the Early Italian Renaissance*. Hanover and London: University Press of New England, 1989.

La Penna, Antonio. "Appunti sulla fortuna di Properzio." In his *L'integrazione difficile: Un profilo di Properzio*, 250–299. Turin: Einaudi, 1977.

Lentzen, Manfred. *Studien zur Dante-Exegese Cristoforo Landinos*. Cologne: Böhlau, 1971.

———. "Le lodi di Firenze di Cristoforo Landino: l'esaltazione del primato politico, culturale e linguistico della città sull'Arno nel Quattrocento." *Romanische Forschungen*, 97.1 (1985): 36–46.

Murgatroyd, P. "Landino, *Xandra* 2.20: a Renaissance Paraclausithyron." *Bibliothèque d'humanisme et Renaissance*, 59.1 (1997): 105–109.

Parker, Deborah. "Commentary as Social Act: Trifone Gabriele's Critique of Landino." *Renaissance Quarterly*, 45 (1992): 225–246.

Thompson, D. F. S. "Propertius." *Catalogus Translationum et Commentariorum*, vol. IX, edited by V. Brown and others. Washington, D.C.: The Catholic University of America Press, forthcoming.

Tonelli, Natascia. "Landino: la *Xandra* e il codice elegiaco." *Giornale storico della letteratura italiana*, 179, no. 586 (2002): 192–211.

Walker, John. "Ginevra de' Benci by Leonardo da Vinci." *Report and Studies in the History of Art, National Gallery of Art* (1967): 1–38.

Index

𝕬𝕾𝕻𝕾

Landino's *Three Books of Xandra* are cited by book, poem, and line number. References to the Earlier Redaction are indicated by "er"; to the Miscellaneous Poems by "Var."; to the doubtful poems by "D."; and to the notes by "n." Lowercase roman numerals refer to page numbers in the Introduction.

Publication of this volume has been made possible by

The Myron and Sheila Gilmore Publication Fund at I Tatti
The Robert Lehman Endowment Fund
The Jean-François Malle Scholarly Programs and Publications Fund
The Andrew W. Mellon Scholarly Publications Fund
The Craig and Barbara Smyth Fund
for Scholarly Programs and Publications
The Lila Wallace–Reader's Digest Endowment Fund
The Malcolm Wiener Fund for Scholarly Programs and Publications